ROUTLEDGE LIBRARY EDITIONS:
WW2

Volume 5

CIVIL LIBERTIES IN BRITAIN DURING THE 2ND WORLD WAR

CIVIL LIBERTIES IN BRITAIN DURING THE 2ND WORLD WAR

A Political Study

NEIL STAMMERS

Routledge
Taylor & Francis Group
LONDON AND NEW YORK

First published in 1983 by Croom Helm Ltd

This edition first published in 2022
by Routledge
2 Park Square, Milton Park, Abingdon, Oxon OX14 4RN

and by Routledge
605 Third Avenue, New York, NY 10158

Routledge is an imprint of the Taylor & Francis Group, an informa business

British Library Cataloguing in Publication Data
A catalogue record for this book is available from the British Library

ISBN: 978-1-03-201217-9 (Set)
ISBN: 978-1-00-319367-8 (Set) (ebk)
ISBN: 978-1-03-207800-7 (Volume 5) (hbk)
ISBN: 978-1-03-207807-6 (Volume 5) (pbk)
ISBN: 978-1-00-321162-4 (Volume 5) (ebk)

DOI: 10.4324/9781003211624

Publisher's Note
The publisher has gone to great lengths to ensure the quality of this reprint but points out that some imperfections in the original copies may be apparent.

Disclaimer
The publisher has made every effort to trace copyright holders and would welcome correspondence from those they have been unable to trace.

CIVIL LIBERTIES IN BRITAIN DURING THE 2ND WORLD WAR

A POLITICAL STUDY

NEIL STAMMERS

CROOM HELM
London & Canberra
ST. MARTIN'S PRESS
New York

Croom Helm Ltd, Provident House, Burrell Row,
Beckenham, Kent BR3 1AT
Croom Helm Australia, P.O. Box 391, Manuka,
ACT 2603, Australia

British Library Cataloguing in Publication Data

Stammres, Neil
Civil liberties in Britain during the Second World
War.
1. civil rights--Great Britain--History
I. Title
323.4'0941 JN906

ISBN 0-7099-2373-2

St. Martin's Press, Inc., 175 Fifth Avenue, New York, N.Y. 10010
First published in the United States of America in 1983

Library of Congress Cataloging in Publication Data

Stammers, Neil.
Civil liberties in Britain during the Second World War.

Bibliography: p.
Includes index.
1. Civil rights--Great Britain--History. 2. World
War, 1935-1945--Law and legislation--Great Britain--
History. I. Title.
KD4080.S72 1983 323.4'0941 83-42999
ISBN 0-312-14129-7

Printed and bound in Great Britain

CONTENTS

TABLES

ACKNOWLEDGEMENTS

I would like to thank the staff at the Public Record Office, Mr. Higgson the archivist of the NCCL records at the Library of the University of Hull and the staff of the Modern Records Centre at the University of Warwick. They all gave me valuable assistance in finding my way through the documents in their care. I would also like to thank the many staff of the University of Sussex Library who put up both with my presence and my frequent questions over the years.

Many people have made useful suggestions but in particular I would like to thank Dr. R.J. Benewick and Dr. John Dearlove who also gave me a good deal of encouragement. Noel Russell, Norman McLeod and Helga Dittmar made valuable comments on the entire text.

Judith Dennison produced the final script which is seen on these pages. Its quality attests to her skill and diligence.

Finally, I would like to thank Chrissy Ethell without whose help I would probably never have started this book, and Noel Russell, without whose help I would certainly never have finished it.

INTRODUCTION

This book deals with three things: civil liberties, crisis government and the idea of democracy. It is based on the view that the practice of government towards civil liberties and the nature of crisis government both have important implications for whether or not a society can be described as democratic. Hardly a novel suggestion, one might think. Yet remarkably there have been few serious attempts to examine these questions through detailed research. This is true both for those who believe that societies like Britain are democratic and for those who argue that democracy cannot be realised in a capitalist society. To explain why this is so and to demonstrate the relevance of this study, the first part of this introduction will examine some of the assumptions and preconceptions of democratic and radical theory.

Democratic theory gives a good deal of weight to the concept of civil liberties. One standard textbook, for example, describes civil liberties as 'perhaps the most vital element in the British political tradition' [1] and it is extensively used to distinguish between democratic and undemocratic societies. It is said that the Soviet Union is undemocratic because civil liberties do not exist there in any real sense. Now the critics of the Soviet Union do not, quite rightly, examine civil liberties in terms of their theoretical existence - say in constitutional arrangements. Their conclusions have been reached by reference to the practice in that society. But democratic theorists have rarely attempted to assess the relationship between theory and practice in their own societies. My research among the vast number of studies of British government and politics from the democratic school failed to uncover a single volume which tries to make a systematic study of government practice towards civil liberties. In other words, it seems that democratic theory does little more than assume and assert that civil liberties are fully developed, protected and operational in societies which they see as democratic.

Equally little attention has been given to the study of

government and the political process during periods of crisis, despite the fact that emergency powers often include provision for the suspension or abrogation of civil liberties. Apparently, democratic theorists see this as of little or no consequence. Emergency powers are rarely mentioned, except occasionally to note that democratic regimes do resort to them during wartime, or to suggest in passing that they are entitled to do so. The nature of crisis government has either been ignored or, at best, given a brief descriptive chapter in the most comprehensive of textbooks. [2] There has been no discussion of whether the nature of crisis government has any implications for theories of democracy.

This omission is symptomatic, for war and crises are seen as aberrations in the history and development of democracy and study has therefore concentrated on the 'normal' - periods of relative peace and stability. But how accurate is it to dismiss war and crises as aberrations? How many times must they occur to make them worth of study? The two world wars cover a period of about ten years in the first eighty years of the twentieth century, and in Britain there have also been various internal crises which have led to the declaration of a state of emergency. There is also the case of Northern Ireland, a part of the United Kingdom which has rarely been free of some form of emergency legislation since its creation. It is far more realistic to see crisis as a recurring historical feature and, if only for that reason, the nature of crisis government merits some attention.

But there is also a more fundamental reason for arguing that democratic theory should have examined crisis government. It seems wholly inadequate to judge the performance of a political system by reference to a partial reality - that is by limiting study to periods of peace and stability. An analogy may highlight this point. When a vehicle is tested to see how it performs the tests do not simply consist of driving the vehicle slowly along a straight road. The vehicle is tested at high speed and under stress. It is in this way that overall performance is assessed and faults, which may have otherwise remained undetected, can be expected to come to light. Political systems are certainly not mechanical systems but a proper assessment of a political system must include studies of that system when it is under stress: during periods of crisis. Such studies could be expected to tell us as much, if not more, about a political system than similar studies during periods of peace and stability.

Democratic theory has claimed a high degree of objectivity through the empirical study of government and politics. But the absence of empirical studies in the areas this book is concerned with has resulted in democratic theory avoiding several fundamental questions. Some of the answers suggested by this book cast doubt on the validity of democratic theory in general.

It could be expected that radical theory would have found the omissions and inconsistencies of democratic theory and sought to expose them through detailed research. But this has not happened. The reasons for this are complex, and detailed discussion of them is far beyond the scope of this introduction. I would however like to make three general points by way of comment.

Firstly, radical theory has become increasingly incestuous in recent years, concentrating on intensely theoretical internal debate. Consequently, radical theorists have tended to ignore or simply denounce the premises and arguments of democratic and, more generally, liberal theory rather than subject them to rigorous scrutiny and criticism. So, for example, civil liberties are sometimes seen as 'nothing more' than bourgeois freedoms, the study of which has no place in radical theory. The apparent reasons for this are that the concept of civil liberties has been incorporated into democratic theory and ideology and that, historically, the development of civil liberties was inextricably bound up with the development of capitalism. Such a view ignores the fact that civil liberties have usually only been established and preserved by protracted struggles against the state. More importantly, it has resulted in a failure to grasp the ambivalent place of civil liberties in democratic theory which I referred to above.

The second point concerns the predominance of economic analysis within radical theory. Many marxist writers have emphasised the role of economic factors in societal development. This has ranged from a crude economic determinism - where the economic base is seen as determining the political, legal and social superstructure - to more refined views which allow various degrees of interaction between the mode of production and political, legal and social forms. But as a result, political, legal and social processes have frequently been seen as subordinate to, or of less importance than, the economic structure of society. In particular, critical research has tended to ignore those issues and areas which do not have an easily traceable economic dimension.

Finally, recent years have seen the rise of theories within marxism, originating with Althusser, which have roundly condemned the empirical study of politics and history and sought to replace it with abstract theory. So for example, despite the fact that the concept of crisis holds an important place in radical thought, there has been no attempt to examine how crisis government functions in practice. Rather, certain behaviour has been presupposed and analysed by reference to abstract theoretical models. Similarly with the study of civil liberties - a point taken up by E.P. Thompson. He has argued that large sections of the left have ignored civil liberties and sunk into a 'pessimistic determinism' because an authoritarian state is seen theoretically as a necessary concomitant of a certain 'capitalist formation'. [3] I would argue that those theorists who see empirical study as worthless have misunderstood the relationship between theory and practice. Theory must be able to explain the concrete reality of society - its practice - in detail. This cannot be done purely abstractly, in the minds of theorists. Empirical study may not always reveal underlying causes and relationships, but without it an understanding of the complex realities of capitalist society is impossible.

Taken in combination, the three tendencies I have outlined explain the serious lack of critical research into the political and ideological processes at work in societies like Britain. The absence of critical studies of crisis government and government practice towards civil liberties only serve to illustrate this more general problem.

The fact that radical theory has failed to provide any detailed analysis of civil liberties has not, of course, prevented some people in Britain taking up the question from a position which does not accept the cosy assumptions of democratic theory. Since the 1930s the National Council for Civil Liberties has acted as a watchdog in this field and, over the years, various studies have shown that civil liberties can be, and have been, curtailed in one way or another. But, despite their merits, the work of the NCCL and others has tended to concentrate on specific, often legal, questions rather than a more general analysis of the practice of government towards civil liberties. In addition they have consistently faced a major difficulty in that they have usually dealt with issues when they have been alive - that is in the arena of public debate. It is usually impossible at that stage to make a thorough study of the factors which determine government policy. This has forced a reliance on assumption and generalisation which has tended to underestimate the complexities involved and has sometimes led to misinterpretation. The one or two studies which have been more wide-ranging have either concentrated on the legal aspects of civil liberties or popular descriptive history.

By dealing with a specific historical period, this book attempts to make a systematic study of government policy towards those civil liberties which had been incorporated into the ideology of democracy at that time. Through this it necessarily examines the way in which government and the political process functioned during the crisis years of the second world war. It is based on the view that the empirical study of crisis government and the practice of government towards civil liberties is not only useful but essential if the nature of government and the state in societies like Britain is to be more fully understood.

So far I have tried to explain the importance of this study in terms of political theory and previous work in the area of civil liberties. But this should not overshadow its relevance as historical research. Until the 1970s the period of the second world war had been covered with a web of largely unchallenged mythology. Central to this mythology was the idea of the British people uniting under a great war leader and a benevolent coalition government to resist and then defeat fascism. Dissent and conflict hardly existed and everyone pulled together for the common good. The origin of this mythology lies in the official ideology of wartime Britain itself, but it has been perpetuated for forty years by uncritical popular historians working from the official histories and the memoirs and diaries of political and military notables.

As a historical study this book is part of a wider movement which has begun to challenge this mythology in recent years. The impetus for this new generation of history comes from the increased availability of primary source material in a number of archives. The most important for this study was undoubtedly the Public Record Office at Kew. The government documents now available proved to be invaluable, but even at a distance of over forty years the veil of official secrecy remains a serious impediment to thorough research.

There were gaps in many of the files consulted either because items remain 'closed to public inspection' or because there was simply no reference at all to documents which should have been included. [4] A far more serious limitation was that certain records which should have been central to this study remain completely closed. Of these, the most important are probably the records of the Home Defence (Security) Executive - a Cabinet committee set up in 1940 and which took executive responsibility for the activities of MI5. From the few documents of this committee which are (perhaps inadvertently) available it is clear that the work of this committee extended into most of the areas covered in this book.

Despite such problems this study has succeeded in assembling a wealth of hitherto unresearched material and is able to analyse the rationale behind many aspects of government policy. It covers almost all those areas which were seen at the time, either by government or organisations such as the NCCL, as major civil liberties issues. The one exception to this is the question of conscientious objection to military service, which had already been the subject of a detailed study before the research for this book began. [5] Each chapter deals with a separate topic but two themes - the effectiveness of Parliament and the government's use of covert and indirect policies - recur in several chapters. The conclusions will attempt to assess government practice towards civil liberties and the nature of crisis government during the second world war, and consider the implications for the idea of democracy.

Introduction: Notes

1. A.H. Hanson & M. Walles, Governing Britain, (Fontana/Collins, 1970) p.285.

2. The one exception to this is Clinton Rossiter, Constitutional Dictatorship, Crisis Government in the Modern Democracies, 2nd Edition, (Harbinger Books, 1963).

3. E.P. Thompson, The Secret State, State Research Pamphlet No. 1, (Independent Research Publications, 1979) p.15.

4. For example, in Home Office files (PRO HO 158) circulars issued in 1944/45 concerning aliens referred back to earlier circulars by their reference numbers. But these earlier circulars were not included in the files and no explanation of their ommision was given.

5. D. Hayes, Challenge of Conscience, (George Allen & Unwin, 1949).

Chapter One

THE NATURE OF EMERGENCY POWERS AND THE LIMITATIONS OF PARLIAMENTARY CONTROL

I have pointed out that in democratic theory it has been assumed that a government is entitled to take special powers in certain circumstances, but that few attempts have been made to examine such powers and how they have been used. A possible reason for this in the British context is that when exceptional powers have been taken they have been invoked and their limitations defined by the normal legislative process, that is by Act of Parliament. Yet this does not take us very far. It does not tell us anything about the process by which special powers are planned and developed, or the extent to which Parliament is able to exercise control over those powers once an Emergency Act has been passed. This raises an important point for, despite their variety of forms, emergencies have tended to exhibit a common political feature, in that the major political parties in Parliament have generally agreed that an emergency exists and that special powers are necessary. In other words, there has generally been some degree of political consensus among the British political elite.

In this chapter then, as well as looking at the 'Emergency Powers (Defence) Acts' and those regulations which curtailed or potentially curtailed civil liberties, I also wish to examine the administrative and political process by which such powers were developed, and the extent to which Parliament exercised control over emergency legislation affecting civil liberties.

THE DEVELOPMENT OF EMERGENCY LEGISLATION

As early as 1924 a 'War Emergency Legislation Sub-Committee' was established as a sub-committee of the 'Committee for Imperial Defence' (CID), its task being to draw up a comprehensive code of defence regulations. [1] The prevailing outlook of the CID until the mid 1930s was that Britain was unlikely to be involved in a major war for at least ten years and, not surprisingly, the sub-committee met only occasionally during its eleven year existence. It did, however, produce draft codes of defence regulations in 1928, 1931 and 1933. In preparing these codes, the sub-committee took the regulations made under the 'Defence of the Realm Acts' (DORA) as a basis and then, by a process of consultation with government departments, considered ways in which those regulations might be improved in terms of their efficiency and usefulness. [2]

In 1925, for instance, the sub-committee considered a report on DORA regulation 46, which had made it an offence to distribute or publish any leaflet concerned with the issues of war and peace unless it had been previously submitted and approved by the 'competent authority'. The report noted that the Home Office felt that the regulation had been too 'unwieldy' and that it prevented any action being taken against a leaflet which had been approved. By 1928, the draft regulation had been amended to remove the requirement of approval (thus perhaps answering the Home Office criticisms) but it still required submission to a competent authority. By 1933, after further consultations, the regulation was tightened by a new clause stipulating that leaflets had to be submitted to the competent authority 72 hours prior to distribution or publication. [3] Although this form of regulation was subsequently dropped and did not appear in the 'Defence (General) Regulations 1939' it was resurrected in 1941 as a possible method of controlling communist propaganda (see Chapter Four). This illustrates the importance of these early discussions and the continuing influence of the DORA regulations.

It should be stressed that the sub-committee's tasks seem to have been purely administrative. The available records suggest that it did not consider, as a matter of general policy, the sort of regulations that ought to be available, or which restrictions on civil liberties might be reasonable in a major emergency. Nevertheless, these deliberations formed the basis for the detailed discussions which took place in the latter half of the 1930s.

In 1935 the Italian-Abyssinian crisis prompted the government to set up an 'Ad-Hoc Interdepartmental Committee' to consider what Bills and regulations might be necessary in the event of British involvement in that crisis. But sometime in the following year it was decided this committee's terms should be expanded to cover all Bills and defence regulations likely to be necessary in a major emergency. [4] In April 1937 the Ad-Hoc Committee produced a comprehensive report which discussed in detail the form an Emergency Act might take and the wording of possible regulations. The Emergency Powers Bill, it argued, ought to include paragraphs providing for detention without trial and the entry and search of premises:

> partly because it is right that Parliament should take explicit responsibility for giving the Executive drastic powers to interfere with personal liberty... and partly because there is always some risk that, in the absence of such specific provisions, the courts might be reluctant to interpret the general words in sub section (1) as sufficient to validate Regulations which involve such interference. [5]

The report also favoured a clause in the Bill to prohibit the introduction of industrial conscription by the use of defence regulations. It is not clear why this recommendation was made, but perhaps the committee felt that any Emergency Bill which did not preclude industrial conscription might be held up in Parliament, preventing the early introduction of other regulations. Other ways of controlling manpower were being considered prior to the war (see Chapter Six) but the most drastic controls in this field were eventually introduced by defence regulations.

Moving on to the draft regulations, the report explained the rationale behind changes that had been made to the DORA regulations. An example relevant to this book was the question of detention without trial. Under DORA regulation 14B the class of persons liable to be so detained was limited to those 'of hostile association or origin' The report states that most of those so interned during the first world war were naturalised British subjects of German extraction. But in a future war, the report pointed out:

> there is a serious danger that attempts to impede the war effort of the nation might be made by persons actuated, not by sympathy with the enemy, but by 'internationalist' affiliations or by disinterested opposition to the war. Moreover, if this country is subjected to frequent and large scale attacks from the air, the need for swift and effective action against persons who are suspected of mischievious activities will be far greater than in the last war. [6]

Thus, with the communist and pacifist movements clearly in mind, and the effect such opposition might have if Britain was subjected to heavy air bombardment, the report argued that there should be no limitation on the provision for detention without trial, such as had been included in DORA regulation 14B.

Another section of the report's analysis dealt with the proposed regulation to control anti-war propaganda, and it argued 'It is desirable that the prohibition against subversive activities of this kind should be stated in terms which are clear and unambiguous.' [7] During the war virtually all anti-government propaganda was considered 'subversive' but the fact that the term should be used in 1937 to describe attempts to influence public opinion suggests that perhaps its broad usage in government circles was not brought about by the pressures of war. That the regulation should be couched in clear and unambiguous terms indicates that the committee was particularly concerned with ensuring that there would be no legal loopholes which could be exploited by defendants or their legal advisers.

A final point of interest concerns the question of strikes in wartime. The report argued that 'no provision should be inserted in the Defence Regulations to limit the freedom of civilians to strike' and added 'So long as it is lawful to strike, those people who promote strikes cannot be properly penalised.' [8] Again there is no explanation for these recommendations but they are important in relation to whether or not regulation 2B was intended to prohibit strikes and stand in contrast to the decisions made to curb strikes in 1940 and to make incitement to strike an offence in 1944. Perhaps the report did not envisage the formation of an all-party coalition government which would make such prohibitions a political possibility.

By the time this report was prepared, the 'no war for ten years' view had been abandoned by the CID and the government was becoming increasingly concerned with what might happen if Britain was subjected to heavy air bombardment on the outbreak of war. Such a 'knockout blow' was anticipated, and the consequences both in terms of casualties, damage, and civilian morale were expected to be catastrophic. [9] It was widely believed that the heavy bombing of cities would lead to panic and hysteria, and that this factor, combined with breakdowns in communications, administration and welfare services might result in a large section of the population calling for an immediate peace, precipitating a dangerous political crisis. The direct impact of these beliefs has already been noted in connection with the drafting of the regulation providing for detention without trial, and it seems likely that other regulations may have been significantly strengthened for the same reasons. The importance of this point is illustrated by a debate which occured in the government committee structure over the timing of the introduction of the Emergency Bill and the regulations.

Some time between July 1937 and June 1938, the Committee for Imperial Defence concluded that the Emergency Bill should not be introduced in peace-time, on the grounds that it would provoke less opposition after hostilities had begun. [10] Such a policy, however, raised a number of other problems, and these were referred back to the re-titled 'War Legislation Sub-Committee' which submitted a further report to the CID in June 1938. This report pointed out that, given the Emergency Bill was not to be introduced in peace-time, there would necessarily be an interval between war breaking out and the

Bill being passed. The report accepted that this interval might be short but warned:

> We must, however, take into account the possibility that the emergency might occur when Parliament was not sitting and that it might develop into an acute crisis within a few hours...if at such a moment an enemy launched an intensive air attack on London, without any preliminary warning or formal declaration of war, it might be impossible for Parliament to meet, for three of four days. [11]

In such circumstances, the report argued, it would be necessary for the executive to take action without parliamentary sanction and that the limits of action to be taken prior to legal powers being obtained should therefore be carefully defined. To this end, the committee appended a draft code of regulations to the report which, it was suggested, could be issued by Royal Proclamation together with an explanatory note from the government. Significantly, those regulations most likely to affect civil liberties were omitted from this draft code. The recommendations were approved by the CID, so it seems that the fear of immediate air bombardment had led to a policy by which the government would take arbitrary powers without reference to Parliament - a procedure which would have been totally unconstitutional.

In April 1939 the Cabinet confirmed that the Emergency Bill should only be introduced after hostilities had begun, [12] but this policy came under scrutiny in July 1939. In correspondence with the Chairman of the sub-committee, the Lord Chancellor said that it might be better to introduce the Emergency Bill in peace-time after all. [13] It seems that he was having second thoughts about the policy of issuing regulations by proclamation. On 20 August, in a Cabinet meeting discussing the introduction of regulations by executive action, the Lord Chancellor stated that 'as a judge he could not approve a procedure which was wholly illegal'. [14] Whether this particular statement closed the issue or whether an extended discussion took place is not revealed. But the decision to abandon the policy and to introduce the Emergency Bill in peace-time must have been taken around this time for, at a Cabinet meeting on 22 August, it was decided to recall Parliament, and by the 25th the 'Emergency Powers (Defence) Act' had become law.

Although I have only traced the development of emergency legislation briefly and in general terms, a number of points can nevertheless be made. Firstly, there is the continuing impact of the DORA regulations on planning. In the deliberations of the 'War Emergency Legislation Sub-committee' 1924-1935 this influence is obvious, but even in 1937 it remained strong, as evidenced by the discussion of the differences between the proposed regulations and the DORA regulations in the report submitted to the CID. Even after the war had begun there were to be examples of the government turning to the DORA regulations for solutions to specific problems.

Undoubtedly though, certain factors did encourage change. I referred to considerations of utility and efficiency, and it would be surprising if such factors were not taken into account. The impact of perceptions of what war would bring is of rather more interest. The proposal to take powers by Royal Proclamation illustrates the importance of this factor, and it is clear that the regulation providing for detention without trial was modified partly in the light of these perceptions. It is a sobering reflection on the predictive power of governments that these perceptions proved to be completely inaccurate. Indeed, the government was to face opposition to aspects of emergency powers not because Britain was being bombarded, but because it was not.

To sum up then, it appears that emergency legislation for the second world war was developed from a reliance on traditional solutions which were modified to the extent that considerations of efficiency, utility and the likely conditions in Britain on the outbreak of war were taken into account.

One final point should be made. Despite the fact that the terms of the defence regulations and Emergency Powers Bill were considered for many years before the war, there was apparently no attempt to discuss the issues involved either in Parliament or with interested parties outside the government. [15] With such drastic powers being proposed it might be thought to be the duty of a democratic government to inform people of its plans, especially since it had always been anticipated that the Emergency Powers Bill would be passed through Parliament either with war imminent or actually in progress. One must conclude that public discussion was intentionally avoided until the crisis had arisen and 'national unity' became the political order of the day, rather than any serious discussion of the issues involved.

THE EMERGENCY POWERS (DEFENCE) ACT 1939 AND THE FIRST DEFENCE REGULATIONS

Clause One of the 'Emergency Powers (Defence) Act', or EP(D)A for short, provided that:

> His Majesty may by Order in Council make such Regulations...as appear to him necessary or expedient for securing the public safety, the defence of the realm, the maintenance of public order and the efficient prosecution of any war... and for maintaining supplies and services

essential to the life of the community. [16]

This was the general enabling clause which allowed the government to introduce defence regulations. But the Act also specified that defence regulations could be made providing for the possession or control of any property other than land, the entry and search of any premise, and 'the detention of persons whose detention appears to the Secretary of State to be expedient in the interests of the public safety or the defence of the realm'. [17] As the 1937 report to the CID had recommended, the imposition of any form of industrial conscription under the Act was prohibited, but the government was allowed to suspend or amend any other legislation as they saw fit, and make any orders or by-laws necessary to expedite the operation of the regulations. In 'The People's War', Angus Calder said that the Act gave the government power 'to act as it liked without reference to Parliament'. [18] This is not strictly true, for the Act provided that any Order in Council containing defence regulations had to lay before Parliament for 28 days, during which time either House could pass a motion annulling that order. But such an annulment was 'without prejudice... to the making of a new Order' [19] and so Calder's comment, if not constitutionally correct, was perhaps a realistic assessment.

Quite clearly, the Act gave the government enormous and unspecified powers, yet its passage through Parliament was completed in less than four hours. [20] In proposing the Bill, Sir Samuel Hoare stressed that the powers provided by it were 'very wide, very drastic and very comprehensive', but that the government would apply them with 'moderation, toleration and common sense'. [21] Arthur Greenwood, replying for the Labour Party, accepted that the government had to 'arm itself with powers which can be swiftly brought into action'. [22] It was left to the Liberal spokesman, Mr Griffith, to sum up the limitations of Parliament's consideration of the Bill. He stated:

> If there was time to consider these matters in detail, if we had time for a long Committee stage, I have no doubt that Amendments would be moved from these benches and from other parts of the House, but we are bound to realise the urgency of the problem as it has been put before us... and, therefore, the necessity is put upon us, in place of moving Amendments, of accepting the assurances ...given. [23]

Thus, after some fifteen years of preparation, the government could say, and the House of Commons could accept, that the circumstances were so urgent that the Bill could not be properly considered by Parliament. A few amendments were proposed during the committee stage, but those put to a vote were defeated and the Bill emerged from both Houses unscathed.

The first defence regulations had been introduced on 25 August, but the Order in Council which introduced most of those regulations designed to restrict civil liberties was signed and published on 1 September. [24] Although many of the regulations had implications for civil liberties the most important can be divided into four categories: those affecting expression of opinion (including propaganda, meetings and censorship), those which allowed restrictions to be placed on individual's movements and activities without reference to the judicial process, those which were specifically directed towards curtailing civil liberties in industry and those which extended police or administrative powers in respect of the gathering of information, arrest and the entry and search of premises.

General Restrictions on the Expression of Opinion. In this first group, regulation 39B clearly had the widest application. Section One made it an offence to 'endeavour to influence, orally or otherwise, public opinion in a manner likely to be prejudicial to the efficient prosecution of the war or the defence of the realm'. [25] It also became an offence to possess any article 'with a view to facilitating such an endeavour'. Section Two allowed the Secretary of State to make an order to prevent or restrict the publication of any matter which 'would or might be' prejudicial to the efficient prosecution of the war or the defence of the realm, including any document, newspaper, book or film. Finally, Section Three allowed the courts to prohibit the publication of any newspaper which had committed an offence under Sections One or Two.

On the face of it this sweeping regulation gave the government almost absolute power to control any propaganda it found odious. Although under Section One a prosecution through the courts was necessary, it was not a defence to show that public opinion had not been influenced. Under Section Two there was not even recourse to the courts, the Secretary of State being the sole arbiter of what constituted prejudicial matter.

Although a general power of censorship was thus provided by regulation 39B, newspapers and other publications were also restricted under regulation 3. Although this regulation was primarily concerned with ensuring that military information did not reach the enemy, Section 1(f) made it an offence to obtain, publish or possess any information regarding 'any matter whatsoever' which 'would or might be directly or indirectly useful to an enemy'. [26]

The expression of opinion through meetings and demonstrations was covered by regulation 39E, Section One of which allowed the Secretary of State to make an order prohibiting public processions or demonstrations in a specific area if he was satisfied that they 'would be likely to cause serious public disorder or to promote disaffection'. [27] Section Two gave the Secretary of State similar powers in respect of public meetings, except in this case these powers could also be delegated to Chief Officers of Police, Mayors or Justices of the Peace. The use of the term 'disaffection' in this regulation related to the civil population rather than the military. Such usage had historical precedent, both in terms of the law of sedition, and DORA regulation 42 which had dealt with incitement to disaffection of both the military and civil population.

The final regulation in this group, regulation 39A, stated that 'No person shall endeavour to cause disaffection amongst persons engaged...in His Majesty's Service.' [28] and that it would also be an offence to possess any documents with intent to contravene or help others contravene the regulation. This regulation appears to have been substantially wider than the 1934 Incitement to Disaffection Act which referred to 'duty and alliegance' rather than 'disaffection', a term with far wider implications.

<u>Restrictions on Individuals' Movements and Activities</u>. A number of regulations provided the government with powers in this respect, but the most important were regulations 18B and 18A. Under regulation 18B the Secretary of State, if he was satisfied that it was necessary 'with a view to preventing' a person 'acting in any manner prejudicial to the public safety or the defence of the realm' [29] could make a detention order or an order restricting that person in respect of his employment or business, his association or communications with others, or his activities relating to the dissemination of news and the propagation of opinions. The only check provided was that aggrieved individuals could make objections to an advisory committee appointed by the Secretary of State, and that it was the duty of the Secretary of State to inform a person of their right to do so.

On the same grounds, regulation 18A allowed the Secretary of State to make an order preventing a person from being in any place or area of the United Kingdom, or requiring an individual to notify their movements to the authorities at such times as specified in the order.

These two regulations gave absolute discretion to the Secretary of State to determine not only what matters were prejudicial to the public safety or the defence of the realm but also who should be restricted or detained under them. The advisory committee had no power to make public pronouncements or reverse the Secretary of State's decisions. As its name suggests, it could only advise and was not a substitute for the judicial process.

Industrial Restrictions. Part One of the defence regulations included regulations dealing with essential services and sabotage. Regulation 1A contained a clause safeguarding workers and trade unions which, in line with the recommendations of the 1937 Report, stated 'that a person shall not be guilty of an offence against this Regulation by reason of his taking part in, or peacefully persuading any other person to take part in, a strike.' [30] But regulation 2B, which also dealt with essential services, contained no such safeguard. Section One of the regulation stated:

> No person shall do any act with intent to impair the efficiency or impede the working or movement of any vessel, aircraft, vehicle, machinery, apparatus or other thing used or intended to be used in His Majesty's service or in the performance of essential services, or to impair the usefulness of any works, structure or premises used or intended to be used as aforesaid. [31]

A strike or picket could have been construed as acts intended to impair the usefulness of a factory or plant, and so strikes and pickets in essential services would seem to have been illegal at the beginning of the war.

Other regulations likely to affect workers and trade union rights in industry were those concerned with 'protected places'. Regulation 12 allowed the Secretary of State to designate factories and other premises as 'protected places', and once so designated it became an offence to enter them without the permission of an approved authority. In the case of industrial concerns this authority was usually the firm's management. Furthermore, under regulation 14, the Secretary of State could make by-laws and directions controlling the activities and behaviour of persons working in a 'protected place' and to restrict the distribution of leaflets, the holding of meetings and other normally legitimate activities of workers.

Finally, Section Two of regulation 15 made it an offence to be in the vicinity of a protected place or other area used for essential services 'for any purpose prejudicial to the public safety or the defence of the realm'. If someone was proved to have been seen in such areas the prosecution could 'adduce such evidence of the character of that person (including evidence of his having been previously convicted of any offence) as tends to show that he was so present for a purpose prejudicial to the public safety or the defence of the realm'. [32] Now while this regulation undoubtedly applied to enemy agents or potential terrorists, it may also have covered picketing. In such cases the prosecution could use evidence of an individual's political affiliations or record of trade union activity to show that the defendant was present for a prejudicial purpose.

The Extension of Administrative and Police Powers. Regulation 80A made it an offence to withhold any information or article from specified officials if they requested it. Regulation 88A extended the right of entry and search of premises and enabled police officers of the rank of superintendent or above to confer the same powers of search and seizure as would be conferred by a warrant issued by a JP in circumstances, such as urgency, which made it impracticable to apply for a warrant. Regulation 88C gave any policeman or member of the armed forces the power to arrest without warrant any person suspected of breaching the defence regulations. Finally, regulation 88D allowed the Secretary of State to make provision for the identification of persons in police custody.

Taken together, these four groups of regulations were clearly very wide in scope. Either by making certain activities an offence, or else by giving the Secretary of State absolute discretionary power, many traditional areas of freedom were subjected to the test of whether they were prejudicial to the public safety, the efficient prosecution of the war, or the defence of the realm. In areas where the Secretary of State had such discretionary power it was up to him, (or in effect the government) to decide what was prejudicial. Even where a regulation required prosecution through the courts, Ministers could argue that only the government was in a position to estimate what matters were, or likely to be, prejudicial.

The majority of the regulations described above were concerned to some effect with ensuring stability for the government itself, either through the maintenance of public and industrial order or through the control of opinions, propaganda or individuals themselves. One can only speculate how these powers would have been used if the anticipated air bombardment had occurred. What now has to be considered here is why, after only three months of war, the government were prepared to significantly restrict the scope of the powers they had taken so recently.

OPPOSITION TO THE DEFENCE REGULATIONS AND THEIR AMENDMENT 1939

If, at the beginning of the war, Britain had been subjected to the sort of attack that had been predicted, it is likely that the Labour and Liberal parties in the House of Commons would have given the government their uncritical support as they had done both for the EP(D)A and the declaration of war. There might even have been a national coalition government formed in the autumn of 1939 had Britain's military position become serious. In other words, a political consensus would have been firmly established at an early date and the powers taken by the government would probably not have been challenged.

As it was, Britain entered the period known as the 'phoney war', and despite a measure of common agreement between the parties in the House of Commons (the electoral truce is another example) the Labour Party in particular remained suspicious of the government. It was possible for both the Labour Party and the Liberals to be patriotic and express support for the war while at the same time remaining critical of government policy. It is in this context that opposition to restrictions on civil liberties needs to be examined.

From the beginning of the war there was a degree of public opposition to the regulations which restricted civil liberties. In September and October 1939 the National Council for Civil Liberties produced a series of leaflets, letters and memoranda analysing and criticising the scope of the regulations. [33] In November they held a conference on 'Civil Liberties in Wartime' which expressed apprehension at:

> the very wide and drastic power conferred on the Government by the Emergency Powers (Defence) Act, 1939 and the Regulations made thereunder - particularly those provisions by which meetings can be suppressed, freedom of expression can be punished and the curfew imposed, - and strongly protests against the power vested in the Secretary of State to detain persons for an indefinite period without charge or trial and without the right of appeal to the Courts of Law. [34]

The resolution also demanded that regulations 12-15 and 2B should not be used against trade unions or those people who take part in peaceful picketing or strikes.

By the time this conference met, however, a more significant event had occured in Parliament. On 31 October 1939 the Liberal MP Dingle Foot, who had been in contact with the NCCL, moved 'a prayer' in the House of Commons 'that the Order in Council amending the Defence Regulations dated the 1st day of September...be annulled.' This was the Order in Council which had introduced most of the regulations discussed in the previous section. Foot said that although it was unavoidable that in time of war the government should be entrusted with extraordinary powers, he argued that some of the regulations were without precedent and 'that some of them go far wider than anything the Government can legitimately need'. [35] He concentrated his attack on three regulations - 18B, 39B and 39A - and argued that their provisions were even wider than in corresponding powers taken under DORA in the first world war. He described regulation 39B as 'one of the most remarkable regulations that can ever have been laid on the Table of the House' [36] since its wording was so wide it could result in the suppression of all anti-war propaganda.

Foot implied that this would be a negation of the very democracy for which, in his view, Britain was fighting.

Several speakers spoke in favour of the motion, but it was the intervention of Herbert Morrison from the Labour Front Bench which made it clear that the government were not just dealing with a small minority of Members. Morrison, too, accepted that during wartime the government should be endowed with exceptional powers, but he argued that the wording of a number of the regulations gave the government extraordinarily sweeping powers. Concluding his speech he stated:

> I think the House is entitled to a statement from the Home Secretary indicating the reasons why he thinks the regulations are essential. It will then be for the House to decide... On the face of the matter I am bound to say that I am exceedingly apprehensive. So are the Hon. Members who sit with me on these benches. [37]

This was a threat that the Labour Party might vote against the government.

In reply, the Home Secretary, Sir John Anderson, stated that the regulations had been prepared upon a careful and systematic review of the regulations that had been in force in the first world war. He claimed that, in general, the powers taken by the government were no more drastic and sweeping than those taken between 1914 and 1918. But when he began to discuss regulation 18B he received a stormy reception and Mr Foot was able to point out that the omission of the phrase 'of hostile association or origin' meant that the new regulation was of much wider application. With regard to regulation 39B, Anderson claimed that, if anything, the corresponding DORA regulation was even wider, but he admitted that the regulation contained a novel provision in so far as it was directed specifically against propaganda. He said such a regulation was essential to deal with modern propaganda techniques, but that he was prepared to reconsider it.

This was the first concession but a more substantial one was to follow. After further critical speeches the Lord Privy Seal rose to say that, since the government wished to have the widest possible measure of agreement on the terms of the regulations, it was willing to consult with the major parties to see how contentious regulations might be amended. This offer was considered to be a major concession by all sides of the House, and the prayer was therefore withdrawn. Following this debate a consultative committee was set up which comprised three Conservative MPs, three Labour MPs, two Liberals, the Home Secretary, his Under-Secretary and a number of civil servants. [38] This committee met on a number of occasions in the first half of November 1939 and appears to have examined all those regulations mentioned in the Commons debate.

As a result of the committee's deliberations the Home Secretary presented a memorandum to the Home Policy Committee on 22 November, submitting his proposals for amending some of the regulations. [39] These can be summarised as follows:

reg. 2B The memo stated that this regulation had never been intended to cover strikes, and a clause such as that included in regulation 1A should be added to the regulation to make this clear.

reg. 18B The class of persons liable to detention should be limited to those who the Secretary of State had 'reasonable cause to believe' to be of 'hostile origin or association' or to have been 'recently concerned in acts prejudicial to the public safety or the defence of the realm'. The clauses allowing the restriction of a person's behaviour or activities should only be applicable to those persons who have been released after detention, and the restrictions in respect of a persons activities in relation to the dissemination of news or propagation of opinions should be dropped altogether. New provisions should be added requiring the Chairman of an Advisory Committee to inform the detainee of the grounds on which a detention order had been made and to give that person sufficient particulars to enable him to present his case to the Advisory Committee. Finally, the Secretary of State should be required to make a statement to Parliament at least once a month about the action taken under the regulation.

reg. 39A The phrase 'to cause disaffection' should be replaced by the phrases 'to seduce from their duty' and 'to cause disaffection likely to lead to breaches of their duty'. The regulation should however be extended to cover employees of a public authority performing functions in connection with the defence of the realm or the securing of public safety.

reg. 39B The memo stated that section one of the regulation had covered all peace/anti-war propaganda but that it should now be limited by adding after the words 'endeavour...to influence public opinion' the phrase 'by means of any false statement, false document or false report', and that it should be a defence to show that the person concerned had reasonable cause to believe the statement, etc. to be true. In addition the general power of censorship conferred by section two should be withdrawn, and section three of the regulation dropped altogether.

reg. 39E The memo pointed out that it had been felt that the powers of delegation under this regulation might be necessary in a serious military crisis, but now that this seemed unlikely to occur, the powers of delegation should be withdrawn.

reg. 80A A provision should be included stipulating that no prosecution could occur without the consent of the Director of Public Prosecutions.

reg. 37 This regulation provided the power to impose a curfew and although MPs on the committee felt it should be withdrawn the Home Office believed that it should be retained in case exceptional circumstances arose. The memo recommended its retention.

The proposals of this memorandum were accepted by the Home Policy Committee [40] and the following day, November 23rd, an Order in Council was made amending the defence regulations. [41]

Thus, with the exceptions of the decision to retain regulation 37 and the extension of regulation 39A, the government went a long way to meet the criticisms made during the debate in the House of Commons and there is no doubt that the scope of the regulations was significantly narrowed. Not surprisingly, the NCCL hailed the changes as an important victory in the struggle to maintain civil liberties. [42] But if a victory had been achieved how had it come about? Why were the government prepared to make significant amendments to the regulations only two to three months after they had been introduced?

Several factors have to be taken into account. Firstly, as we have seen, the government had anticipated an immediate crisis in the form of air bombardment, and at least some of the regulations had been formulated in this context. When no such crisis materialised it may have been felt that such drastic powers were no longer necessary or for that matter justifiable. Secondly, it is possible that some Ministers themselves came to think that some of the regulations were too wide. In the Home Policy Committee meeting of 22 November, for example, the Attorney General stated that in his view the limitations were an improvement.

But although these points are of relevance, the role of the political opposition should not be underestimated. Although there was no chance that the government would have been defeated on the prayer to annul the Order in Council, a combined vote of Labour and Liberal MPs would have re-asserted party divisions and threatened the fragile political consensus. We may take the Lord Privy Seal's assertion that the government wanted the widest possible measure of agreement on the emergency powers as a statement of the government's desire to maintain a consensus, and the amendments to the regulations can therefore be seen as a practical expression of that desire. As long as the Labour and Liberal parties remained outside the government, consensus could only be maintained by a degree of compromise. Once these parties joined the government, compromises were no longer necessary. In this context it is significant that this was the only occasion throughout the entire war when parliamentary opposition to restrictions on civil liberties achieved any real success.

One final point needs to be made for, as we shall see later, the success of the opposition had two results beyond the actual amendment of the regulations. Firstly, the establishment of a consultative committee including MPs from the major political parties appears to have set a precedent for future years. Although this committee was not always reconvened to discuss new regulations or amendments likely to affect civil liberties, on one or two of the occasions when it was, it seems to have wielded some influence and contained some of the more extreme measures that were to be proposed. There was no constitutional reason why the setting up of this committee should set a precedent, but it appears that both the government and the House of Commons saw it as such. Similarly, when in later years the coalition government examined the possibility of extending the scope of the regulations into areas which had been subject of criticism in the October debate, the point was often made in government documents that parliamentary pressure had forced the government to abandon certain powers in November 1939, and that therefore such powers could not properly be restored. It is difficult to explain why such views should be propounded. There was no legal reason why abandoned powers could not be reintroduced, and the political position had changed significantly with the formation of the coalition - the House of Commons being in reality a different body after May 1940. Perhaps such views were a recognition of this fact - a recognition that only the pre-coalition House of Commons was able to fulfil what was conceived as its proper role.

THE MILITARY CRISIS AND NEW POWERS

The months from April to August 1940 were a period of acute military crisis in Britain. The Nazi war machine, after walking through Scandanavia and the rest of Western Europe, was expected to launch an immediate invasion, and it was seriously doubted in government circles whether the armed forces had the capability to resist a German onslaught. In these circumstances it was perhaps not surprising that the government should seek to extend the scope of the regulations and retrieve the powers it had ceded the previous autumn.

Through the first months of 1940 there had been demands for action to be taken both against enemy aliens and anti-war organisations. The Home Policy Committee, however, had not decided on any specific policy and appear to have been reluctant to take further powers directed against anti-war propaganda. [43] But on 23 April the Home Policy Committee invited the Lord Chancellor to:

> consider as a matter of urgency in what direction the existing provisions of the law could be properly strengthened so as to enable action to be taken against organisations or individuals seeking to hinder the war effort of this country. [44]

Unfortunately, it is not clear whether this change of attitude was a result of military disasters in Norway or intelligence information indicating that a Nazi offensive in the West was imminent.

At a further meeting on 30 April the Home Policy Committee approved a number of amendments to the regulations but also agreed that consultations with representative MPs (i.e. the consultative committee) should take place before an Order in Council was made. [45] As a result of these consultations one of the proposed regulations, which was to become regulation 2C, was significantly amended to limit the restrictions on freedom of expression. In a memorandum in 1941, the Home Secretary stated that this regulation as originally drafted would have made it an offence to 'endeavour to hinder the efficient prosecution of the war...by discouraging the will of the people, or any section of the people to achieve victory'. [46] But this draft was never made public or communicated to the House of Commons because in the course of discussions with the representatives it became apparent 'that there would be no chance of securing agreement on such a Regulation' and that, therefore, 'In view of the strong desire of members with whom discussion took place to limit more closely any provision restricting expressions of opinion, Regulation 2C was ultimately drafted.' [47] The consultative committee do not appear to have objected to any of the other regulations and, on 9 May, Orders in Council were signed which included the following additions and amendments to the defence regulations:

reg. 39A was amended to make it an offence both to incite persons to evade the duties and liabilities under the National Service Acts and to incite persons to abstain from enrolling voluntarily in His Majesty's Services, civil defence organisations or the National Fire Service.

reg. 2C This new regulation gave the Secretary of State power to warn any person or organisation who, in his opinion, was engaged in the systematic publication of matter calculated to foment opposition to the war. Once such a warning had been given future publication of such matter would be an offence. Subsequent to the warning it also became an offence to possess any document etc. which if published would constitute an offence. The regulation however provided that it should be a defence to show that there was no intention to foment opposition and no reasonable cause to believe that the matter published was calculated to foment such opposition.

reg. 94A Another new regulation which stated that any printing press which had been used in the production of any document in respect of which a conviction had been obtained under either 2C, 39A, or 39B could be closed or seized by order of the Secretary of State until such time as the High Court gave permission for that press to be used.

When the Home Secretary explained these new measures to the House of Commons on 9 May he stated that:

> in view of the situation with which we may be faced, it is necessary that further powers should be taken to enable the responsible authorities to deal more effectively with subversive activities [48]

and added that he believed public opinion would recognise that the additional powers were 'in no way disproportionate to our present circumstances'. [49]

The circumstances had indeed begun to change rapidly. On 7 May, the famous debate which resulted in the fall of the Chamberlain government had taken place, and the next few days witnessed not only the formation of the Churchill coalition but also the beginning of the Nazi offensive in Western Europe. But if the formation of the coalition government made the extension of emergency powers that much more of a practical possibility, it was the rapidly deteriorating military position that led to many of the measures that were adopted in the next few weeks.

On 18 May the War Cabinet considered a memorandum entitled 'The Invasion of Great Britain and the possible co-operation of a 5th column'. [50] In general the memo argued against further action being taken either against enemy aliens, British fascists or the Communist Party. But Churchill, summing up the Cabinet discussion, said that he felt that the War Cabinet as a whole wanted tougher action to be taken. [51] On 22 May therefore, the Cabinet agreed to amend regulation 18B in order to detain leading members of the British Union. [52] The same day the Cabinet also agreed a much wider measure which was immediately put before Parliament and received its support. The 'Emergency Powers (Defence) Act, 1940' filled the important gap left by the 1939 Act by providing the government with power to make defence regulations 'requiring persons to place themselves, their services, and their property at the disposal of His Majesty'. [53] Industrial conscription was thus provided for and, on the night of 22 May, regulation 58A gave the new Minister of Labour, Ernest Bevin, many of the powers necessary for the control of employment and the direction of labour.

The next step, which occured around the time of the Dunkirk evacuation, was to make further provision for the control of propaganda. On 28 May the Home Secretary asked Ministers to consider further powers to control the press. He said that he had been considering newspapers such as the British Union's 'Action' and the Communist Party's 'Daily Worker', and pointed out that under regulation 2C action could only be taken in successive stages, culminating in a prosecution through the courts. He therefore proposed a new regulation - 2D - which conferred on the Secretary of State the power to suppress any newspaper which he felt was systematically fomenting opposition to the war. A further regulation, 94B, would allow the closure or seizure of any printing press concerned in the production of a newspaper suppressed under regulation 2D. [54] No consultations with representative MPs took place in connection with these regulations, but the Cabinet approved them and they were introduced the following day.

On 11 June the Minister of Information reported to the Home Policy Committee that the intelligence services were very concerned about the spreading of rumours of German landings, which it was claimed was bad for national morale. He therefore recommended the introduction of a new regulation which would make it an offence to make any report or statement connected with the war which was likely to cause 'alarm and despondency'. The committee accepted these recommendations and regulation 39BA was made that evening. [55]

I mentioned that regulation 18B was amended in May to allow the detention of leading members of the British Union and, on 25 June, the Home Policy Committee agreed the Home Secretary's recommendation that a new regulation should be made by which this organisation could be banned altogether. [56] Regulation 18AA, which was introduced the next day, did not however refer to the British Union specifically. It allowed the Secretary of State to ban any organisation if he was satisfied that it was either subject to foreign influence or control, or that its leaders had associations with persons in the government of, or had sympathies with the system of government of, any power with which Britain was at war and that in either case there was a danger that the organisation might be utilised for prejudicial purposes. Once the regulation was applied to an organisation no-one could legally summon a meeting, or invite support for, or have any financial connection with that organisation. Furthermore, the courts were empowered to dissolve and wind up the organisation and make arrangements for disposing of its property.

One other regulation made during this period should be mentioned although its introduction was probably a result of the political changes that had taken place rather than what were seen as defence requirements. After discussions between the government and both sides of industry, regulation 58AA was introduced in July 1940. This allowed the Minister of Labour to make orders providing for the compulsory arbitration of trade disputes and the prohibition of strikes and lock-outs. Such an order - Order 1305 - was made shortly afterwards.

By the end of July the government had acquired far greater powers than its predecessor had taken at the beginning of the war, and most of the limitations imposed on the regulations by the November amendments had been by-passed by further amendments or new regulations. But whereas in 1939 opposition to restrictions on civil liberties had managed to persuade the government to limit the more extreme provisions of the regulations, no such success was achieved during 1940. Indeed many of the new powers went unchallenged apart from an occasional parliamentary question. The potentially most extensive measure, the 1940 EP(D)A, was a case in point. As with its predecessor, the Bill was passed through both Houses of Parliament in the space of a few hours and although some MPs enquired whether wealth would be conscripted as well as labour, no division was forced. [57] Perhaps one of the reasons why the changes made on 9 May were not questioned was that representative MPs had been consulted, but it is not clear whether the amendment to regulation 18B on 22 May, or the introduction of regulation 18AA were the subject of similar consultations. We know, on the other hand, that regulations 2D and 94B were introduced without consultations and this is perhaps one reason why they were an exception to the rule and were challenged in the House of Commons.

On 31 July 1940, Sidney Silverman moved a prayer to annul regulations 2D and 94B. He was supported by a number of other MPs, including Sir Richard Acland, Emmanuel Shinwell, and the Communist MP Willie Gallacher. [58] The general drift of their argument was that these regulations were so sweeping that they gave the Home Secretary powers akin to those of Goebbels in Nazi Germany, and that regulation 2D should at least be amended to allow a subsequent appeal to a court of law. Replying for the government, Sir John Anderson said that these powers had been taken because of the threat of imminent invasion and that, if it came about, the more cumbersome powers under regulation 2C might not be sufficient. He dismissed the possibility of a subsequent appeal to a court of law by arguing that drastic action ought to be judged by the House of Commons rather than a court. This brought an immediate response from Mr Pickthorn who reminded MPs of the nature of the coalition government when he said 'To some of us, it seems that the real danger in which our general liberties are involved at present is precisely that the Executive controls some 99/100ths of this House.' [59] When the House divided, 60 MPs voted for the motion and 98 against. In terms of the majority, this was the closest division over a civil liberties question during the war, but the small government voting figure suggests that the government only mobilised sufficient numbers to ensure that the motion was defeated. Certainly no concessions were offered or extracted.

The only other regulation introduced during this period which provoked any serious or significant challenge was regulation 39BA, the 'alarm and despondency' regulation. But even then it was not so much the regulation that was questioned as the way in which it was used. Instead of being used exclusively against anti-war propagandists, as might have been expected, many ordinary people were prosecuted for remarks contained in their casual conversations. For example on 17 July, the 'News Chronicle' reported that a man had been sent to prison for one month for saying to a woman in a fish-and-chip shop that Britain had no chance of winning the war. [60] On 23 July, Churchill, in a reply to a question, announced that the Home Secretary was to make a review of all the sentences imposed under this regulation. But he refused to consider withdrawing it altogether, saying that the government desired to 'curb, as it is their duty to do, propaganda of a persistent, organised and defeatist character'. [61]

In general then, there was little parliamentary opposition to further restrictions of civil liberties during 1940, and that which did occur was firmly resisted by the government. The reasons for this are straightforward. Firstly, Britain's military position in 1940 was undoubtedly very grave, and for that reason few MPs believed that such measures were unnecessary at the time. Secondly, the political climate was hardly conducive to forcing a change of policy. Not only was the coalition government new and popular, it also completely dominated the House of Commons. Any successful attempt to force a change in government policy would have required a massive revolt among backbench MPs. In the circumstances of 1940, this was hardly likely.

THE RESISTANCE TO CHANGE

By the end of 1940 the vast majority of the regulations which concern this study had reached their final form and the areas of civil liberties likely to be affected were already clearly delineated. Many of these regulations had been made or amended in the context of the military crisis in 1940, and had been accepted in this context and spirit by the House of Commons. But by mid-1941 the danger of immediate invasion had receded and from 1942 the likelihood of Britain becoming a military front progressively diminished. In these circumstances it might be expected that the government would have been prepared to rescind some of the more rigorous aspects of the regulations, perhaps returning to a position akin to that of the regulations as amended in November 1939. But this was not the case. Between 1941 and the end of the European war not one of the regulations I have described was revoked or had its scope reduced. In other words, having introduced 'crisis measures', the government retained those measures after the crisis had passed. Furthermore, this was clearly a deliberate policy, since the government had to resist pressure from the House of Commons in favour of liberalising amendments. As the war progressed a significant number of MPs became increasingly frustrated by their inability to force a change in government policy, not only in respect of the regulations affecting civil liberties but with respect to defence regulations in general. It is this apparent impotence and the reasons for it that I wish to examine in this section.

From the legal point of view there was an important constraint on MPs who wanted regulations amended or revoked, which was a function of the terms of the original 'Emergency Powers (Defence) Act'. Apart from the possibility of annulling an Order in Council within 28 days there was no other mechanism by which Parliament could revoke a specific Order after that time. The only procedural course left open was for Parliament to reject a government motion requesting a continuation of the EP(D)A, whereupon all the regulations made under the Act would be automatically repealed.

But Parliament is, of course, more than a legislative body, and as such can normally influence government policy in ways other than simply by passing or rejecting legislation. In the Autumn of 1939 the threat of the opposition to divide the House, combined with the government's desire to maintain the existing degree of political consensus, were sufficient for the government to agree to some significant amendments of the regulations. In later years there were many similar attempts to have certain regulations amended or revoked: there was also a more general demand that the House of Commons should be able to investigate delegated legislation.

Some of the cricicisms and suggested amendments arose out

of the specific application and use of the regulations. But the set opportunity for criticism was when the motion for continuing the EP(D)A was put before Parliament. In 1942 this motion was passed without discussion but in other years a variety of criticisms and suggestions emerged. In 1941 discussion concentrated on regulation 18B, although it was also suggested that regulation 2D and regulation 88A should be amended. Herbert Morrison, by then Home Secretary, simply reminded critical members of the government's majority. [62]

By 1943 criticisms had become more generalised and questions were being raised regarding Parliament's control over delegated legislation. Some MPs argued that a select committee should be established to examine regulations and orders. The Home Policy Committee decided that this proposal should be resisted, although it was agreed that the government should make time for a debate on the subject. [63]

The 1943 debate on the motion to continue the EP(D)A was wide ranging, with some MPs questioning regulations which infringed rights of property, others continuing the demand for a select committee and others raising the question of regulation 18B. The general tenor of the criticisms was that, since the country was no longer in as much danger as it had been, the time had come when the government could relax many of the restrictions that had been imposed. The government spokesman did not accept these arguments and once again no concessions were offered. [64]

It was not until 1944 that the government moved to dispel some of the criticism that had developed. In May 1944, 140 MPs signed a motion calling for the establishment of a select committee to examine delegated legislation. Seconding the motion, Commander Bower said that it had originated with the small number of MPs who, three years previously, had seen that regulations such as 18AA, 18B and 2D were 'something of a menace to the liberties of our people' [65] and that although at the time their activities had been unpopular, their views had subsequently received wider acceptance. Replying for the government, the Home Secretary said that the government was prepared to provide for the establishment of a select committee, although it would not be able to send for Ministers or examine departmental papers. [66] This proposal was accepted and the motion was withdrawn.

It had taken well over a year for MPs to persuade the government to adopt what was hardly a radical suggestion, and still there had been no success in persuading the government to amend or revoke any of the regulations we are concerned with. Throughout the war as a whole, there only appears to have been one instance of a defence regulation being annulled by the House of Commons - a particularly widely worded traffic regulation which the government had already agreed to withdraw. [67]

To understand the inability of MPs to elicit changes of

policy from the government it is necessary above all to appreciate the continuing strength of the coalition government and the relative weakness of the opposition. It is clear that the vast majority of MPs not only supported the war effort, but accepted the view that during an emergency the government were entitled to take exceptional powers. From this it followed that there was always a degree of ambivalence in demands for the amendment or revocation of specific regulations. Thus, even during the later years of the war when a considerable number of backbench MPs had become frustrated with their inability to get the government to change its policy, the motions to continue the EP(D)A were always passed without a division. When the government was under pressure it could always force the issue by calling or threatening to call a formal vote. This brings us to another important factor, party discipline. Although the government parties held the vast majority of seats in the House of Commons, the 'whipping' system appears to have been used whenever the government came under pressure. Just as in a peace-time Parliament, Members ignoring the party whips threatened their political careers. Although a few were consistently prepared to take that risk, they remained a tiny minority. Providing that the government could either convince, cajole or bully their backbenchers into support, they retained unfettered powers.

COMMENTARY

In this chapter I have shown that while emergency legislation was prepared well in advance of the war, the 'Emergency Powers (Defence) Act' and the initial regulations were only brought into public view once the crisis had materialised and it was likely that a political consensus could be established. The fact that the war did not develop along expected lines resulted in that consensus not being fully established until 1940. In the intervening period the government had to shore up consensus through compromise. Once the military position deteriorated and the consensus became structurally based with the formation of the coalition government, the parliamentary constraints on government policy were drastically diminished, and many more restrictive regulations were introduced. Even after the military crisis had passed, the continuing structural consensus enabled the government to retain the powers that had been taken in spite of parliamentary opposition. In this context Parliament does not appear to have acted as a check on the executive in so far as the making of, and retention of, regulations was concerned.

In terms of the scope of the regulations, it is apparent that from the earliest discussions of emergency legislation until the end of the war it was accepted in a general and abstract way that government could legitimately curtail fundamental civil liberties during wartime. As we have seen the regulations that were made encroached a long way into traditional freedoms, either by making normally legal activities illegal or by giving Ministers discretionary powers. In both cases civil liberties could be affected in two ways. Firstly, there was the extension of prohibitions and powers as such, which can be seen as a legal encroachment on traditional rights. Secondly, there was the way in which those powers and prohibitions were used or enforced. In this chapter I have concentrated on the scope of the regulations themselves. In the following chapters I shall examine how these regulations were used. It should also be stressed that the powers taken under the Emergency Acts were not the only way in which restrictions on civil liberties could be imposed: a point that is graphically illustrated in the next chapter.

Chapter One - Notes

1. PRO CAB 52/1.
2. PRO CAB 52/2.
3. PRO CAB 52/2, see 1925 report on DORA reg. 46 and the draft codes of regulations 1928 & 1933.
4. PRO CAB 52/3, WEL 99, 'Report of the Interdepartmental Committee on the Emergency Powers (Defence) Bill and Defence Regulations', dated 21 April 1937.
5. Ibid.
6. Ibid.
7. Ibid.
8. Ibid.
9. R. Titmuss, Problems of Social Policy, History of the Second World War (U.K. Civil Series), (HMSO, 1950), Chapters 1 & 2.
10. PRO CAB 52/5, WL 15, Fourth Report of the War Legislation Sub-Committee dated 17 June 1938.
11. Ibid.
12. PRO CAB 23/99, CM(39)22 & CM(39)23.
13. PRO CAB 52/6, Memo from Lord Chancellor to Claude Schuster, Chairman of the War Legislation Sub-Committee.
14. PRO CAB 23/100, CM(39)39.
15. The TUC did request and obtain a meeting with Ministers to discuss 'labour questions' the day before the Emergency Bill was passed, but this cannot properly be termed consultation. See v.351 H.C.DEB 5s cols. 65-66.
16. 2 & 3 Geo 6 Ch. 62 'Emergency Powers (Defence) Act 1939'.
17. Ibid.
18. A. Calder, The People's War, (Panther, 1971) p. 36.
19. 'Emergency Powers (Defence) Act 1939'.
20. v. 351 H.C.DEB 5s col. 63-110. The Bill was first introduced into the Commons at 6.45pm and received the Royal

Assent before 10.20pm.

21. v.351 H.C.DEB 5s cols. 64-5.

22. v.351 H.C.DEB 5s col.69.

23. v.351 H.C.DEB 5s col.70.

24. See SR & O 927 dated 25 August 1939 and SR & O 978 dated 1 September 1939.

25. Def. Reg. 39B, SR & O 978.

26. Def. Reg. 3 in *Defence Regulations Vol. I.*, 15th Edition, (HMSO), 24th March 1944.

27. Def.Reg. 39E, SR & O 978.

28. Def. Reg. 39A, SR & O 978.

29. Def. Reg. 18B, SR & O 978.

30. Def. Reg. 1A, in *Defence Regulations Vol.I.*

31. Def. Reg. 2B, SR & O 978.

32. Def. Reg. 15, SR & O 927.

33. see NCCL Archives, Filing Case No. 4, 'Wartime', section 6, 'Emergency Powers (Defence) Regulations' and Filing Case No. 32, 'NCCL 1937-49', section 3, 'Articles for the Press 1939-41'.

34. NCCL Archives, Filing Case No. 1, section 2, 'Report of the Delegate Conference on Civil Liberty in Wartime'.

35. v.352 H.C.DEB 5s col. 1830.

36. v.352 H.C.DEB 5s col. 1833.

37. v.352 H.C.DEB 5s col. 1852.

38. PRO CAB 75/3, Memo WL(39)27 to Sub-Committee on War Legislation.

39. PRO CAB 75/3, Memo HPC(39)103.

40. PRO CAB 75/1, HPC(39)17th Meeting.

41. SR & O 1681, dated 23 November 1939.

42. NCCL Archives, Filing Case No. 4 'Wartime', section 6, 'Emergency Powers (Defence) Regulation', letter dated 30 November 1939.

43. see PRO CAB 75/4, HPC(40)9th Meeting and HPC(40)10th Meeting.

44. PRO CAB 75/4, HPC(40) 13th Meeting.

45. This was recommended by the Home Secretary see PRO CAB 75/7, Memo HPC(40)87.

46. PRO CAB 98/18, CA(41)5, Memo to Committee on Communist Activities.

47. Ibid.

48. v.360 H.C.DEB 5s col. 1385.

49. Ibid.

50. PRO CAB 67/6, WP(G)(40)131.

51. PRO CAB 65/7, WM 128.

52. PRO CAB 65/7, WM 133.

53. 3 & 4, Geo 6, Ch. 20, 'Emergency Powers (Defence) Act 1940'.

54. Def. Regs. 2D and 94B in *Defence Regulations Vol. I.*

55. PRO CAB 75/5, HPC(40)19th Meeting.

56. PRO CAB 75/5, HPC(40)22nd Meeting.

57. The Bill passed through all its stages in the House

of Commons in under two hours. See v.361 H.C.DEB 5s cols. 154-185.

58. for the debate see v.363 H.C.DEB 5s cols.1307-50.
59. v. 363 H.C.DEB 5s col.1323.
60. 'News Chronicle', 17 July 1940, p.2.
61. v.363 H.C.DEB 5s col.598.
62. for the debate see v.373 H.C.DEB 5s cols. 941-1024.
63. PRO CAB 75/15, HPC(43)5th, 6th, 9th & 10th Meetings.
64. for the debate see v.391 H.C.DEB 5s cols. 425-536.
65. v.400 H.C.DEB 5s cols. 212-3.
66. v.400 H.C.DEB 5s col. 269.
67. v.386 H.C.DEB 5s cols. 996-1022

Chapter Two

THE INTERNMENT OF ENEMY ALIENS

Of all the changes and developments in government policy during the military crisis of 1940, none had such a dramatic effect or was to provoke such widespread opposition as the policy of general internment of enemy aliens. Until May 1940 about 2,000 of these people had been detained and interned, but by June 1940 this figure was to rise to about 27,000. Several thousand were to remain in detention for long periods of time and, during the summer of 1940, many of them had to endure wretched conditions and face deportation to internment camps established in Canada and Australia. Even when some releases began to occur, the process involved was often complex and mainly applicable to those people who should not have been interned in the first place, or who were considered useful to the war effort.

In this chapter I shall examine the changes in government policy towards enemy aliens, concentrating in particular on the policy of general internment - why it was adopted and its effects - and the extent to which parliamentary opposition to general internment was able to influence policy making.

PRE-WAR PLANNING AND THE ALIENS TRIBUNALS

The question of what measures should be taken against enemy aliens had, like other aspects of emergency planning, been considered well before the outbreak of war. In February 1939, a sub-committee of the Committee for Imperial Defence on the 'Control of Aliens in War' was told that it might become necessary to intern up to 18,000 male enemy aliens and that the rapid internment of such numbers would place great strains on the authorities responsible. [1] In the sub-committee's report to the CID in April 1939 it was stated:

> it is not proposed to undertake an automatic internment of male enemy aliens immediately on the outbreak of war, but we concur in the Home Office view that some measure

> of general internment would become inevitable at a very early date. The War Office has accepted this view and accommodation for 18,000 civilian internees has been earmarked. [2]

The view that general internment would quickly become inevitable stemmed from the anticipation of an immediate German offensive which would generate public hostility towards enemy aliens. In the event such circumstances did not arise, but it is important to recognise that the possibility of general internment had been given serious consideration well before September 1939 - even to the point of making some preparations for it.

On the outbreak of war there were some 74,000 German and Austrians in Britain, all of whom were technically 'enemy aliens'. But the vast majority were refugees who had fled from Nazi Germany and many were only staying in Britain until they could find a country in which to settle. Regulations under the Emergency Powers Act were not necessary to restrict or detain enemy aliens, for such powers were available under the Aliens Acts of 1914 and 1919. [3]

According to government figures, 415 enemy aliens were arrested and interned in the first few days of the war. [4] These arrests were based on a list prepared by MI5. Some were undoubtedly supporters of the Nazi Party, but it has been suggested that a substantial proportion were either Jewish or anti-Nazi and were considered suspicious simply because they were businessmen or journalists. [5] Nevertheless, the vast majority of Germans and Austrians in Britain were treated with rather more consideration in the first few months of the war.

In a statement published in the press on 4 September, all aliens were told to report to the police with their passports and identity papers. Subsequently it was announced that a system of tribunals was to be set up to examine the cases of all those Germans and Austrians still at large in Great Britain. [6] The tribunals, 120 in all, began their work in late September and had completed their task by the end of the year. They classified enemy aliens in two ways: firstly in relation to their status as refugees, either as a 'refugee from Nazi oppression' or as a 'non refugee', and secondly in relation to what was to happen to them. In this second classification there were three categories, 'A', 'B' and 'C'. Those placed in category 'A' were to be interned, and those in category 'B' subject to certain restrictions (normally that they could not travel more than five miles from their home without police permission). Those people placed in category 'C' were to be left unrestricted and, if they were also classified as a 'refugee from Nazi oppression', could have this phrase stamped on their documents rather than the words 'enemy alien'. The Home Office issued confidential instructions to the tribunals which pointed out that it would be wrong to treat all Germans and Austrians as enemies of Britain, [7] and it was also suggested that only those people considered dangerous should be interned. [8] Nevertheless, the aliens' tribunals often interpreted their tasks in peculiar ways.

Francois Lafitte, writing in 1940, said that some tribunals placed all enemy aliens they did not intern into category 'B', while others placed all domestic servants in that category. He added that some tribunals had difficulty in understanding that a non-Jew could be an anti-Nazi refugee, and that such refugees were also often placed in category 'B'. [9] There were problems too for those enemy aliens who had been connected with the political left. The NCCL archives indicate that such people were often classified 'A', and then interned in the same camps as Nazi sympathisers. [10] A letter from Ronald Kidd to Sir Richard Acland on the subject points out that 'All the cases have a family likeness and in many instances the reason for the internment has apparently been that the internee has in some way, often very remotely, been connected with the left wing movement.' [11] How many cases of this sort there may have been is unclear, but Lafitte argued that 'class prejudice and snobbery' lay behind the internment of enemy aliens with left wing connections and that the same factor also ensured that some suspicious and dubious Germans and Austrians were placed in category 'C' because of their high social connections. [12]

Despite these criticisms, the government's scheme was, in general, considered to be fair and efficient [13] and it certainly stood in sharp contrast to the policy that was to be adopted in May and June 1940. Out of approximately 73,000 enemy aliens examined by the tribunals some 64,000 were placed in category 'C', about 6,800 in category 'B', and only 569 in category 'A'. [14] For those enemy aliens interned prior to April 1940, an advisory committee was established to review cases referred to it by the Home Secretary. By February 1940 this committee had examined 162 cases, and in 45 instances this had led to the release of the internee concerned. [15]

Although the tribunals were designed to deal with the bulk of the cases, the government did not depend solely on this procedure. A Home Office circular to Chief Constables in September 1939 made it clear that there were grounds on which the police could detain an enemy alien either prior to, or subsequent to, a tribunal hearing. [16] The grounds cited in the circular were

(i) on receipt of information from MI5
(ii) if a Chief Constable had reason to believe that internment was necessary on the grounds of national security.

A further 900 enemy aliens were detained in this way by March

1940 for, on 21 March, the Home Secretary stated that the total number of enemy aliens who had been interned stood at 1,959. [17]

Thus, although there was a significant number of arbitrary detentions in the first six months of the war, the majority of Germans and Austrians were allowed to remain at liberty without any major restrictions being imposed upon them.

THE POLICY OF GENERAL INTERNMENT

Until the early months of 1940, both the press and public opinion had viewed the plight of the many enemy aliens who were refugees with sympathy and consideration. But by March enemy aliens, as a collective group, were beginning to be portrayed in a new light - as a potential fifth column and a threat to national security. Sections of the press demanded that they should be subjected to far greater restrictions, [18] and a number of backbench Tory MPs echoed these demands in Parliament. On 1 March, for instance, the Home Secretary was asked about the number of enemy aliens still at large, and it was suggested that German and Austrian domestic servants in the Aldershot area were a particular threat to national security. [19] In reply, Sir John Anderson stated:

> I think it is a mistake to assume that every German domestic servant is a menace to the security of this country; and, in my view, there would be no justification for a policy under which all aliens of German and Austrian nationality were treated alike, without regard to the fact that the majority of them are refugees from Nazi oppression and are bitterly opposed to the present regime in Germany. [20]

Despite the fact that the pressure for harsher measures came predominately from the conservative press and political supporters of the government, Anderson's reply appears to typify the government's attitude to such pressure up until May 1940. There is no evidence to suggest that these demands were seriously discussed within government circles until then. But by the beginning of May the fifth column scare was making itself felt in an important quarter: among the military and security authorities. In the weeks that followed, they were to play a crucial role in the formation of government policy.

The first time the possibility of general internment was raised at Cabinet level was after the fall of the Chamberlain government and - more significantly - after the German invasion of the Low Countries had begun. The question was discussed at a special meeting on 11 May consisting of Churchill, Halifax, Chamberlain, and a number of military chiefs. The minutes of the meeting record that the Vice Chief of the Imperial General Staff, Sir John Dill, advised that all enemy aliens in a coastal belt from Nairn to Hampshire should be interned, and that Sir John Anderson, who had been consulted earlier, had said 'that if the case were pressed on military grounds he would agree to it'. [21] The meeting accepted Dill's advice and also instructed Chamberlain to set up a small committee to consider what further measures might be necessary.

The following day, instructions were issued to the police to detain all male enemy aliens in the coastal zone. On 16 or 17 May these instructions were extended to cover all males in Britain aged 16-60 who had been placed in category 'B' by the aliens' tribunals. Sir John Anderson announcing these moves on 23 May, described them as a 'precautionary measure'. He stated that the position would be reviewed as soon as possible. [22]

A few days earlier the Cabinet had considered the memorandum 'The Invasion of Great Britain and the possible co-operation of a 5th column'. [23] This memo, drawn up by the Home Secretary in conjunction with Attlee and Arthur Greenwood, discussed the potential threat posed by enemy aliens in some detail. The memo stated that the intelligence services had not revealed any Nazi plans to plant enemy agents among German and Austrian refugees coming to Britain and that - even if any such a plan existed - it should have been thoroughly disrupted by the measures taken in the previous few days. The memo went on, 'there are very strong objections to wholesale internment' for while it would be welcomed in the short term, 'the inevitably poor treatment' of internees would lead to a sympathetic backlash. Furthermore, wholesale internment would have to be based on the principle that all Germans and Austrians were potentially dangerous which, the memo argued, was not the case. [24]

At least three Ministers supported the views expressed in this memo, but they did not prevail. At a Cabinet meeting on 24 May a demand from the War Office that all enemy aliens should be interned was accepted in principle. It was agreed however that this policy should be implemented in stages. [25] The first step was the detention of all class 'B' German and Austrian women aged 16 - 60 and class 'B' males aged 60-70. Even these measures were not sufficient for the Chiefs of Staff. In a memo prepared for the next Cabinet meeting they warned that alien refugees were 'a most dangerous source of subversive activity' and that 'The most ruthless action should be taken to eliminate any chances of Fifth Column activities'. [26] At the same Cabinet meeting Chamberlain received approval for the establishment of the Home Defence (Security) Executive which, it has been suggested, took control of the policy towards enemy aliens and ensured the dominance of the views of the military and security authorities. [27]

On 10 June, following Italy's entry into the war, the Home Office instructed the police to detain all male Italians aged 16-70 with less than 20 years residence in Britain as well as those Italians, male or female, on MI5s suspect list. Finally, in the last week of June, internment was extended to German and Austrian males aged 16-70 who had been put in category 'C' by the aliens' tribunals.

So, by the end of June, the only collective exceptions to general internment were non-suspect Italian women and non-suspect German and Austrian women in category 'C'. The police, however, had been given special instructions not to detain the 'invalid or infirm', and Anderson stated that special consideration was to be given to male Germans and Austrians in category 'C' who had specialist knowledge useful to the war effort. Altogether it seems that during period May to July 1940 about 22,000 Germans and Austrians and 4,000 Italians were interned. [28]

From the evidence of the Cabinet minutes it is clear that the policy of general internment was introduced because the War Office, the military chiefs and the security services advocated it as a military necessity. This necessity appears to have been based on three main beliefs which can be summarised as follows:

(i) enemy agents could have been planted among Germans and Austrians who had come to Britain
(ii) enemy aliens constituted a serious military threat as a potential 5th column
(iii) pressure could be brought to bear on enemy aliens who had friends and relatives in Germany to act as in (i) or (ii)

Early public explanations of the new policy concentrated on the grounds of military necessity without being specific [29] but from July 1940 a new factor was introduced to justify the adoption of general internment.

On 10 July, when the Under-Secretary of State at the Home Office, Osbert Peake, explained the policy to the House of Commons, he appeared to undermine the argument of military necessity and laid greater emphasis on the role of public opinion. He began by defending enemy aliens, saying that they had been thoroughly screened since entering Britain, and that:

> I can only say, on behalf of the Home Secretary and myself, that I wish we knew half as much about many of the neutral aliens and many British subjects as we know about the enemy aliens now in this country. [30]

Praising their behaviour as a group whilst they had been in Britain he said that although there had been one or two petty incidents, 'there have been no serious cases of acts hostile to the State which can be attributed to these people'. [31] He went on to argue that throughout the winter until early May the government were able to 'resist the clamour to "intern the lot"', [32] but that when the military authorities had asked for the removal of enemy aliens from the coastal belt, it was felt that the more humane policy was to intern the male enemy aliens from these areas temporarily rather than send them as strangers to different regions of the country where they might have received a hostile reception. The switch from temporary internment to a more long term policy was made, he claimed, because a number of new factors emerged. Firstly, the rate of unemployment among enemy aliens was rising because few employers would give them work. Secondly, the government feared physical reprisals against enemy aliens. Thirdly, some enemy aliens had asked to be interned because of growing hostility. It was only as his final point that Peake mentioned that such a move was strongly advocated by the military authorities.

In August 1940, Sir John Anderson also tried to explain the basis for general internment to the House of Commons. While he laid greater stress on the military factors than Peake had done the previous month, he also argued that one of the reasons why the policy was adopted was the government's fear of public hostility towards enemy aliens erupting into physical violence in the event of air raids or invasion. [33]

Anderson and Peake were almost certainly correct in saying that by May and June public opinion had swung against enemy aliens. But was public opinion really a factor in policy making? Lafitte accepts that it was, and argued that the government should not have bowed down to what amounted to a concerted smear campaign by reactionary newspapers. [34] Some MPs, the NCCL and many of the refugee organisations also believed that the government had been stampeded into general internment by public opinion whipped up by the press, and this point was continually raised in documents and speeches criticising government policy.

Yet is seems plausible to see the 'public opinion' explanation as a red herring, intentionally floated by the government to draw public debate away from the question of military necessity. It might even be that Home Office spokesmen were so unconvinced by the military arguments for general internment that they felt unable to defend government policy solely on this basis. The fact that this explanation was not raised until July, and does not appear at all in the available records of government discussions at the time, suggests that it was an afterthought. Also, some aspects of Peake's statement on 10 July are inconsistent with the available records. In relation to the initial internment measures, Peake stated that the military authorities had requested that all aliens be removed from the coastal belt, while the minutes of the meeting on 11 May clearly state that the military had called for the internment of all enemy aliens from the coastal belt. Similarly, Peake claimed that the internment of male enemy aliens from the coastal belt was the most humane policy possible, but the minutes show Anderson only accepting internment if the course was pressed on military grounds.

The military arguments for internment can be reduced to two distinct notions, which by July and August would have looked more like military panic than military strategy. Firstly, there was the notion that all enemy aliens were potentially dangerous. Although this view had been paraded in the press and was a fashionable prejudice in the early months of 1940, it could not stand up to critical analysis. Anderson made this point categorically in the memo submitted to the Cabinet on 18 May, [35] and Home Office spokesmen repeatedly stressed that the vast majority of enemy aliens were refugees from the Nazi regime: the people least likely to aid a Nazi invasion of Britain. Secondly, there was the notion that it was better to intern thousands of innocent people rather than risk a few enemy agents being left at large. Dubious from every point of view except the purely military, this justification must have begun to look brutal and callous as the appalling conditions endured by many internees became known during the summer of 1940.

The available evidence suggests that general internment was adopted solely because the military and security authorities had demanded such actions for the reasons given above. The fact that they should do so is not particularly surprising since their role is to look for potential threats, no matter how improbable, and then suggest solutions satisfactory from the military point of view. What is more important is that the Cabinet were prepared to accede to such demands, despite the fact that senior Ministers had argued that the threat posed by enemy aliens was minimal. So, in the crisis of May - July 1940, it seems that the views of the military and security authorities dominated policy making in this area and that all other considerations were for the time being ignored. Ministers had been warned that if general internment were adopted 'inevitably poor treatment' would follow, but they chose to ignore this warning.

CONDITIONS, CHAOS AND DEPORTATIONS

On paper, the process of interning large numbers of enemy aliens appeared straightforward. The police, with the help of the army, would arrest and detain those groups of people specified in their instructions. Those detained would be passed into the custody of the War Office which would then send them to internment camps on the Isle of Man where their conditions 'should be as little oppressive as possible'. [36] But having adopted general internment as a military expedient the Cabinet do not appear to have seriously considered the enormity of the task to be undertaken or questioned whether the War Office was the most suitable government department to ensure that internees were reasonably treated.

The problems began as soon as the police and army started rounding up the various groups. Sir John Anderson claimed that the police were instructed to give people reasonable facilities to make the necessary arrangements for their detention, [37] but often such facilities were not provided or allowed. Lafitte gives many examples of people being detained without being allowed to contact friends or relatives, or being given only a few minutes to pack and whisked off in the middle of the night. [38] He claims that the police often acted in a manner reminiscent of the Gestapo and contemporary newspaper reports back up this allegation. [39] As I mentioned above, instructions had also been issued that the invalid and infirm should not be detained and that certain category 'C' men with special skills should be exempted, but these instructions, too, seem to have been largely ignored.

The detention of the invalid and infirm was to create long term problems in the internment camps, and the extent to which such detentions occurred can be illustrated by reference to a report by Lord Snell on conditions at the Huyton Camp in Liverpool. The report states that no less than 33 per cent of the inmates were 'unfit in one way or another' and that even cripples and people with serious mental disorders had arrived at the camp. The police, he concludes, should have done better! [40]

Once detained, people were gathered at 'collecting stations' and it was at this point that the administrative chaos, which was to be one of the hallmarks of general internment, began. Because record keeping was neglected, War Office officials did not always know who was in their custody. Personal effects were frequently bundled together and might then be sent to the wrong camp. [41] Furthermore, no-one tried to sort out those people who should not have been detained and have them sent home.

Although all internees were eventually to be sent to permanent camps in the Isle of Man, from May until August 1940 they were being held in various places all over the country. Women were usually sent to prisons which were the responsibility of the Home Office, and their physical environment was generally no worse than that of normal prisoners. Men, on the other hand, were sent to transit camps under the control of the War Office. It was these camps that were to become notorious for their wretched conditions.

Of the twenty or so transit camps set up around the country, several consisted of little more than tents surrounded by barbed wire and armed guards. Others were established in disused factories and racecourse stands. Conditions varied from camp to camp, but Lafitte gives some graphic accounts based largely on the testimony of the internees themselves. The Wharf Mills camp, which Lafitte says was one of the worst, is described as a rat-infested disused factory with a broken glass roof. Eighteen water taps supplied 2,000 internees, and the toilets consisted of sixty buckets in the factory yard. Internees slept on boards, although some of the chronically sick were given straw mattresses. There were no tables or chairs. [42] Other camps were similar, and Lafitte says that there was a dire shortage of bedding, furniture, food and medical supplies everywhere.

Conditions in all camps were at their worst from May to July, but even in August when - according to the Home Office - conditions were being rapidly improved, a tent camp was opened in Sutton Coldfield which Lafitte describes as follows:

> In mid-August, when 800 men were there, there were only plates and cutlery for 300. Men slept directly on ground sheets on the damp earth, without even straw sacks; many of these men were over fifty. [43]

At the same camp medical facilities apparently consisted of a hospital tent, a stethoscope and a supply of aspirin.

Lafitte was a severe critic of both the camp conditions and the policy of general interment, and it might be thought that his description of conditions was exaggerated. But comparison with the description of Huyton Camp in Lord Snell's report to the Cabinet reveals a startling similarity, [44] especially if one considers that the camp was probably cleaned up prior to the official inquiry. The report states that internees were placed in two types of accommodation. A number of small houses slept three or four per room, and were supplied with running water. The rest of the accommodation consisted of tents, each of which housed four internees. Ground sheets were supplied but in wet weather the ground between the tents became muddy and, as the report succinctly states, 'much of it' found its way into the tents. Sanitary arrangements were described as 'unsatisfactory', and under a sub-heading 'furniture', the report notes simply that, at first, there was none. At one point there were 340 beds for 4,000 internees, the rest of the bedding consisting of straw mattresses and blankets. Camp officials apparently tried to get tables and chairs but failed because there 'was a lack of furniture throughout Western Command'. The report states that food was poor and in short supply and that there was a severe shortage of drugs and other medical supplies. There was only one medical officer for the whole camp despite the large number of sick inmates.

Lord Snell's report differs from Lafitte's description to only a minor degree, and during 1940 few people disputed that the conditions in the camps were appalling. The War Office denied that things were as bad as was being suggested, and claimed that the transit camps reached the standard laid down by the Prisoners of War Convention. [45] Lafitte argued that this was manifestly not the case, but even if the War Office had intended this to be so they had missed the crucial point. Firstly, interned enemy aliens were not prisoners of war. But secondly, and more importantly, civilian internees as a population could not be compared with captured soldiers, since a large proportion of them were elderly (up to 70 years old) and many were chronically sick. Lord Snell's report says that 40 per cent of the internees at Huyton Camp were over 50, and many were over 60. The report goes on to say that, although conditions at Huyton were generally in accord with the standards laid down by the Prisoners of War Convention, and that this may be tolerable for healthy soldiers, these conditions 'may well be insupportable to elderly internees (who formed the large majority) even when healthy'. [46] The report concludes:

> the War Office should have been able to foresee the presence of large numbers of elderly people and should have provided greater corresponding amenities. Even when this was appreciated, the Army machine appears to have been unable to adjust itself quickly to changed circumstances. [47]

In the language of government reports, this was a severe indictment of the War Office and makes it clear that conditions could have been much better had the War Office applied itself to serious consideration of internees' welfare.

What makes this far worse is that as early as April 1939 plans were being prepared to intern 18,000 male enemy aliens. So the lack of organisation and the appalling conditions can hardly be ascribed to the rapid adoption of a policy which had never been previously considered. The only credit which emerges from this sordid account is that conditions in the permanent camps on the Isle of Man were better than those described and most internees had reached them by the end of August 1940.

So far, I have only considered the physical conditions which internees faced during the first months of general internment, but other aspects of their treatment both in the transit camps and in the permanent camps on the Isle of Man led to severe criticisms. While some of these stemmed from the difficulties of implementing the policy, others were caused by the government's continuing concern with security.

I mentioned the administrative chaos that occurred at the collecting stations, and this followed detainees into the camps. With changing camp populations, officials failed to keep up-to-date records and often had no idea of who was in their charge. [48] The result was that central government departments were unable to trace specific individuals and the Home Office admitted this on a number of occasions. [49] For internees this meant that communication with the outside world was very difficult. Sometimes only the internee was able to tell relatives and friends where he was. Even then letters sent back to him might be returned or re-directed because officials were not aware that he was at the camp. More disconcerting were cases of internees whose release had been authorised but who remained in detention simply because they could not be found. Such confusion existed in most camps to a greater or lesser degree in the summer of 1940 and was often cleared up only after the internees themselves had sorted out personal details and set up record systems.

The difficulty of communication was compounded by the system of censorship. Internees were allowed to send two letters a week and receive any number, but all correspondence had to pass through the censor, resulting in long delays. In August, Osbert Peake admitted that over 100,000 letters were held up at the censorship offices in Liverpool, some of which had been posted three to four weeks previously. [50] This was a problem which was never satisfactorily solved for even in 1941 complaints were still being made in Parliament about undue delays.

Another long-term problem was the mixing of Nazi sympathisers and anti-Nazi refugees who were often Jewish. This had first arisen when some refugees had been placed in category 'A' by the aliens' tribunals. The government had promised that this would be rectified, but when general internment was adopted further groups of refugees were placed in camps and prisons with predominantly pro-Nazi internees. Again complaints were still being made in 1941 that the government had failed to implement their policy of separation.

In line with Anderson's assurance that the treatment of internees should be as little oppressive as possible, some camps, particularly those on the Isle of Man, allowed internees a degree of freedom of movement and they soon set up a variety of recreational and educational groups. But, in one important area, blanket restrictions were imposed. Until July 1940, newspapers, radios and books were prohibited and this, together with the operation of the censorship, imposed a total news blackout. The decision to impose this ban was taken by the Cabinet on 24 May on the grounds that internees (and thus perhaps enemy agents) should not have access to information through which national security could be threatened. [51] Lafitte argued that this ban was a particularly cruel measure which led to wild rumours in the internment camps and severely depressed the morale of refugees. He claims that many refugees saw the ban, together with the shortages and conditions, as indications that Britain had already been invaded and they feared that a surrendering British government might return them to the Nazis. Lord Snell's report confirmed that the blackout at Huyton had a bad effect on morale and describes it as both 'unwise and unnecessary'. [52] Once again it appears that the Cabinet were prepared to sacrifice the welfare of internees for a minimal - if not illusory - benefit in terms of national security.

One final aspect of the treatment of internees which requires discussion is the policy of deportation. The policy was introduced after Lord Swinton, head of the Home Defence (Security) Executive, had warned Chamberlain of the dangers of keeping so many enemy aliens in the country. [53] In 'Collar the Lot', the Gillmans imply that Swinton's committee was largely responsible for the decision and say that the Cabinet were effectively presented with a fait accompli on 11 June when Chamberlain informed them that Canada had agreed to take 7,000 men. [54] The original intention appears to have been to deport those civilian internees considered most dangerous. The reality was quite different. By 15 July, 2,700 category 'B' and 'C' internees had arrived in Canada and many more were to arrive in Australia after enduring the Dunera voyage. [55] Some people volunteered, but the remainder were selected at random and compulsorily deported. Some were sent overseas without being given the chance to inform their relatives, and Lafitte says that scores of boys aged 16 and 17 who had 'volunteered' were deported without their parents even being informed. [56]

Ironically, it was the sinking of a ship carrying so-called dangerous enemy aliens which came to highlight not only the plight of reluctant deportees from the 'B' and 'C' categories but also the plight of internees in general and the administrative chaos surrounding them. On 2 July, the 'Arandora Star', carrying about 1,500 deportees to Canada, was torpedoed and sunk in the Atlantic. Out of 1,900 people on board only 600 survived. The announcement on the radio the next day was the first public admission that internees were being shipped overseas, but it was claimed that all those internees on board were Nazi sympathisers and Italian fascists, a claim that was to highlight the incompetence of War Office administrators.

After some probing questions in the House of Commons, it was firstly established that many of the Germans and Austrians on board were category 'A' enemy aliens, [57] which did not necessarily mean that they were Nazi sympathisers. Lafitte gives a list of prominent 'anti-fascists' who had been shipped on the 'Arandora Star', some of whom had died. [58] Suspicions were also raised about the selection of 'Italian fascists' when reports filtered through that a number of apparently respectable non-fascist Italians were amongst the dead.

On 10 July, Peake admitted that the War Office, who were responsible for arranging deportations, had only a nominal roll of those who were supposed to be on board, [59] and in August Attlee told the Commons that Lord Snell had been asked to undertake an inquiry into the selection of aliens for the 'Arandora Star'. The report, which was submitted to the Cabinet in November 1940, [60] pointed out that Cabinet instructions regarding deportation had not been specifically limited to 'dangerous characters' but that, of the 473 Germans and Austrians on board, 123 were captured merchant seamen and the other 350 had either been interned as Nazis or had been classified category 'A' by the aliens' tribunals. The report did not criticise this form of selection but did question the form of selection of Italian deportees. It stated that, since Italians had not gone before the aliens' tribunals, selection had been based on MI5s list of 'dangerous characters' which was based mainly on membership of the Italian fascist party. According to the report, 26 Italians shipped on the 'Arandora Star' had not been on MI5s list and a number of Italians who had been on that list had not been members of the fascist party. The numbers involved in this latter category were not specified, but the example was given of one man who had lived in England for 20 years and was Secretary of the Italian section of the League of the Rights of Man. He was not a member of the fascist party but was on MI5s list. He was shipped on the 'Arandora Star' and drowned. Despite cases such as this, the report concluded that the errors that occured were not cause for major criticism. The Cabinet minutes record that MI5s method of picking dangerous Italians was noted and that the meeting was reminded that Swinton's committee had executive responsibility for MI5. The meeting concluded, however, that since no undertaking to publish the report had been given, publication should not occur in order to avoid a revival of interest in the matter. [61]

THE GROWTH OF OPPOSITION AND THE GOVERNMENT RESPONSE

The various stages of general internment were initially welcomed both by the press and in Parliament. During May and much of June only a handful of MPs, the NCCL and refugee organisations questioned the ethics of interning thousands of people, most of whom were known to be refugees. But as reports of camp conditions and individual hardship emerged, and then the 'Arandora Star' was sunk, more and more people began to criticise and question government policy. In Parliament, much of the criticism took the form of questions and it became unusual for question time to pass without at least one reference to the internment of aliens. [62]

The first major challenge to the government's policy came on 10 July, just a week after the 'Arandora Star' had been sunk. During question time Peake was asked whether the Home Office would take over total responsibility for internees, and whether there was to be a review of the government's general policy. The Under-Secretary answered both questions in the negative, [63] but the same day Major Cazalet and Eleanor Rathbone were able to raise the whole issue on the Adjournment of the House. [64] They launched an attack both on the principle of general internment and the treatment of internees. Miss Rathbone pointed out that a number of Members had wanted to raise the issue for some time but had been restrained, partly by a realisation of the strain and pressure the government faced, and partly by a reluctance to raise an issue which reflected unfavourably on the country's reputation. She said however that the matter now had to be raised because of the:

> mass of evidence pouring in upon all of us of the widespread misery and fear suffered by refugees, many of them anxious to serve our country's cause, and also the waste of labour and talent and the clogging of the machine, which arises from the present system. [65]

Many speakers referred to evidence relating to the way in which people had been detained, the conditions and treatment in the camps and the policy of deportation, but two particular themes of criticism can be isolated. Firstly, although the necessity of security measures was recognised and accepted, there was a widespread belief that internment should be limited to those enemy aliens against whom there was some specific suspicion, and that there was no possible rational basis for interning people who were known to be loyal to the allied cause, or were refugees. The second theme concerned the role of the War Office. It was known that the military authorities had strongly advocated general internment and it had become apparent that the War Office were also responsible for the management of the internment camps and thus the treatment of male internees. It was argued not only that this department had panicked, but that it was also insensitive to the needs of internees who, being mostly refugees, should not be subjected to conditions similar to Nazi concentration camps.

Two Under-Secretaries of State replied for the government: Peake from the Home Office and Sir James Grigg from the War Office. Peake, as I mentioned earlier, tried to justify the policy of general internment more in terms of hostile public opinion than military necessity, but he accepted that hardship and suffering were being caused and argued that the government were trying to implement the policy as fairly and humanely as possible. Grigg, on the other hand, while reiterating the government's concern for the welfare of refugees, took a harder line. He expressed his amazement that MPs could consider the question of enemy aliens with such detachment, and asked members to put themselves in the place of the men who were responsible for the security of the country. He implied that some of the critics of the government were trying to create 'alarm and despondency', and that enemy aliens had no more to complain about than many other sections of society which had been inconvenienced during the course of the war. In conclusion he stated:

> Although thousands have been interned, the number of really hard cases is very small. The system, I admit, has of necessity been rough and ready but, unfortunately, that is a hard necessity in war. We shall try to make it less rough. I am sure the House will agree that it is better, in a situation of the kind in which the country now finds itself, to be rough and ready, than to be soft and unready. [66]

Although no concessions were offered during the course of the debate Attlee was prompted to raise the matter at a Cabinet meeting the next day. He reported that there had been 'some disquiet' in the House, and questioned whether the War Office might be relieved of the responsibilities for the internment camps. [67] More importantly perhaps, some Ministers appear to have been shocked when they received information concerning conditions in some of the camps. Chamberlain told the Cabinet, for instance, that he was disturbed by the large number of complaints reaching him about conditions. He specifically mentioned the lack of bedding, the problems of the chronically sick and the question of maladministration, arguing that the policy must be rectified. [68]

On a more personal note, Sir Archibald Sinclair, the Secretary of State for Air, said in an interview with W.P. Crozier:

> I know that many dreadful things have happened; I know of some of them myself. There's a family that my wife and I know personally. A boy belonging to it was taken from school and interned. His mother, distracted, did not know where he had gone and appealed to my wife. My wife rang up Osbert Peake...who was very decent and promised to get the boy out. After a fortnight the mother rang up again and said they had heard nothing more about the boy. My wife got Peake again and he said 'I'm frightfully sorry, I can't tell you how sorry, but, you know, we can't find the boy. He's lost'. [69]

Between 17 and 22 July, the Cabinet reconsidered their policy [70] and as well as hearing Chamberlain's reference to camp conditions, they were also told by Sir John Anderson that the policy of not interning the invalid or infirm had gone wrong and that the War Office were at their wit's end in trying to find accommodation for internees. Discussion at these meetings, however, was concentrated on two memoranda from Attlee [71] which argued that only those enemy aliens whose usefulness outweighed the security risks involved should be released, and that the principle of general internment should be maintained. To deal with the problems of conditions and treatment of internees, Attlee suggested that two advisory bodies should be established to help the Home Office in respect of welfare and morale.

On 18 July the Cabinet agreed that the management of the internment camps should be transferred to the Home Office and that an inquiry should be set up to examine the selection procedure for the 'Arandora Star'. On the 22nd they approved the proposals for the two advisory bodies and agreed to an inquiry into the conditions at the Huyton Internment Camp.

In a statement to the House of Commons on 23 July, Anderson announced most of these measures. An advisory committee, later known as the 'Asquith Committee', was:

(i) to keep under review the application of the principles laid down in regard to the internment of enemy aliens and to make to the Home Secretary such suggestions and recommendations thereon as they think fit.
(ii) to advise the Home Secretary on such proposals for modifying the internment policy as he may refer to them from time to time; and
(iii) to examine, and make recommendations upon, such individual cases or groups of cases as may be referred to them...by the Home Secretary. [72]

The other body, an 'Advisory Council', was to advise the Home Office on arrangements for the welfare of internees, to suggest measures for maintaining the morale of aliens and to investigate the problem of finding occupations for aliens in internment camps. When this council was set up in August 1940 it was headed by Lord Lytton, and included prominent opponents of the government's policy including Eleanor Rathbone and Graham White. [73]

On the face of it, the committee and council seemed to have considerable scope both in terms of the general policy and the welfare of internees. But they were only advisory and the Home Secretary stressed that, although mistakes were to be rectified and the categories of persons eligible for release might be enlarged, the policy of general internment was to be maintained. [74]

The extent to which these changes were of a consolidating nature rather than a dramatic reversal of policy is clearly illustrated by a White Paper published at the end of July. It dealt with the categories of persons eligible for release and the procedures to be followed in applying for release. [75] A number of categories simply restated exemptions which should have applied in the first place. Persons under 16 and over 70 years of age were eligible as were 'the invalid or infirm' and people who occupied key positions in industries engaged in work of national importance. Most of the other categories specified particular skills useful to the war effort, such as doctors, dentists, skilled agricultural workers and employers who employed more than twelve British subjects. The few exceptions to this 'usefulness' approach were little more than common-sense additions. Persons who had a British-born or naturalised son serving in the Armed Forces were eligible for release as were 'Persons who having served in His Majesty's Forces...have been discharged...on grounds not reflecting on their loyalty to this country or their personal character'! [76] The only general category of eligibility provided for the release of an internee who had been accepted for enlistment in the Auxiliary Pioneer Corps, but here again the importance of 'usefulness' is apparent.

It should be stressed that all of these categories were only applicable to class 'C' Germans and Austrians, so that even internees over 70 years old or chronically sick could not apply for release if they were Italian or a category 'B' internee. Thus, the White Paper was not even aimed at rectifying all the mistakes that had been made. Furthermore, it stated 'It must be understood that the release of a person who falls within one of the categories may nevertheless be refused on security grounds.' [77]

Even if an internee fell into one of the categories of the White Paper and had his case cleared by the Security Services, this did not necessarily mean that he could expect an early release from internment. Some of the procedures for release were not only cumbersome but laid down provisions which either restricted eligibility further or simply could not be met. Take for example the procedure set out in relation to category six - that is, persons who occupied key positions in industries engaged in work of national importance. The White Paper stated that:

> application for release should not be made direct to the Home Office. The firm concerned should certify that the work in which the alien was engaged was work of national importance, that he cannot be replaced by a British subject, and that his detention prejudicially affects the national war effort. This certificate should be presented to the Divisional Controller of the Ministry of Labour who will arrange for the necessary enquiries to be made, with a view to a report being furnished to the Government Department concerned with the industry. The Department will inform the Home Office of the result of enquiries, and will state whether or not the alien comes within this category. [78]

Even in the later months of 1940 it was difficult for internees to contact their relatives by letter. To correspond with one's former employer and persuade him to apply for a person's release through this complicated procedure would seem to have been a difficult - if not impossible - task.

The utilitarian nature of the provisions for release should not detract from what appears to have been a genuine desire on the part of at least some Cabinet Ministers to make rapid improvements in the physical conditions in the camps. But how far these rapid improvements were actually achieved is open to question. The measures agreed by the Cabinet in this area - the transfer of control of camps to the Home Office and the establishment of the Advisory Council - did not automatically guarantee that conditions would improve, and there is some evidence to suggest that even by August and September not all internees enjoyed the facilities of the permanent camps on the Isle of Man, or that their treatment had become 'as little oppressive as possible'.

The whole question of general internment was debated again by the House of Commons on 22 August, and criticism of the government's policy came from MPs of all parties. [79] While it was accepted that improvements in conditions were being made, it was argued, particularly by Sir Richard Acland, that the government were dragging their heels. Why, he asked, were men of 60 and 70 still sleeping on ground sheets in tented accommodation? And why were food and medical supplies still totally inadequate two months after the last batch of enemy aliens had been detained? He suggested that if Britain captured 20,000 prisoners of war they would be fed in accordance with standards for prisoners of war within a week. Why could this not be done with friendly internees? The Conservative MP, Major Cazalet, also mentioned that elderly men were living under canvas at Sutton Park and Pree's Heath, and criticisms were also made of the continued mixing of pro-Nazi sympathisers and Jewish refugees, the difficulties of communicating with internees and restrictions still imposed in some camps on books, newspapers and wirelesses.

Answering these accusations, Peake claimed that, although such complaints were undoubtedly pertinent six or seven weeks previously, by and large MPs' information was out of date and conditions had improved enormously. He admitted however that the two camps at Sutton Coldfield and Pree's Heath were inadequate and said that they were to be evacuated. He added that conditions would be further alleviated by a substantial number of releases which he anticipated in the next few weeks.

In making this latter suggestion the Under-Secretary was addressing himself to the main criticisms of government policy, for the majority of the speakers concentrated their attention on the overall policy of general internment and the provisions for release made in the July White Paper. The arguments made in the previous debate - that the policy of general internment should be reversed and that only those people against whom there was particular suspicion should be detained - were restated, and a number of speakers attacked the over-riding concern with 'usefulness' in the White Paper. Major Cazalet did not object to releasing internees according to categories, providing those categories actually applied to people who were interned. His general position, which probably commanded the support of a majority of MPs and public opinion by August 1940, was that all those internees whose honesty, patriotism and loyalty were beyond question should be released. He concluded:

> Frankly, I shall not feel happy, either as an Englishman or as a supporter of this Government, until this bespattered page of our history has been cleaned up and rewritten. [80]

Sir John Anderson refused to accept that the policy of general internment should be abandoned, resurrecting the view that there might be a few enemy agents masquerading as friendly aliens, and implying that the military authorities still felt that general internment was necessary if the threatened invasion occured. He stated:

> So long as the danger of invasion is a reality - and we have been told that it still is - we must maintain, in substance, the policy of general internment.

But he added:

> That does not mean that we ought not to do, and do speedily, all we can to alleviate the situation. [81]

Anderson then announced a number of amendments to the release policy which had been recommended by the Asquith Committee. These were incorporated in a new White Paper published before the end of August. [82] The main points of the amendments were that:

(i) persons over the age of 65 became eligible for release.

(ii) Category 'B' Germans and Austrians could be released under the White Paper categories providing that, after application, an advisory committee re-classified them into category 'C'.

(iii) Italians could apply for release under the categories of the White Paper, their cases to be examined by another Advisory Committee.

(iv) A new category for release was included which stated that a person might be released if:

'enough is known of his history to show that by his writings or speeches or political or official

> activities he has consistently, over a period of years, taken a public and prominent part in opposition to the Nazi system and is actively friendly towards the Allied cause'. [83]

Although these amendments extended eligibility for release to class 'B' Germans and Austrians and interned Italians, there was little attempt to go beyond the principles of the earlier White Paper - that is to rectify mistakes and to release some of those internees who would be useful to the war effort. The new category, which appears to be an exception to this rule, was worded to ensure that its application was extremely limited, and communists were specifically excluded from its scope. [84] In fact, up to 8 February 1941, only 145 internees were released under this category. [85]

Before moving on to consider the next step in government policy it is worth considering where the policy of general internment had gone between May and October 1940 simply in terms of the numbers involved. This is not an easy task since the figures given by government spokesmen by no means tally with each other. For convenience I will start by taking one of the more comprehensive sets of figures given to the House of Commons by the Home Secretary on 10 October 1940. [86] He stated that approximately 22,000 Germans and Austrians had been interned in this country, some 6,600 of whom had subsequently been deported. Almost 4,600 Germans and Austrians had been released, leaving about 11,000 interned in Britain. We know that about 4,000 Italians were also interned, and on 17 October Morrison stated that altogether some 5,200 internees had been released. Thus, out of a total number of internees of about 26,000 it seems that about 20 per cent had been released by mid-October 1940, fewer in fact than had been deported. On the basis of these figures it is difficult to understand Peake's claim on 22 August that he expected a substantial number of releases in the next few weeks.

By the Autumn of 1940 it seems the Cabinet were prepared to adopt a more flexible policy towards releases, continuing the utilitarian approach, but providing loopholes to enable most internees to at least apply for release. On 21 November, the new Home Secretary, Herbert Morrison, submitted a memorandum to the Cabinet on policy towards releases. [87] The memo noted that the Joint Intelligence Sub-Committee and the Home Defence (Security) Executive believed that there should be no relaxation of the principles of general internment and that, in cases where release was proposed, security and military considerations should remain the first priority. It added however that these considerations were difficult to reconcile with the wellbeing of friendly enemy aliens. The memo stated that the Asquith Committee had been considering these matters and had recommended that men over 50 should be eligible for release as well as any enemy aliens who had been rejected from service in the Pioneer Corps on medical grounds but had shown some friendliness towards the allied cause. The Cabinet agreed that the 'rough and ready' measures of the summer could be relaxed and approved the recommendations. [88]

When Morrison announced the new measures to the House of Commons the logic of this new approach was revealed. [89] Although the principle of general internment remained, internees over the age of 50 would become eligible for release and the upper age limit for enlistment in the Pioneer Corps was fifty. The way those people under the age of fifty could demonstrate their friendliness to the allied cause was to apply for enlistment in the Pioneer Corps. Those who were accepted could be transferred to vital war work and those who were rejected on medical grounds would be eligible for release since, by applying for the Pioneer Corps, they could be considered to have demonstrated their friendliness to Britain and the war effort. In the debate on the King's Speech, Morrison said 'I will sort them out and get them out as quickly as I can.' [90] The reality was, however, somewhat different.

Firstly, the release policy was still essentially based on the concept of rectifying mistakes and on an individual's usefulness. Secondly, releases could still be refused on security grounds. In February 1941 it was announced that just over 11,000 enemy aliens had been released, an increase of about 6,000 over the figure given in October 1940. But of these 11,000, almost 5,000 had been released under category 3 of the White Papers as invalid or infirm. [91] Out of 27,000 internees, nearly 60 per cent remained in detention in February 1941. A proportion of these, probably about 3,000, were classified as category 'A', and no doubt some internees were unwilling to apply for release via the Pioneer Corps because they were pacifists. But this still left many thousands of internees who were not specifically considered dangerous and who, according to Morrison's announcement in November, should have been able to apply for release. In fact many had, but approximately 7,000 applications had been refused as 'not falling within the categories'. [92]

The explanation for all this would appear to be that MI5 exercised a veto over individual releases and that their view of a security risk was far wider at this stage than that held by tribunals established to consider cases for release. I noted previously that the Security Executive had argued against any relaxation of the principle of general internment and practical effect may have been given to this view by the consistent opposition to release on grounds of security. In January 1941, after Lord Lytton, Chairman of the Advisory Council, had twice offered his resignation because his Committee's recommendations for release were being over-ridden by MI5, [93] Churchill wrote:

I have heard from various quarters that the witch-finding activities of MI5 are becoming an actual impediment to the more important work of the department. I am carefully considering certain changes, not only in MI5 but in the Intelligence and Secret Service control...It would be a great pity if Lord Lytton's resignation had to be accepted...and it seems altogether wrong that his judgement and that of his Committee should not have been made effective, in the majority of cases...I have no doubt that there is a certain amount of risk that some bad people may get loose but our dangers are so much less now than they were in May and June... that I am sure a more rapid and general process of release from internment should be adopted. [94]

Unfortunately, because the activities and control of the Security Services remain shrouded in secrecy, there is no evidence available to indicate whether their influence in respect of releases was reduced from 1941. What is apparent, however, is that by then the government no longer accepted that the principle of general internment was a military necessity and that, as Churchill put it, a more rapid and general process of release should be adopted.

There was a good reason why this should be so. Not only had the threat of invasion receeded, another factor - the potential shortage of manpower for industrial production - was becoming increasingly important and enemy aliens were a significant pool of untapped labour. Like millions of British citizens, those enemy aliens who had been released from internment could, from 1941, be called to register at employment exchanges and directed to jobs in war industries. [95]

By November 1941, 3,695 enemy aliens remained interned in Britain according to figures given to the House of Commons. [96] But even then this was not the full picture. About 5,000 or so male enemy aliens were still interned in the Dominions in November 1941, approximately half of whom were either category 'B' or 'C' Germans and Austrians, or Italians. As releases in Britain proceeded the refugee lobby in Parliament concentrated its attention on deportees, trying to ensure that those internees, who would have been released had they been in Britain, were either released in the Dominions or could return to Britain if they so desired. Deported internees could apply for release under the categories of the White Papers but, up to February 1941, only 411 such releases had occurred, [97] and it seems that a return to Britain was a pre-requisite for release. The problem was that although the British government were ostensibly responsible for the policy towards internees in the Dominions they did not expect the Canadian or Australian governments to release internees into those countries. The government's policy therefore seems to have been that those people most eligible for release would gradually be returned to Britain when shipping was available. In July 1941 the House of Commons was told that 891 internees had returned from Canada or Australia, and 579 of these had already been released. A further 481 were to be returned and in addition, 196 were on their way from Australia. [98] It was not until January 1942 that the Australian government announced a scheme whereby certain internees could be released in that country to help with the war effort. [99]

With the exception of the policy towards deportees, by mid-1941 most MPs were reasonably satisfied both with the treatment of those enemy aliens who remained interned and with the speed with which internees were being released. Specific questions were still raised concerning such things as delays and censorship of mail, but far less parliamentary time was devoted to the issue in general than in the preceeding fourteen months. But to what extent had the government's policy been influenced by opposition in Parliament when it had been at its strongest, and how had this occurred?

It seems from the evidence available that, by their barrage of parliamentary questions, criticisms in debates, and the passing on of dossiers and reports, certain MPs had made Ministers face up to the conditions internees faced between May and August 1940 and examine the extent to which administration had broken down during the period. In so far as some Ministers appear to have been shocked by these revelations and the government tried to begin rectifying physical conditions and the administrative chaos, parliamentary criticism certainly had an impact. The importance of this should not be underestimated, for it seems that some of the worst aspects of conditions and treatment were alleviated more rapidly than would otherwise have been the case.

On the other hand, the effect of parliamentary opposition in terms of the government's general policy was limited. Once the principle of general internment had been adopted it was never really abandoned. Even after Morrison had announced that he would sort them out and get them out quickly, releases were still based on certain categories, and the government were not forced to revert to the pre-May 1940 policy whereby only those people who were individually regarded as suspicious or dangerous should remain interned.

COMMENTARY

It could no doubt be argued that the release policy embodied in the White Papers and the establishment of the advisory bodies were a significant advance which had been forced by parliamentary opposition. But I would suggest that they can be more realistically assessed as palliatives:

designed to appease opposition, but to have a relatively minor effect. As I said earlier, most of the White Paper categories were either aimed at rectifying mistakes which should not have occurred in the first place, or providing a means by which some of those internees most useful to the war effort could be released.

In Chapter One I discussed the political difficulties which opposition to the coalition government had to face, and these were equally applicable to this issue. They were, however, compounded by an added factor which must be taken into account - the pressure on Ministers from the military and security wings of the government to maintain the policy of general internment.

The influence of the military and security authorities cannot be underestimated. Not only were they the prime advocates of general internment between May and July 1940, they also argued and fought for a continuation of that policy until at least the end of 1940. The military justification for general internment was always of dubious validity but, between May and July 1940, it could be seen as a panic reaction to the dire circumstance of the time. Yet the argument of military necessity continued to be pressed after the crisis of the early summer had passed, and after there had been both the time and the opportunity to make further investigations into the background and credentials of any individual enemy alien considered suspicious. It would seem therefore that, in the autumn of 1940, the military and security authorities were prepared to advocate a long term policy of general internment on the basis that there might be enemy aliens who might act as enemy agents but who could not be detected by the security forces, despite the detailed information available. Such an argument is so tenuous as to suggest that there were other reasons involved. The most likely candidate is prejudice. Quite clearly the military and security authorities shared the views expressed in the press campaign in the spring of 1940 and believed that all enemy aliens should be interned on principle. Perhaps their attitude was best summed up by Lord Swinton, speaking on the question of aliens in the House of Lords in 1946. He referred to his 'considerable responsibility and experience' in this area and stated 'As for the scum, quite rightly we put lots of them inside at the critical time, but a great many of them did not really matter very much.' [100]

As for the Cabinet, the decision to adopt general internment must again be placed in the context of the panic that was rife between May and July 1940. Government spokesmen always denied that it was a panic measure, but at least one Minister admitted privately that this was more or less the case. [101] This does not of course excuse the lamentable treatment of internees, especially in view of the pre-war plans for general internment. It is a sobering reflection that a government can, without resorting to the use of emergency powers, incarcerate thousands of innocent people, having been warned that such steps would cause suffering and hardship. But what is perhaps of greater significance is that the government were not prepared to reverse their overall policy after the immediate panic had passed. Beyond the demands of the military and security authorities there were probably more complex reasons for this stance. If the government had abandoned general internment in the late summer of autumn of 1940, this would have been interpreted by many as an admission that the policy had been wrong in the first place and that the government had indeed panicked. Furthermore, such a move would have also raised doubts about the credibility and sanity of the military authorities. For this reason alone the government may have wished to avoid a rapid change of policy. Thus, internees may have become pawns in a process of maintaining the image of both the government and the military chiefs.

Criticism of detention without trial has usually centred on the point that individuals should not be detained on grounds of suspicion or for political or other reasons. In the case of enemy aliens however the government went far beyond this. Only a small minority of enemy aliens were ever detained because they, as individuals, were regarded with suspicion. The vast majority of enemy aliens were never suspected of anything and it was accepted that they were largely innocent refugees. They were detained simply because they were German, Austrian, or Italian - detained, not as individuals, but part of that collective group: enemy aliens.

Chapter Two: Notes

1. PRO CAB 16/211, Memo CAW 12, February 1939.
2. PRO CAB 16/211, Memo CAW 21, April 1939.
3. 4 & 5 Geo. 5 c.12 'The Aliens Restriction Act 1914' and 9 & 10 Geo 5 c.92 'The Aliens Restriction (Amendment) Act 1919'.
4. v.356 H.C.DEB 5s cols. 1270-1.
5. P and L. Gillman, Collar the Lot, (Quartet Books, 1980) pp. 30 & 33.
6. see 'The Times', 4 September & 26 September 1939.
7. B. Wasserstein Britain & The Jews of Europe 1939-45 (Institute of Jewish Affairs/Oxford U.P., 1979) p. 85.
8. For more details see Gillmans, Collar the Lot, pp. 43-5.
9. F. Lafitte, The Internment of Aliens, (Penguin, 1940) pp. 62-5.
10. NCCL Archives, Filing Case No. 17, Section 2, 'Aliens'.
11. Ibid.

12. Lafitte, *Internment of Aliens*, p. 64
13. Ibid, p. 63
14. v.357 H.C.DEB 5s cols. 2410-1.
15. v.356 H.C.DEB 5s cols. 1270-1.
16. PRO HO 158/31, circular to Chief Constables referenced 'Internment (EA)'.
17. v.358 H.C.DEB 5s col.2107.
18. Lafitte, *Internment of Aliens*, discusses this campaign pp.165-177. So too does A. Stevens, *The Dispossessed - German Refugees in Britain*, (Barrie and Jenkins, 1975) pp.171-6.
19. v.357 H.C.DEB 5s cols.2410-1. For a similar question see also v.358 H.C.DEB 5s col.2107.
20. v.357 H.C.DEB 5s col.2410-1.
21. PRO CAB 65/7, WM 119A.
22. v.361 H.C.DEB 5s cols. 293-4.
23. Meeting, PRO CAB 65/7, WM 128 and Memorandum PRO CAB 67/6, WP(G)(40)131.
24. PRO CAB 67/6, WP(G)(40)131. The evidence from this memorandum, and the minutes of the meeting of ministers on the 11 May, makes nonsense of the claim that it was Anderson who pressed for the internment of aliens. See R. Skidelsky, *Oswald Mosley*, (Macmillan, 1975) p.446.
25. PRO CAB 65/7, WM 137.
26. quoted in Gillman's, *Collar the Lot*, p. 141. They cite CAB 66/7, WP(40)168.
27. Ibid. p.145.
28. It is extremely difficult to establish how many German and Austrians were interned in total, since figures given by government spokesmen varied considerably. This is probably accounted for by the administrative confusion which existed throughout the summer months and I have therefore taken this figure from a comprehensive breakdown given in Parliament in October 1940. see v.365 H.C.DEB 5s col. 488. The figures given by Lafitte only exceed this figure by about a thousand. Lafitte, *Internment of Aliens*, p.74. It should also be borne in mind that many refugees had re-emigrated between September and May 1940. The figures for the number of Italians interned was given in the House of Commons v.400 H.C.DEB 5s col. 1064.
29. see for instance v.362 H.C.DEB 5s col.222 and col.1016.
30. v.362 H.C.DEB 5s col. 1236.
31. Ibid.
32. v.362 H.C.DEB 5s col. 1237.
33. v.364 H.C.DEB 5s col. 1546.
34. Lafitte, *Internment of Aliens*, pp.165-177.
35. PRO CAB 67/6, WP(G)(40)131, 'The Invasion of Great Britain and the Possible Co-operation of a Fifth Column'.
36. v.362 H.C.DEB 5s col.1318.
37. v.362 H.C.DEB 5s col.1016.

38. Lafitte, Internment of Aliens, p.71 and pp.75-6, and see also Stevens, The Dispossesed, pp. 183-5.

39. see for instance 'The Times', 17 May 1940.

40. PRO CAB 66/13, WP(40)463. Report to the Cabinet from Lord Snell regarding the conditions at the Huyton Internment Camp. Submitted to the Cabinet 28 November 1940.

41. Lafitte, Internment of Aliens, p.97-8.

42. Ibid, pp.101-2.

43. Ibid, p.104.

44. PRO CAB 66/13, WP(40)463.

45. v.362 H.C.DEB 5s col.1370.

46. PRO CAB 66/13, WP(40)463.

47. Ibid.

48. Lafitte, Internment of Aliens p.98.

49. See for example the interview between W.P. Crozier and the Secretary of State for Air, cited below and v.363 H.C.DEB 5s col.1385.

50. v.364 H.C.DEB 5s cols.1580-1.

51. PRO CAB 65/7, WM 137.

52. PRO CAB 66/13, WP(40)463.

53. PRO CAB 66/13, WP(40)432. Report by Lord Snell on the method of selection of deportees to be shipped on the 'Arandora Star'. Submitted to the Cabinet 7 November 1940.

54. Gillmans, Collar the Lot, Ch. 15.

55. Ibid, Ch. 22.

56. Lafitte, Internment of Aliens, p.134.

57. See v.362 H.C.DEB 5s cols. 1074-6 & v.363 H.C.DEB 5s col. 12-13 & col.1178.

58. Lafitte, Internment of Aliens, pp.126-8.

59. v.362 H.C.DEB 5s col.1244.

60. PRO CAB 66/13, WP(40)432.

61. PRO CAB 65/10, WM 284, 7 November 1940. A carefully revised copy of the report was eventually published see Cmd. 6238.

62. v.366 H.C.DEB 5s, 'General Index', Heading 'Aliens', sub-heading 'Cases'.

63. v.362 H.C.DEB 5s cols.1155-6.

64. for debate see v.362 H.C.DEB 5s cols. 1207-1306

65. v.362 H.C.DEB 5s col.1211.

66. v.362 H.C.DEB 5s col.1302.

67. PRO CAB 65/8, WM 200.

68. PRO CAB 65/8, WM 207.

69. W.P. Crozier, Off the Record - Political Interviews 1933-43, edited by A.J.P. Taylor, (Hutchinson, 1973) pp.172-3.

70. see PRO CAB 65/8, WM 206, WM 207 & WM 209.

71. PRO CAB 67/7, WP(G)(40)187 and WP(G)(40)195.

72. v.363 H.C.DEB 5s col.588.

73. The records of the activities of the Advisory Committee & Advisory Council are not open in Home Office Records, but some minutes of their meetings are available in Foreign Office files: see PRO FO 371/29172-29192.

74. v.363 H.C.DEB 5s col.587.

75. Cmd. 6217, 'German and Austrian Civilian Internees, Categories of Persons Eligible for Release from Internment and Procedure to be Followed in Applying for Release', Home Office, July 1940.

76. Ibid, category 11.

77. Ibid.

78. Ibid, category 6.

79. for the debate see v.364 H.C.DEB 5s cols.1525-1586.

80. v.364 H.C.DEB 5s cols.1537-8.

81. v.364 H.C.DEB 5s col.1547.

82. Cmd. 6223, 'Civilian Internees of Enemy Nationality - Categories of Persons Eligible for Release from Internment and Procedure to be followed in Applying for Release', Home Office, August 1940.

83. Ibid, category 19.

84. On 22 August 1940, Sir John Anderson was asked whether, in releasing those enemy aliens hostile to fascism, he would ensure that he was not releasing people whose devotion to the cause of communist world revolution was a great a menace to world peace and our institutions as fascism. Anderson replied: 'Yes Sir, I can give the assurance asked for.' v.364 H.C.DEB 5s cols.1435-6.

85. v.368 H.C.DEB 5s cols. 1503-4.

86. v.365 H.C.DEB 5s cols. 488-9.

87. PRO CAB 67/8 WP(G)(40) 309.

88. PRO CAB 65/10, WM 293.

89. v.367 H.C.DEB 5s cols.78-81.

90. v.367 H.C.DEB 5s col.446.

91. v.368 H.C.DEB 5s cols.1503-4.

92. Ibid.

93. PRO PREM 4 39/3, Minute from Churchill dated 25 January 1941.

94. Ibid.

95. See H.M.D. Parker, *Manpower*, History of the Second World War, (UK Civil Series), (HMSO, 1957) pp.345-7.

96. these figures are taken from statistics given to the House of Commons v.374 H.C.DEB 5s cols.2073-4.

97. v.368 H.C.DEB 5s cols.1503-4.

98. v.373 H.C.DEB 5s col.1547.

99. v.377 H.C.DEB 5s cols.925-6.

100. v.140 H.L.DEB 5s col.55.

101. W.P. Crozier, *Political Interviews*, p.172. Interview with Sir Archibald Sinclair.

Chapter Three

THE DEBATES OVER REGULATION 18B

As we saw in Chapter One, defence regulation 18B provided the Secretary of State with powers to detain people without trial, and it was to be a constant feature of the emergency regulations available to the government from September 1939 to the end of the European War.

Both the scope and use of the regulation provoked a good deal of criticism and opposition in Parliament, and in this chapter I shall again examine the attempts by parliamentary opposition to change government policy. In relation to this issue, however, the nature of the parliamentary opposition is itself of interest, for the political complexion of that opposition underwent a number of changes during the course of the war. The importance of this is that is shows the extent to which the concept of civil liberties can be highly relative - both in terms of the people who use it and the circumstances in which it is used. But before going into these questions, it is necessary to consider how the regulation was used during the course of the war, and what detention without trial was to mean in practice.

REGULATION 18B AND ITS USE

During the first two months of the war, when regulation 18B had its widest potential scope (see Chapter One p.15), about 30 people were detained. By March 1940, after the regulation had been amended, only about 40 people were held under it, according to figures given to the House of Commons. [1] Many of these people appear to have been of enemy origin - although technically British subjects - but a few may have been suspected members of the IRA, and Colin Cross says that a few minor members of the British Union had also been detained. [2]

As with the policy towards enemy aliens, the government's attitude towards the use of 18B took a dramatic turn during the invasion crisis of May and June 1940 and, in part, this change was directly linked to the government's policy towards Oswald Mosley's British Union. In the memo submitted to the Cabinet on 18 May regarding potential fifth columnists it was pointed out that there was no evidence to indicate that the British Union would assist the enemy, and that it would be a mistake to strike at the organisation at that time. [3] Churchill, summing up the Cabinet's deliberations, had said he felt that the War Cabinet as a whole wanted things tightened up. [4] Four days later, therefore, the Cabinet returned to the question of the British Union. The Home Secretary had discussed the British Union with two officers from MI5 and could only repeat that there was no apparent connection between Mosley's organisation and fifth column activities. But he said that if the Cabinet wanted to curtail fascist activities, the internment of 25-30 leading members of the British Union could be an initial step to see if this was sufficient to cripple the organisation. In such circumstances, he continued, it would be necessary to amend regulation 18B since, under the terms of the regulation as it stood after November 1939, he could only intern people who he had reasonable cause to believe were of hostile association or origin or, as 'a question of fact', had recently been concerned in prejudicial acts. [5] The War Cabinet concluded that regulation 18B should be suitably modified and that the Home Secretary should take such action as he saw fit, on the principle that such action should cripple the British Union. [6]

Within a few hours of the government's decision, a new paragraph - 1A - was added to regulation 18B. It allowed the Secretary of State to detain anyone who he had reasonable cause to believe was, or had been, a member of, or active in the furtherance of the objects of, any organisation which was either subject to foreign influence or control, or whose leadership had associations with persons in the government of, or had sympathy with the system of government of, any power with which Britain was at war, and that, in either case, there was a danger that the organisation might be utilised for prejudicial purposes. The following day, Sir Oswald Mosley was detained and, in the following week, so too were a number of the leading British Union members, including Mosley's wife.

At about the same time, two equally notable characters were detained under the other sections of the regulation. Admiral Sir Barry Domvile, a former director of Naval Intelligence who was closely involved with a right wing organisation called 'The Link', was detained because of his 'hostile associations', and the Conservative MP for Midlothian and Peebles, Captain Ramsay, was detained on the basis of his recently being concerned in acts prejudicial to the public safety and the defence of the realm.

Ramsay's case was discussed at the same Cabinet meeting which took the decision to amend 18B, and the minutes note that Ramsay had been involved in 'treasonable practices' with an employee of the United States' Embassy. [7] This employee, Tyler Kent, and Anna Wolkoff were later tried and convicted under Section One of the Official Secrets Act, but at the Cabinet meeting the Home Secretary pointed out that if Ramsay were interned he could be interrogated freely: something which would not be possible if he were prosecuted. In their recent book on enemy aliens, Peter and Leni Gillman suggest that it was no accident that this case came to light when it did. They claim that MI5 had been aware of the case since April, and allege a political conspiracy designed to force the government into further measures against potential fifth columnists. [8]

Although paragraph 1A had initially been added to 18B for the specific purpose of detaining leaders of the British Union, in the following months over 700 people were to be detained because of their connection with that organisation: [9] apparently in line with the policy adopted in July 1940 that the British Union should be totally suppressed (see Chapter 4). But it was not just this section of the regulation that was to be used extensively, and it is by no means clear that the majority of those detained under 18B were sympathisers either with German or British fascism.

According to figures given in Parliament, over 1,450 detention orders had been made by July 1940 and, by July 1941, this figure had risen to almost 1,800. [10] In relation to this latter figure, the Under-Secretary of State said that just under 800 orders had been made under paragraph 1A, a small number on the grounds of individuals concerned in prejudicial acts, and the rest on the basis of peoples' 'hostile association or origin'. [11] Unfortunately this was to be the standard method by which government spokesmen broke down the figures for detentions, since the Secretary of State was not obliged to disclose what constituted hostile associations or origins, or prejudicial acts. So we still cannot say with any degree of certainty what sort of people made up the 1,000 or so detentions which were not connected with the British Union, or why they were detained.

In one case detailed by Richard Croucher in 'Engineers at War', John Mason - a Sheffield shop steward - was detained in August 1940 for 'impeding the war effort'. A campaign to secure Mason's release continued throughout 1940,and Croucher notes that while many activists were victimised, the use of 18B against shop stewards was unusual. [12] It is not clear whether it was Mason's case or a similar one which was raised in Parliament in February 1941. Again a shop steward seems to have been involved, and Willie Gallacher suggested that the man had been detained because he was a communist. In a rare specific statement the Home Secretary said that the man was detained because he had been 'involved in attempts to slow down war production'. [13] From this answer alone it was clear that prejudicial acts were not limited to treason and espionage but could extend to all sorts of political and industrial activities.

Turning to the grounds of 'hostile association or origin', it was often suggested that most people so detained were of enemy origin although technically British subjects. [14] Apart from the fact that someone of enemy origin was not necessarily a fascist, it also seems likely that some British communists, pacifists or other radicals were detained on these grounds. For example, Sybil Morrison - in her history of the Peace Pledge Union - noted that a well known seller of 'Peace News' was detained and held in Holloway for 3 months without being charged. [15] Government spokesmen were also noticeably reluctant to answer questions regarding the detention of communists. The set response was that nobody had been detained on the basis of their membership of the Communist Party, linked with a refusal to say how many detainees were in fact communists. [16]

Once arrested, 18B detainees were initially housed in prisons but the majority had been transferred to a camp on the Isle of Man by 1941, with the exception of a few important detainees - such as Mosley and Captain Ramsay - who remained in Brixton prison. In January 1940 a White Paper from the Home Office had set down the conditions under which detainees were to be kept in custody. [17] While in general these conditions were similar to those for prisoners awaiting trial, certain extra facilities were specifically provided for. Detainees were allowed to wear their own clothes, arrange to have their meals varied or supplemented at their own expense, and to be treated by a medical practitioner of their own choice. They were to be allowed considerable scope for association with other detainees and, although communications were subject to censorship, there was no limitation imposed on the number of letters that could be received or sent. The White Paper also stated that detainees were to be given full opportunities to make representations in writing to the Secretary of State regarding their case or treatment.

The extent to which conditions and treatment actually matched up to those specified in the White Paper is unclear. Skidelsky says that in the early days the authorities made little attempt to comply with these conditions, and that it was not until Mosley and others threatened to prosecute the prison governor that freedom of association was permitted. He dismisses the stories in some newspapers that top fascists were revelling in idle luxury as 'wildly exaggerated' and says that the women detainees 'languished at Holloway in conditions of unbelievable filth'. [18] In January 1941 the Home Secretary claimed that, the conditions laid down in the White Paper were being applied at Brixton with the exception of providing mealtimes in association. [19] As for the tales of high living, even if Mosley and one or two others were allowed to live extravagantly, it is unlikely that the majority of 18B detainees enjoyed such opportunities. I shall refer to a number of criticisms that were made in Parliament below. But at this point it should be stressed that there is no evidence to show that 18B detainees had to endure the barbarous conditions faced by many enemy aliens between May and August 1940.

Under the terms of the regulation amended in November 1939, detainees could make objections to an Advisory Committee appointed by the Secretary of State, and it was the duty of the Chairman to inform the detainee of the grounds on which the detention order had been made and to furnish him with sufficient particulars to enable him to present his case. The findings of an Advisory Committee were not communicated to the detainee and the Secretary of State was not obliged to accept them. Under paragraph 6 of 18B, however, the Secretary of State was required to report to the House of Commons the number of cases in which he declined to follow the advice of the Advisory Committee.

Not surprisingly, the vast majority of those detained under 18B did make appeals to the Advisory Committee, and in most cases the Home Secretary was prepared to accept its findings. But such a hearing was no guarantee of release. Just as with the internment of enemy aliens, the process of release took far longer than the time taken to carry out large numbers of detentions.

In terms of the numbers detained under 18B at any one time, the peak occurred in August 1940 when about 1,450 people were being held but, by December 1940, this figure had fallen to 1,258. By July 1941, when the total number of detention orders had approached 1,800, the number of people in detention had dropped significantly to 762, and by July 1942 the figure was down to 529. [20] The number was to continue falling steadily until the end of the European war, when the last few detainees were released.

It is apparent that, after the detentions of the summer of 1940, the figure for the total number detained held fairly steady for a few months, dropped fairly rapidly until about July 1941 and then declined at a slower rate in later years.

There does not appear to have been any intentional pattern of releases, although in the later years of the war the number of people detained on the grounds of 'hostile association of origin' became a larger proportion of the total number detained, indicating that persons detained under paragraph 1A were released more quickly. In November 1944, for instance, it was stated that, of the 90 or so people still detained, the great majority were of hostile association or origin and only technically British subjects. [21]

As we saw in Chapter One, 18B also allowed restrictions to be placed on peoples' movements and activities. Prior to

November 1939 such restrictions could be imposed as an alternative to detention, but after the amendment of the regulation they could only be applied after a person had been released from detention. No details are available regarding the extent to which these restrictions were used prior to November 1939 but, in November 1944, it was stated that of the 1,753 people who had been released from detention, restrictions had been imposed in 934 cases, although in 207 cases these had subsequently been cancelled. [22]

Between 1942 and 1945 the number of fresh detentions made was small, probably less than 100 in total. Thus the criticism of the government's policy in respect of 18B, which continued in some form for most of the war, was clearly related to either the terms of the regulation itself, or to the policies adopted towards those people who, by and large, were detained in 1940 and 1941. It is to the nature and development of this opposition that I now wish to turn.

THE DEVELOPMENT OF UNITED OPPOSITION

From the outbreak of war until the autumn of 1940, parliamentary criticism of 18B was almost exclusively confined to those MPs outside the Conservative Party. During the debate which led to the amendment of the regulation in October 1939, the Liberal MPs Dingle Foot and K. Griffith led the attack on this and other regulations, and a number of leading Labour MPs attacked the principle of detention without trial and the provisions of 18B. They had the support of the ILP members and apparently the Communist MP, Willie Gallacher. [23] During the phoney war period party government still prevailed at Westminster and, in this sense, the Labour, Liberal and other groups were the natural opponents of a Tory government which had taken these exceptional powers. Significantly, however, the predominance of Labour/Liberal/ILP criticism of 18B continued after the formation of the coalition government, and after it had become apparent that many of those detained were connected with British fascism.

During the autumn of 1940, a large number of questions were raised in the Commons concerning the treatment of detainees and the workings of the Advisory Committee, and most of these were put by Labour and Liberal members. Even in the case of the detained Conservative MP, Captain Ramsay, a majority of those MPs who initially questioned whether a Member of Parliament should be detained or whether a breach of privilege had occurred stood outside the Conservative Party. [24]

But by December 1940 things had begun to change and one or two Conservative MPs started questioning the government's policy. In the following year this group of Conservative critics was to grow and, in alliance with certain Labour and

Liberal members, they were to form an important parliamentary opposition. Before discussing this in detail, however, we must examine the developments which occurred during the winter of 1940.

On 21 November the new Home Secretary, Herbert Morrison, submitted a memo to the Cabinet on the detention of fascists. [25] It is not clear whether this memo had been prepared in response to Labour and Liberal criticisms or simply because Morrison was new to the job. But it did provide a substantial assessment of previous and proposed policy, with particular reference to the role of the Advisory Committee. The memo reminded Ministers that about 750 people had been detained because of their connections with the British Union, and said that by the end of October 1940 the Advisory Committee had dealt with 317 objections and had recommended release in 199 cases. It was noted that the Advisory Committee believed that many members of the British Union were entirely patriotic and held no pro-Nazi sympathies, and a case was cited of a man who had been detained because he was the only member of the organisation in a certain locality, and had therefore appeared on lists of BU members as a local leader. Of those cases recommended for release, the Security Services had opposed 100 on the grounds that they were BU officials and might encourage activity among the rank and file. But, the memo pointed out, after this question had been discussed by the Security Executive, it was agreed that the Advisory Committee's recommendations could be accepted. The memo concluded that, in general, the advice of the Advisory Committee should be followed. One of the reasons given for this conclusion was that the Home Secretary had to report to Parliament the number of cases in which the recommendations of the Advisory Committee had been rejected, and that any substantial deviation from those recommendations could cause trouble in Parliament, for it would be argued that the safeguard which had been provided was, in fact, illusory. The Cabinet approved Morrison's memorandum and at the meeting he said he expected the Advisory Committee to recommend release in about sixty per cent of cases and proposed to abide by those decisions as far as possible. [26]

Interestingly, despite this decision and the fact that there were to be relatively few instances of the Home Secretary rejecting the Committee's recommendations, a good deal of trouble was nevertheless caused in Parliament over this question.

On 10 December 1940, the Labour MP, Donald Stokes, raised the question of 18B detainees on the Adjournment of the House. He attacked both the principle of detention without trial and the treatment of detainees. [27] He disassociated himself from the political views of many of the detainees, but said that he had raised the issue as a matter of principle because he felt the administration of the regulation had been hopelessly bad and savoured too much of the Gestapo and the Court of Star Chamber. He gave instances of individuals who had little or no connection with the BU but who had been detained under paragraph 1A. When he moved on to the case of Mosley, he produced evidence to suggest that British Union members were no longer being detained as a potential danger to the state, but because it was believed that their political views might undermine civilian morale. He quoted the following exchange between Mosley and the Chairman of the Advisory Committee, Norman Birkett.

Mosley: There appear to be two grounds for detaining us - (1) a suggestion that we are traitors who would take up arms and fight with the Germans if they landed and, (2) that our propaganda undermines the civilian morale.

Birkett replied:

> Speaking for myself, you can entirely dismiss the first suggestion. [28]

Moving on to the role of the Advisory Committee, Stokes argued that many people had been detained for months before their cases had been heard, and that even when release orders had been signed following an Advisory Committee recommendation, it had sometimes taken weeks for this order to be executed. Why, he asked, were legal advisors not allowed to argue a detainee's case before the Committee? And why were detainees not informed of the Committee's findings? In respect of conditions, he claimed that facilities for female detainees at Holloway had been primitive: there having been no washing water for a week, and only two toilets for 170 detainees. Some male detainees, he said, were being kept in solitary confinement for long periods. In these and other ways he claimed that the treatment of detainees seemed to be punitive rather than preventive.

During the course of the debate Stokes was supported by several members including the Conservative MP, Sir Irving Albery, who argued that the regulation had been made at a time of acute crisis, and that the time had come for it to be modified.

Replying for the government, Morrison opened with an attack on what he called the arguments of 'classical liberalism', suggesting that any country which tried to uphold the liberal principles during a war would almost certainly lose. He went on:

> In situations of war, and situations of revolution, if you are to be soft and preserve meticulously liberal doctrines and principles which may be, and are,

> ordinarily right and defensible...I would...say... Take my advice, do not be a Minister in those circumstances, because it will be exceedingly dangerous for the security of the state or the success of the cause. [29]

His argument in a nutshell was that liberal values could be abandoned wherever the security of the state was threatened, an interesting observation for a man who was said by his recent biographers to have upheld the classic principles of liberalism during his period as Home Secretary (see below Chapter Five). Having made it clear from the outset that the government were not prepared to make any major modification to 18B, Morrison went on to question the allegations made by Mr Stokes and to defend the government's administration of the regulation. He said that conditions at Holloway had been brought about by the non-cooperation of detainees, and he implied that, in general, the provisions laid down by the White Paper were being adhered to. Consequently, he made no offer to alter existing procedures.

During his defence of government policy Morrison indicated on a number of occasions that the vast majority of those detained were fascists. This claim foreshadowed an assumption that was to become prevalent from 1942 although, as I have suggested, it was not necessarily the case.

The growth of Conservative interest in the administration of 18B was not the exclusive preserve of a few MPs outside the government. Whether for the same reason as a few of his backbenchers, or perhaps because of them, Churchill took an interest in the administration of the regulation in December 1940, and wrote a memorandum to Morrison. [30] The memo reminded the Home Secretary that detainees had not committed any offence but were being held in custody because of the public danger and the conditions of war. Churchill expressed distress at being responsible for actions 'so utterly at variance with all the fundamental principles of liberty, habeas corpus and the like'. But much of the memorandum was concerned with the details of the Mosleys' treatment 'as well as others of that category'. Churchill questioned whether many of the restrictions imposed were necessary - would it be wrong to allow a bath every day, he asked: Are detainees allowed wireless sets? What arrangements have been made to allow husbands and wives to see each other? and what 'arrangements have been made for Mosley's wife to see her baby, from whom it was taken before it was weaned?'. The memo concluded by asking for Morrison's views. Unfortunately, there is no record of the reply.

On 11 December 1940, the Commons considered a report from the Committee of Privileges which concluded that the detention of Captain Ramsay had not been a breach of parliamentary Privilege. [31] Without going into the technical details of the debate, we may note that a number of MPs argued that the report should be rejected. They included the Conservatives, Captain Shaw, Sir Irving Albery and Sir Archibald Southeby, the ILP MP, James Maxton, the Labour Member, Mr Henderson and the Liberal, Mr Mander. Here were the first indications of a basic unity amongst a small number of MPs from all parties which was to put further pressure on the government.

In the early months of 1941 the questioning of the Home Office Ministers continued unabated, but the first real opportunity to challenge the government did not come until July, when the government had to put forward a motion to continue the 'Emergency Powers (Defence) Acts'. [32] Anticipating that 18B was a contentious issue, Osbert Peake, opening the debate for the government, said that, although the regulation was repugnant, it remained a necessary safeguard and could not therefore be revoked. He pointed out that many people had been released and claimed that there had been hardly any complaints from detainees themselves over the role of the Advisory Committee. He admitted, however, that the Home Secretary had disagreed with the findings of the Advisory Committee on 132 occasions.

In attacking the government's policy, some Members drew attention to specific cases while others concentrated on general criticisms and proposals for reform. James Maxton referred to a case he had taken up of a man who had waited twelve months for an Advisory Committee hearing, after which he had been released. Maxton claimed that the worst that could be said about him was that he was a lapsed member of the Labour Party, had taken a holiday in Germany and corresponded with a member of the German Social Democratic Party. Maxton also referred to the detention of a republican Member of the Northern Ireland Parliament and suggested that the detention had been ordered solely on the basis of the man's political beliefs. On a more general level, Sir Irving Albery directed his attention to the functioning of the Advisory Committee and, after arguing that it was difficult for a detainee to make a case, he questioned the usefulness of a tribunal which the Home Secretary could ignore. He concluded by suggesting that a committee of the House of Commons should be established to consider the case of Captain Ramsay. Mr Mander endorsed Albery's argument, saying that detainees should be given every consideration and all the rights of appeal that could be devised. He also argued that a new all-party conference should be established to examine this and other regulations.

In reply, Morrison gave nothing away. [33] He admitted that the decisions of the Advisory Committee had sometimes been delayed due to a divergence of views between the Committee and the Security Services but argued it was fundamentally wrong to assume that because someone had been released after two or three months' detention they should not have been detained in the first place. He firmly rejected the idea of new all-party talks, but was more careful in dismissing Albery's proposal that a committee of the House should examine the case of Captain Ramsay.

Perhaps Morrison's reticence on this latter point was because it had obtained substantial support among Conservative MPs. In September 1941, Morrison submitted a memo to the Cabinet [34] which pointed out that there was a strong feeling in the House of Commons that a detained MP ought to have his case investigated by a committee of the House rather than by the Advisory Committee. But the memo argued that this demand should be resisted since, if a committee of the House made a recommendation for release which was rejected by the Home Secretary, it would then be necessary to give a full explanation of the circumstances to the whole House. The War Cabinet agreed that no changes in procedure should be made. [35]

The opponents of 18B did not confine themselves to questions and speeches in Parliament, and during 1941 a number of cases involving the regulation were brought before the courts. The most well known of these, 'Liversidge vs. Anderson and another', was concluded in the House of Lords in November 1941 [36] and was principally concerned with establishing whether or not a person's detention could be challenged in the courts and whether the Secretary of State could be required to disclose the specific grounds for detention. The left-wing counsel, D.N. Pritt, who fought the case for Liversidge, notes in his autobiography that other detainees had applied for writs of Habeas Corpus, but had failed because the courts had accepted affidavits from the Home Secretary stating that he had 'reasonable cause to believe' that a person was, for instance, of hostile association. In the Liversidge case, therefore, it was claimed that the plaintiff had been falsely imprisoned, in an attempt to get the Home Secretary to specify the basis for detention. [37] What the courts had to decide was whether the insertion of the phrase 'reasonable cause to believe' in November 1939 required the Home Secretary to disclose the basis of his belief and that the courts could then decide whether it was reasonable. The High Court and the Court of Appeal both decided in the government's favour. When the case was brought to the House of Lords the Attorney General contended that authority had been intended to, and in fact did, rest solely with the Secretary of State. Four of the five Law Lords accepted this submission, but Lord Aitkin argued in a dissenting speech that, both traditionally and in other defence regulations, 'reasonable cause' was testable in the courts. He said that from the government's submission it would follow that the phrase 'if the Secretary of State has reasonable cause to believe' meant the same thing as 'if the Secretary of State thinks he has reasonable cause to believe' - a view he could not accept. [38]

The judgement in the Liversidge case caused considerable discussion in legal circles at the time [39] and has subsequently been discredited. Indeed, a recent edition of Wade's 'Administrative Law' says of the case:

> the decision of the House of Lords is to be regarded as an isolated exception attributable solely to the exigencies of wartime government and the grave national danger of 1941. It would be surprising if a decision like the latter were ever given again. [40]

While seeing the judgement as wrong, these comments avoid any discussion of the role of the judiciary in crisis government even though they seem to question the traditional notion of judicial independence.

At the time, though, Lord Aitken's dissenting judgement acted as a spur to the parliamentary opponents of the regulation. On 10 November the Prime Minister was asked whether the government were prepared to amend 18B in the light of Lord Aitkin's views. When he replied in the negative, preparations were made to challenge the government by putting an amendment to the King's Speech.

This challenge prompted further Cabinet discussions and there is evidence to show that Churchill was prepared to consider relaxing certain provisions connected with the regulation. In a memo to the Home Secretary dated 15 November 1941, Churchill pointed out that feeling against 18B was very strong, and asked whether the possibility of releasing some detainees on parole had been considered. The memo referred specifically to the fact that Lady Mosley had been imprisoned and separated from her husband for eighteen months, and suggested that some way ought to be found to allow married couples a reasonable degree of association. The memo asked Morrison to 'make proposals to the Cabinet before the debate in the House takes place'. [41] Despite Churchill's position the Cabinet decided on 20 November that no concessions should be made and that Morrison should make the point that 'reasonable cause' was not challengeable in the courts. [42]

Two Conservatives, Sir Irving Albery and Sir Archibald Southeby, proposed and seconded the amendment, but were supported in speeches by the Labour MPs, Ernest Evans and Sydney Silverman, as well as the pro-communist D.N. Pritt. [43] Albery apologised for the fact that he had not questioned the powers under 18B in earlier years, and praised those Members (i.e. Labour and Liberal Members) who had consistently fought for an amendment of the regulation. He said that following the amendment made in November 1939 most MPs had been fairly satisfied, but that anxiety had developed, especially as it became apparent that the Home Secretary was rejecting the advice of the Advisory Committee in about ten per cent of cases. He complained that MPs were unable to find out information relevant to specific cases and called on the government to modify the regulation. Other speeches criticised different aspects of the regulation. Sir Archibald Southeby and Ernest Evans said that the judgement in the Liversidge case had given the Home Secretary unchallengable powers which had never been the intention of the House of Commons. D.N. Pritt suggested that the Home Secretary could publish the general grounds or reasons for specific detentions and the reports of the Advisory Committee. The Conservative, Bob Boothby, returned to the fundamental question of parliamentary control when he stated that 'it is a complete fallacy to suggest that any real power is exercised by Members of this House over the Executive'. [44]

The first reply for the government was made by the Attorney General, who described the legal history of the regulation and argued that the phrase 'reasonable cause to believe' had been added to the regulation simply to stress the Home Secretary's personal involvement with individual cases. Later, the Home Secretary reiterated this point and gave a statistical breakdown of the use of the regulation. He pointed out that over 1,000 people had been released from detention and said that in the vast majority of cases he had accepted the advice of the Advisory Committee. On concluding his speech he challenged the opponents of the regulation to divide the House, but added that the government were not prepared to allow a free vote. With no possibility of a government defeat, and realising that they had failed to wring any concessions, the movers did not force a division and the amendment fell.

This debate was the last major attempt to force a change in government policy during what can be termed the period of united opposition. We have seen that, from the autumn of 1940 to the autumn of 1941, the Labour and Liberal opponents of the regulation were joined by a number of Conservative backbenchers, and it would appear that this united opposition enjoyed a considerable degree of support in the House. Certainly few backbench MPs opposed their arguments, and senior Ministers accepted that parliamentary opposition was strong. But although Churchill was prepared to suggest certain reforms, the government as a whole were not prepared to consider any major modification of the regulation which would have limited the power of the Secretary of State.

One question which arises out of these events is why Conservatives should begin to question the use and scope of 18B in the autumn of 1940, when they had shown little concern with the regulation in the previous year. Unfortunately, the reasons are far from clear. Perhaps there had been a latent dissatisfaction among some Conservatives which had not been expressed because they felt that, during the crisis of 1940, criticism would be unpatriotic. Possibly some Conservatives had friends who had been detained, and information regarding their appeals and treatment led to the Conservative intervention. The detention of the Tory MP Captain Ramsay almost certainly had some effect, and perhaps it is also significant that the first major Conservative speech against 18B occurred shortly after Herbert Morrison took over as Home Secretary.

An important feature of the debates during this period was that they took place on a technical rather than a political level. The regulation and the way in which it had been used were the issues discussed, rather than the wider and potentially more explosive question of who, in political terms, was detained. The only exception to this rule were certain aspects of Morrison's speeches in December 1940 and November 1941, when he laid emphasis on the fact that many of those detained were fascists. This was the point that, from 1942, was to lead to the disintegration of united opposition.

THE DISINTEGRATION OF UNITED OPPOSITION

In contrast to 1940, when opposition to 18B had come more or less exclusively from a few Labour and Liberal MPs, from 1942 such opposition was supported by an increasing number of Conservatives. At the same time some Labour and left-wing members who had been involved in the earlier opposition began to back the continued existence and use of the regulation. These developments can be most easily seen if we briefly summarise the debates that occured between 1942 and 1944.

In July 1942 a Conservative MP, Commander Bower, raised the question of 18B and a number of the earlier opponents supported him including Ernest Evans and James Maxton. [45] Many of the by-now familiar arguments were raised. But what distinguished this debate from its predecessors was the inclusion in some speeches of a markedly political slant and the defection of a few left-wing MPs from the opposition camp. Opening the debate, Commander Bower said that it was no accident that the Home Secretary was a left-winger while the majority of those detained held right-wing views. He added that this was not a personal attack on the Home Secretary since a right-wing Home Secretary would be just as likely to detain people from the left. But he made his own position clear when he went on to argue that the threat of fascism did not come from the British Union but from the left. As we have seen, the pro-communist MP, D.N. Pritt, had been closely involved with the opposition to 18B, both in Parliament and in his professional capacity as a King's Counsel. But when he spoke in this debate his line had changed radically. He argued that, if there was public unease about the regulation, it was based not on the fact that too many people had been detained but because too few had been dealt with in that way. He said that there was too much pro-fascist feeling in the country and that public opinion would be reinforced if it were discovered that the Home Secretary was:

> sternly putting an end to any mollycoddling of the people who are interned and seeing whether...some more people were interned to keep them company.

He concluded:

> In general I support the policy that has been applied by the Home Secretary, except that I hope it will be a little firmer, and if the matter is pressed to a Division, I shall vote for it. [46]

It was left to the Labour MP Donald Stokes to make the point that probably only a small proportion of those still detained were fascists. Although figures given by the Home Secretary in the debate substantiated this point, [47] it had little impact, either on the vote or on the continued existence of the assumption. In this debate 25 MPs voted against the government but only 7 of these (including the ILP member James Maxton) were from the Labour benches. There were a number of abstentions from what had been previously been the Labour opposition to the regulation, and Pritt and the Communist MP Willie Gallacher voted with the government.

The view that the majority of those detained were fascists was being fostered particularly in the left press, and the point came up in Parliament again in February 1943, in a debate over the question of whether Sir Barry Domvile, who was still in detention, should be allowed to send a letter to 'The Times'. The Cabinet had decided he should not be allowed to do so, [48] but when their decision was made public Sir Irving Albery raised the matter on the Adjournment of the House. [49] The debate expanded to cover other aspects of 18B, and the criticism of the treatment of detainees came from a number of Conservative MPs and the Labour member Sydney Silverman. But Tom Driberg argued that many more important liberties had been lost during the war and that, after all, most of the detainees were people who would gladly have led the Nazis into London. He said that the liberties that had been fought for in the past were the very liberties which would have been destroyed 'if the philosophy of the friends of the 18B detainees had prevailed in this country'. [50]

It is not clear whether Driberg was referring to the Nazis or to the people who had opposed regulation 18B, but by this time there was undoubtedly some suspicion on the left regarding the motives of Conservatives who were criticising the use of the regulation. In this debate such a sentiment was most clearly expressed by Willie Gallacher, who questioned whether the Tories who were so concerned with 18B would have been equally concerned if he, a communist, had been detained.

Although political divisions were clearly emerging over the issue from 1942 they reached their logical conclusion in the autumn of 1943 when a major political storm blew up over the release of Sir Oswald Mosley. The matter was discussed by the Cabinet on 17 November [51] and Morrison recommended that Mosley and his wife should be released, since Mosley was suffering from thrombo-phlebitis and a conference of doctors had said there was a danger of an extension of the trouble and even a danger to life if Mosley remained in detention. The Cabinet minutes note that Bevin opposed Mosley's release on the grounds of undermining morale and endangering industrial negotiations, but Morrison pointed out that he could not take such factors into account. The Cabinet, with Bevin dissenting, agreed that Mosley and his wife could be released. [52]

Under the terms of their release the Mosleys were subjected to most of the restrictions provided for in regulation 18B. They were to reside at a specified house and were prohibited from travelling more than seven miles from that house. They were to report to the police monthly, and were not to communicate or associate with anyone (other than their immediate family) who had been a member of the British Union. Association or communication with anyone for the purpose of promoting political objects was forbidden, as was any attempt to publish any book, newspaper, article, leaflet etc. Finally, they were not to make any public speeches or give interviews to journalists or others for the purpose of publication.

Although Morrison announced these restrictions and said that he was quite prepared to redetain Mosley if necessary, his statement to the House of Commons was greeted with a storm of protest from Labour and left-wing MPs. Attlee promised that time would be made for a debate.

Protests were not confined to the House of Commons and feelings against Mosley's release were expressed up and down the country. The General Council of the TUC and the National Council of Labour indicated their disapproval, the Communist Party organised meetings and demonstrations, and sections of the press, which had formerly criticised the government over the scope and use of 18B, condemned Mosley's release. Perhaps more interestingly, the National Council for Civil Liberties took a similar view and called for Mosley to be re-interned. [53] At the root of all this opposition were two complementary strands of thought which were closely allied to the more general reasons for the growth of the left's disinterest in arbitrary detentions. Firstly, Mosley was Britain's leading fascist, and it was argued that there was no reason to be lenient with him. Secondly, there was the question of class and privilege, for it was argued that Mosley had been released because of his high social and political connections rather than on medical grounds. Both of these reasons can also be related to general suspicions on the part of the left, prevalent in these later years of the war, as to what Britain was actually fighting for, and who, in terms of classes, was going to benefit from an allied victory.

On 1 December, the promised debate took place in the House of Commons. [54] Most of the critics of the government's decision came from the Labour benches and restated the reasons given above, with added warnings about the impact of the decision on international opinion and the re-birth of fascism in Britain. Mr Parker, seconding the amendment, argued that 'full democratic rights should not be given to Fascists and other groups which attempt to overthrow the Constitution'. [55] Willie Gallacher said that if Britain had been at war with the Soviet Union there would have been no chance of the government letting him out of jail or for the Tories to be advocating such a course of action.

Defending the government's decision, Morrison repeated that medical grounds had been the sole basis for the decision to release Mosley, and that he was to be subjected to severe restrictions. He said, however, that Mosley's release could not be divorced from the general question of the application of 18B and attacked those sections of the press which, having earlier denounced the brutality of 18B, had then, 'joined the mob'. Later in his speech, the following comments are recorded in Hansard:

> Mr Morrison: A lot of people have walked round the clock on this. This regulation was denounced by the Communist Party earlier on.
>
> Mr Gallacher: No.
>
> Mr Morrison: Yes. I wish I had time to go into it. It was denounced by the National Council for Civil Liberties. That is an amazing organisation. They switched right round, and so did a lot of other people. [56]

In essence Morrison was quite right.

When it came to a division, 62 MPs voted against the government the vast majority of whom were either from the Labour Party, the ILP or the Communist Party. They included prominent left-wing Labour MPs such as Bevan and Shinwell, as well as James Maxton, Sydney Silverman and D.N. Pritt, all of whom had previously opposed the principle and use of detention without trial. On the other hand, the Conservatives who had criticised 18B voted solidly with the government.

By mid-1944, about 200 people still remained in detention and, on 16 June, Sir Irving Albery and Sir Archibald Southeby moved a motion which proposed that a judicial tribunal should be set up to examine the cases of those people still detained, and that Captain Ramsay should be released unless his continued detention was justified to the House of Commons.

[57] The criticisms of government policy were much the same as they had been from 1940 to 1942, with the addition that Britain's position was now much more secure, and that some people had by this stage been detained without trial for over four years. The government's position also remained the same in the sense that no concessions or changes in the terms of the regulation were offered, and it was stressed that the vast majority of those detained had at some point been released. When the House divided, 31 MPs voted for the motion, most of whom were Conservatives. Two ILP members and two members of Commonwealth also supported the motion, but the only official Labour Party member to do so was Donald Stokes - who, it seems, was the only member of Parliament who had consistently opposed 18B from the early months of 1940.

In summing up this section the first point that should be made is that the predominantly Conservative opposition fared no better than its predecessor in terms of getting any major modifications to 18B, even though at times Churchill appears to have been sympathetic to such demands. [58] The essential character of the regulation remained unchanged from May 1940 until it was revoked at the end of the European war. For most of this section, though, I have been primarily concerned with the changing composition of parliamentary opposition to the regulation and opposition to the government's decision to release Sir Oswald Mosley.

At the end of the last section I put forward some possible explanations for the growth of Conservative opposition to the regulation. Now it is necessary to explain why some Labour and left-wing MPs who had previously opposed the regulation reversed their position. To do this we must start from the widely accepted view among MPs from all parties that the vast majority of those detained were pro-fascist. In addition, and partly because of the re-emergence of party politics in the later years of the war, some Labour and left MPs became suspicious of the motives of Tory opposition to the regulation.

It seems that sections of the left - the Communist Party in particular - came to see the need to destroy fascism as an issue to which all other considerations were subordinate. Thus, in so far as pro-fascists had been detained, the principle of detention without trial should be supported. It was a position which mirrored the view that, in times of emergency, the government is entitled to take exceptional powers. But for the Communist Party it was also a logical outcome of their change of line in 1941, and fits with their policy of full support for the Churchill coalition.

The suspicion of Tory opposition was an amalgam of at least two factors. Firstly, it was believed that some, if not all, conservatives were the 'friends' of fascism both on a political and class basis and that Tory opposition to 18B was not due to a principled concern with arbitrary detentions but was motivated by a desire to get their friends out of jail. Secondly, there was the view that Conservatives were using the question of 18B as a political stick with which to beat the Labour Home Secretary.

Although these suspicions were probably exaggerated to make a political point, they can be understood. As I said at the end of the previous section, Conservative opposition to 18B did only emerge after Morrison had become Home Secretary and, from the 1930s onwards, there had been numerous examples of the quasi-fascist views of some Tory MPs. The question of class affinity can most easily be seen in relation to the case of Mosley. Churchill had taken a particular interest in Mosley's case and, on 6 October 1943, he wrote a note to Morrison which stated 'I have received privately some rather serious medical reports about him, but they are of course unofficial.' [59] Morrison did suggest to the Cabinet that Mosley should be released, but prior to this he had been interviewed by W.P. Crozier. It is recorded that Morrison said there had been 'a good deal of agitation behind the scenes about Sir Oswald Mosley' and that although Mosley was ill:

> there were doctors who didn't take so serious a view, and he himself was afraid lest there be some sort of 'frame-up' to get M. out of prison...There was also, he said, a fashionable lady, some sort of relation of Mosley's wife, 'fluttering about' and trying to use her influence in important quarters. [60]

Even if there was some sort of upper-class plot to get Mosley released this does not necessarily reflect on the activities of the Conservative opponents of 18B, but it does illustrate the atmosphere within which the left reached their conclusions.

The main problem with the analysis made by some Labour and left MPs, and organisations such as the Communist Party and the NCCL, was the first premise from which their arguments flowed - that the vast majority of those detained were fascists. Although Morrison maintained this was the case: as I said in the first section of this chapter it is difficult to say with any certainty who the majority of detainees were. To associate detainees with the Nazis and fascism might simply have been a convenient way for the Home Secretary to justify government policy. The left do not usually take the claims of Ministers at face value: that they should do so in this case suggests that it was also convenient for them.

COMMENTARY

In this chapter I have examined the way in which regulation 18B was used by the executive, and the way in which the powers under this regulation were criticised and challenged in Parliament. There is little doubt that, even in its amended form after November 1939, the executive had enormously wide powers under the regulation. After the Liversidge case it became apparent that there was no way in which a decision to detain a person could be effectively questioned or challenged in law. It is interesting, therefore, that legal forms continued to be a question considered by the government. In 1941, for instance, the Attorney General pointed out that the detention of a person on the grounds of opinions he had expressed could be challenged in the courts, but this would have only been the case if the government had admitted that these were the grounds for detention. Had they simply stated grounds contained under the terms of the regulation these could not have been questioned. Similarly, it seems possible that members of the British Union could have been detained on the grounds of hostile association, but this was not considered sufficient, and paragraph 1A was therefore added to the regulation.

Having said this, it should be stressed that detentions do not appear to have been made or continued solely on the basis of what was considered a direct threat to security. Take the case of British Union members. Although their initial detention was probably motivated by the fear that they were a potential fifth column, the continued detention of some of these people clearly had a political aspect - to prevent the resurgence of fascist propaganda.

The parliamentary opposition to 18B always accepted that some form of detention without trial was necessary on security grounds during an acute crisis. What they questioned was whether such powers were necessary when an immediate crisis did not exist, and the lack of safeguards under the terms of the regulation. As we have seen, opposition existed in some form throughout the war, yet its only success was in the autumn of 1939, for the reasons discussed in Chapter One. After the formation of the coalition government, and the extensive use of the regulation in 1940, the opposition failed completely in all attempts to force the government to change its policy, although during the period of united opposition there was probably substantial support for reform in the House of Commons. The best that can be said of this opposition is that its existence may have dissuaded the government from using its powers even more widely and, as with the internment of aliens, individuals may have benefited from MPs taking up their specific case.

The changing composition of the parliamentary opposition is an important example of the relativity of the concept of civil liberties. Although virtually all shades of political opinion would have agreed, in the abstract, that detention without trial was a serious infringement of civil liberties, in terms of political reality the extent to which sections of the political spectrum were prepared to take up this question was mediated by other factors. In part these other factors may have amounted to a sincere conviction that civil liberties could be overidden by other considerations. But there is at least a hint that many politicians felt that principles of civil liberties could be taken up or abandoned as required, depending upon political expediency.

Chapter Three: Notes

1. See v.352 H.C.DEB 5s col.1592, v.353 H.C.DEB 5s col.403 and v.358 H.C.DEB 5s col.2138.
2. C. Cross, The Fascists in Britain, (Barrie & Rockcliff, 1961) p.193.
3. PRO CAB 67/6, WP(G)(40)131, Memo 'The Invasion of Great Britain and the Possible Co-operation of a Fifth Column'.
4. PRO CAB 65/7, WM 128.
5. PRO CAB 65/7, WM 133.
6. Ibid.
7. PRO CAB 65/13, WM 133.
8. P. and L. Gillman, Collar the Lot, (Quartet Books, 1980) Ch.12.
9. This was stated to the House of Commons on a number of occasions and see PRO CAB 67/8, WP(G)(40)308.
10. v.363 H.C.DEB 5s col.991 and vol.373 H.C.DEB 5s col.946.
11. v.373 H.C.DEB 5s col.946.
12. R. Croucher, Engineers at War, (Merlin, 1982) pp. 92-3.
13. v.369 H.C.DEB 5s col.273-4.
14. see for instance v.376 H.C.DEB 5s col.848.
15. S. Morrison, I Renounce War - The Story of the Peace Pledge Union, (Sheppard Press, 1962) pp.51-2.
16. for example see v.361 H.C.DEB 5s col.671 and v.374 H.C.DEB 5s col.1478.
17. Cmd.6162, 'Defence Regulation 18B'.
18. R. Skidelsky, Oswald Mosley, (Macmillan, 1975) p.456.
19. v.368 H.C.DEB 5s col.658-9.
20. See v.367 H.C.DEB 5s col.642, v.373 H.C.DEB 5s col.946 and v.381 H.C.DEB 5s col.1516.
21. v.404 H.C.DEB 5s cols.951-2.
22. v.404 H.C.DEB 5s col.1525.
23. see v.352 H.C.DEB 5s cols.1866 and 1868.
24. The ILP Member James Maxton took the lead in raising questions regarding the detention of Captain Ramsay.
25. PRO CAB 67/8, WP(G)(40)308.
26. PRO CAB 65/10, WM 293.
27. for the debate see v.367 H.C.DEB 5s col.836-884.
28. v.367 H.C.DEB 5s col.839.

29. v.367 H.C.DEB 5s col.868.

30. see W. Churchill, *The Second World War* Vol.II, (Cassell, 1949) p.627.

31. for the debate see v.369 H.C.DEB 5s cols.933-991.

32. for the debate see v.373 H.C.DEB 5s cols.941-1024.

33. for Morrison's speech see v.373 H.C.DEB 5s cols.993-1015.

34. PRO CAB 66/17, WP(41)213.

35. PRO CAB 65/19, WM 19, 8 September 1941.

36. see *The All England Law Reports*, 1941, Vol. 3, pp.338-387.

37. D.N. Pritt, *The Autobiography of D.N. Pritt, Part One, From Right to Left* (Lawrence & Wishart, 1966) pp.232-3 and 305. Pritt says the grounds for detention were that Liversidge was (1) suspected of having been engaged in commercial frauds, (2) suspected of being in touch with persons who were suspected of being enemy agents, (3) the son of a Jewish rabbi.

38. see Lord Aitkin's judgement in *The All England Law Reports*, Vol. 3, pp.349-363.

39. see for example, Dr. C. Kemp Allen, 'Regulation 18B and Reasonable Cause' in *The Quarterly Law Review*, vol.58, 1942, pp.232-242, and G.W.Keeton, 'Liversidge vs. Anderson' in *The Modern Law Review*, vol. 5, 1941, p.162-173.

40. see. H.W.R. Wade, *Administrative Law* (4th edition) (Oxford, 1977) p.386-7. One recent commentator has, however, argued that the judgement may have been technically correct. See R.F. Heaston, 'Liversidge vs Anderson in Retrospect', in *Law Quarterly Review*, vol. 86. January 1970, pp. 33-68.

41. Churchill, *Second World War*, Vol.III, p.749-50.

42. PRO CAB 65/20, WM 116

43. for the debate see v.376 H.C.DEB 5s cols.776-862.

44. v.376 H.C.DEB 5s col.829.

45. for the debate see v.381 H.C.DEB 5s cols.1426-1519.

46. v.381 H.C.DEB 5s col.1475.

47. Morrison said that, of the 529 people still detained, 322 were detained on the grounds of hostile association or origin, 141 under paragraph 1A, and 66 on the grounds of being recently concerned in prejudicial acts.

48. PRO CAB 65/33, WM 12.

49. for debate see v.386 H.C.DEB 5s cols.1375-1412.

50. v.386 H.C.DEB 5s col.1387.

51. The minutes of this meeting were placed in the Secretary's Standard File PRO CAB 65/40, WM 156.

52. Ibid.

53. The Executive Committee of the NCCL issued a statement on 19 November deploring the release. They argued that fascism was the ultimate threat to civil liberties and that therefore Mosley should remain in detention. This statement brought many protests from groups who had previously been in close contact with the NCCL, such as branches of the

Peace Pledge Union. The NCCL claimed that their position on Mosley was a logical outcome of their policy on 18B adopted in July 1942. See NCCL Archives, Filing Case No.41 'Fascism and Anti-semitism', sections 3 and 4, 'The Release of Mosley'.

54. for debate see v.395 H.C.DEB 5s col.395-478.

55. v.395 H.C.DEB 5s col.403.

56. v.395 H.C.DEB 5s col.474.

57. for debate see v.400 H.C.DEB 5s cols. 2137-2420.

58. I noted Churchill's interest with the regulation earlier and on the question of the release of Mosley he wrote a number of Memos to Morrison. One of these, dated 25 November 1943, began 'I am convinced that 18B should be completely abolished as the national emergency no longer justifies abrogation of individual rights of Habeas Corpus and trial by jury on definite charges.' The same day, however, he wrote another memo to Morrison and Attlee which said that in case of another parliamentary attempt to terminate reg.18B, the government should say that the time had not yet come when those powers could be dispensed with. See Churchill, _Second World War_ Vol. V, Appendix F, 'The Release of the Mosleys'.

59. Ibid.

60. W.P. Crozier, '_Off the Record - Political Interviews 1933-43_', (ed.) A.J.P Taylor (Hutchinson, 1973) p.385.

Chapter Four

THE CONTROL OF POLITICAL ACTION

So far I have discussed areas which were necessarily open to public debate. But in moving on to consider the control of political action it is sometimes necessary to delve beneath the level of publicly taken action to get a full picture of government policy. As I shall show, the government were involved in a process designed to stifle forms of political opposition more or less continuously throughout the war, but their activities in this field rarely came under close public scrutiny. Only on odd occasions, when the government resorted to the use of emergency powers or instituted major prosecutions, were such actions publicly acknowledged. For the most part the government were concerned, in terms of public policy, to stress a liberal approach in so far as this was compatible with the success of the war effort.

The control of political action is a particularly complex area to examine for, as well as explaining action taken by the government, it is also necessary to assess the limits of this action. Despite a consistent desire to control, there were a number of restraints on government policy. It was, for instance, clearly difficult to suppress political propaganda which was not in itself illegal, but to prohibit it by law would raise questions about the extent of democracy in Britain. Account also had to be taken of the potential political and industrial repercussions within Britain and on Britain's image abroad, both with the United States and the Soviet Union.

The task of analysis is made more difficult because of the limitation on research in this area. Important government files including the records of the Home Defence (Security) Executive, the 'Committee on Communism 1941-5' and most of the records of the Metropolitan Police remain closed to public inspection at the Public Record Office. In particular there is virtually no information from official sources regarding the relationship between central government and the police.

Having entitled this chapter 'The Control of Political

Action', it will be useful to consider briefly the most important political groupings which stood outside the pro-war consensus of the Tory, Labour and Liberal parties and which, at various times and in various ways, opposed many of the fundamental assumptions of government policy.

Firstly there was Mosley's fascist organisation - the British Union - which until its suppression in 1940 maintained a public policy of loyalty to Britain while at the same time calling for a negotiated peace. In their paper and propaganda they kept up a constant criticism of the British government, arguing that there was no need for war and that it had been brought about by a conspiracy of Jews and their supporters.

Another group who called for an immediate peace were the pacifists who were mainly organised around the Peace Pledge Union. Initially their political activities tended to centre around informing conscripts to military service of their rights to claim a conscientious objection. Although 'Peace News' was published throughout the war, pacifist influence dwindled as the war progressed.

Undoubtedly the most important political opposition - both in terms of numbers and influence - was the Communist Party of Great Britain, the party affiliated to the Communist International. Its position on the war underwent a number of changes, but it was always viewed with the greatest suspicion in government circles. In the first few days of the war the party had pledged its support for whatever measures were necessary to destroy fascism, but at the beginning of October it adopted the Comintern line and denounced the war as imperialist. From then until mid-1941 the party campaigned to stop the war and to establish a 'People's Government'. Its propaganda during this period was directed largely towards exposing the class nature of the war and was bitterly opposed both to the Tory government and the coalition which replaced it. Following the Nazi invasion of the Soviet Union the party's line was changed again: this time to support for the anti-fascist war and the coalition government. The party became closely involved in the campaign for a second front but in the vital field of industry they denounced all strikes which impeded production.

Another marxist grouping which came into the public eye in the later years of the war were the British trotskyists. Until 1944 they were split into two small organisations, but then combined to form the Revolutionary Communist Party. Throughout the period the trotskyist position was that the war was imperialist, but their attention and activities were generally aimed at exposing the class nature of British society, particularly in industry. The trotskyists gained some support after the Communist Party's change of line in 1941 and so too did the remnants of the Independent Labour Party whose politics were a mixture of marxism and pacifism.

Finally, there was the group of anarchists around the

regular 'Freedom' paper who succeeded in publishing 'War Commentary' and who had the dubious distinction of being involved in one of the last political prosecutions of the war. They also denounced the war and tried to expose the continued existence of class privilege in wartime Britain. It should be stressed that the trotskyist and anarchist groupings were very small - numerically tiny compared with the communist, pacifist or fascist organisations.

THE CHAMBERLAIN GOVERNMENT AND ANTI-WAR PROPAGANDA

Despite the scope of the original defence regulations, the government adopted a cautious approach to anti-war propaganda at the beginning of hostilities which was maintained until April 1940. Early in the war a member of the British Union was prosecuted under 39B and the Public Order Act, [1] but there was no immediate spate of prosecutions for 'endeavouring to influence public opinion in a manner likely to be prejudicial to the efficient prosecution of war or the defence of the realm'. The most obvious public measure that was taken in the first few weeks of the war was a ban on 'processions of a political character' imposed under regulation 39E. On 1 September such a ban was applied to the East End of London. Two days later it was extended to cover the whole of the Metropolitan Police area for a period of three months. It was apparently renewed at the beginning of December. [2]

But it would be wrong to assume that, because the full power of the emergency regulations was not invoked, opponents of the war were allowed to pursue their political activities unhindered. Benewick says that the police were 'more diligent at fascist meetings' after the war had begun, [3] and the NCCL archives contain a substantial amount of material relating to instances of the police, and occasionally local authorities, interfering with the activities of anti-war groups in the period from October 1939 to February 1940. [4] The form of this interference varied - ranging from prohibiting or stopping meetings to threatening distributors of leaflets with prosecution under the defence regulations. But apparently there were few prosecutions and when they did occur they were for relatively minor 'public order' offences such as obstruction, or 'insulting words and behaviour likely to cause a breach of the peace'.

This sort of activity seems to have peaked in October 1939 according to Ronald Kidd, the General Secretary of the NCCL. In a letter to Stuart Morris of the Peace Pledge Union dated 13 October 1939, Kidd wrote that there 'is a wave of police interference at the present time, not with the PPU alone'. [5] Towards the end of October the NCCL drew up a dossier of cases of interference which was presented to the leader of the Labour Party, Mr Attlee. [6]

Contemporary newspaper reports corroborate the evidence from NCCL sources. On 12 October, the 'News Chronicle' reported that the police in some areas had stopped the distribution of a leaflet issued by the Peace Pledge Union entitled 'Stop the War' and that the organisation's London headquarters had been visited by the police. The following day the 'Daily Herald' noted that a PPU meeting in Bournemouth had been prohibited on the grounds that it might cause a disturbance. Finally, in the 'Manchester Guardian' of 7 October, a local Communist Party alleged that the police were trying to stop all its meetings. [7]

The Executive Council of the NCCL believed that the activities of the police were directed by central government. In a memo dated 30 October, they suggested that interference with anti-war activities was 'an example of the methods of the Executive when they seek to suppress minority opinion but fear to have the propriety of their actions tested by the judiciary'. [8] It seems more likely that the government feared the political repercussions of drastic action rather than any attitude which might be taken by the judiciary. But it is not clear whether the police action was directed by central government or initiated independently.

The question of anti-war propaganda was raised in the Cabinet on 16 October, in the middle of the wave of police activity described by Kidd. But instead of discussing the opportunities for covert suppression of propaganda, which one might expect if police interference had been centrally directed, a memorandum from the Home Secretary and the ensuing discussion concentrated on the possibilities of prosecutions under regulation 39B.

The memo simply entitled 'Anti-War Propaganda' [9] stated that consultations between the Home Office and the Attorney General had already taken place with regard to the distribution of leaflets and small posters and that the question to be considered was not simply whether a prosecution under 39B would succeed 'but also whether it is expedient on grounds of policy for a prosecution to be taken'. [10] It was pointed out that, if prosecutions were brought against anti-war groups such as the PPU or the Communist Party, those groups might attract a good deal of sympathy, since dictatorial methods were disliked even in wartime. Reference was also made to the undesirability of prosecuting members of the PPU - which was generally regarded as a respectable organisation - without prosecuting members of the Communist Party, even though it was admitted that the CP had not at that stage produced any anti-war leaflets! The memo argued that it might be better to wait until communist anti-war material was produced and then prosecute members of the CP, the PPU and the British Union at the same time. Such a course of action, it was suggested, would have the advantage of indicating government impartiality while at the same time showing that 'proceedings are being taken as a means of giving a general warning to members of the public'. The memo concluded that this would probably be the best form of action and that 'there are no sufficient grounds of policy why such proceedings should not be taken'. [11]

The Cabinet, however, felt that anti-war propaganda had been relatively harmless up to that time and that prosecutions might do more harm than good. On the other hand, it was agreed that if there were signs of such propaganda having any success then proceedings ought to be brought. The Cabinet also agreed that it was undesirable to prosecute the PPU and not the Communist Party, and thus finally concluded that it was not desirable to institute proceedings under 39B at that stage, but that developments should be closely watched. [12]

With its concern for public opinion and the success of anti-war propaganda being the yardstick for determining a prosecution strategy, the tactical dimension of this debate is explicit and shows that Ministers saw the law as a political weapon. But it remains unclear how this discussion related to the wave of police interference that was taking place at the time. The nature and timing of the Cabinet discussion might have been related to pressure on the Home Office from Chief Officers of Police who wished to take proceedings under 39B, for under the terms of the regulation the consent of the Attorney General had to be obtained before a prosecution could be instituted. During September such consent had apparently been requested on a number of occasions for, in a strongly worded circular to Chief Constables dated 28 September, the Home Office stated that the reason the consent clause had been included in the regulation was to ensure that proceedings would not occur in cases of a 'trivial or unimportant character' or without the 'fullest consideration in cases raising political issues'. [13] If this circular did not dissuade the police from requesting consent, the Home Office may have felt it necessary to take the issue to the Cabinet for a decision.

If such an explanation were accurate it would be plausible to suggest that the police may have used those powers which did not require sanction from a higher authority in order to restrict anti-war propaganda. The evidence of harrassment and threats of proceedings, but only a few minor prosecutions, would be compatible with this theory, as would certain statements made in Parliament at the end of October.

In the parliamentary debate on the defence regulations on 31 October, Dingle Foot referred to the banning of pacifist propaganda in some areas, and George Lansbury offered to give the Home Secretary details of police interference with anti-war activities. Sir John Anderson did not deny that pacifist leaflets had been suppressed, but stated that the Home Office had not instructed the police to report people distributing anti-war leaflets and admitted that the police could misuse the defence regulations. He assured the House that he was prepared to take action to prevent such misuse and offered to look into the cases mentioned by Lansbury. [14] The Home Secretary's statements cannot be taken as an admission that the police had been taking independent action. But it may be significant that Kidd noted that after the NCCL dossier had been presented to Attlee (which coincided with the Commons debate) police interference ceased almost completely - at least for a time. [15]

These points favour the view that police activities in October 1939 were independent of central government, but a case can also be made out for the opposite view, which would raise the question of whether the government were pursuing a dual policy - a liberal approach on the level of public policy (e.g. agreeing to amend the regulations) but also a covert policy designed to limit the scope of anti-war propaganda. The Home Office memorandum and the Cabinet discussion could be seen as a debate over the question of whether to turn a covert policy into a public policy, which the use of 39B would certainly entail. Similarly, the Home Secretary's statements in the Commons and the subsequent decline in police activities could be seen as an attempt to keep such a policy undercover when there was some danger that it might be raised to the level of public debate by interested MPs and the NCCL.

It seems unlikely that the Home Office could have been unaware of the police activities in this field, since they were receiving weekly reports from a number of sources. Furthermore, if such activities had been contrary to government policy, one would expect there to have been some attempt to curtail them. Also, there is the point that Kidd's use of the term 'wave' indicates co-ordinated activity throughout much of the country. It is unlikely that Chief Officers of Police could plan a common strategy without the Home Office being aware of what was happening. But then what Kidd saw as a 'wave' could have simply been regional police chiefs reacting in a similar manner to the refusal by the Home Office and the Attorney General to authorise prosecutions under 39B. Although the evidence supporting the view that police action was centrally directed is relatively slim and largely circumstantial, it must be borne in mind that evidence showing this link may be closed to public inspection at the Public Record Office or witheld or destroyed by the department concerned.

If this episode were taken in isolation the balance of evidence would suggest that the wave of police action was initiated independently. But there is evidence to show that, a few months later, central government was pursuing a covert policy against anti-war groups and at least on one occasion the Cabinet agreed that the police should be instructed to suppress a Communist Party leaflet. If only for these reasons it would be unwise to dismiss the possibility that the wave of police action was centrally directed, or at least condoned.

By January 1940, police action against anti-war activities had recurred to such an extent that Ronald Kidd, in a letter dated 8 January, referred to continual police intimidation of people trying to hold meetings and distribute literature. [16] Again it is impossible to specify where responsibility for such a policy lay, but it is clear that during the early months of 1940 the government were coming under increased pressure to take a tougher line with anti-war activities. In Parliament a series of questions were directed at the Home Secretary, the implications of which were that such activities should be prohibited by the use of the law. For example, on 22 February, the Home Secretary was asked whether he was aware that the Peace Pledge Union were picketing employment exchanges in order to induce people to become conscientious objectors. Anderson replied that there was a general agreement that the defence regulations should not interfere with the ordinary propagation of opinion, although it was widely believed that the activities described were an abuse of that freedom. He said that the PPU were being watched carefully, and that the question of whether further measures were necessary would be kept in view. [17] On 21 March a similar question was asked in relation to the activities of the Communist Party, and again the Home Secretary stressed the point that ordinary propagation of opinions should be allowed, but that the activities of the CP were being watched. [18]

But almost certainly of more importance than this sort of parliamentary pressure was information reaching the government from localities and regions. The Home Office and other government departments received regular reports from various official and unofficial bodies up and down the country, and these were usually compiled into numerous weekly reports which could be studied by Ministers and senior civil servants. In the first few months of the war those reports which are now publicly available mention the activities of anti-war groups but show little concern either about the nature of these activities or their effect. Between January and April 1940, however, the tone of such reports changed significantly.

Reports from the Ministry of Information Regional Offices for February and March 1940 were concerned about an increasing level of communist and pacifist activity and the degree of support these groups seemed to be obtaining. [19] The Civil Defence Report for the period 18 February to 3 March said that widespread activity on the part of the PPU and the CP had been reported [20] and, at a meeting of the Civil Defence Committee on 28 February, both the Minister of Supply and the Minister of Labour mentioned that they had received reports from local bodies expressing concern over the growth of communist propaganda. The Home Secretary stated he 'was receiving from all quarters expressions of concern at the growth of various kinds of subversive propaganda'. [21] It is difficult to say whether these reports reflected a real growth in the activities of anti-war groups, or whether the authors were worrying more about their activities because of the Soviet invasion of Finland or attacks on anti-war activities in the press. Nevertheless, such reports prompted the government to review their policy and strategy.

At the meeting of the Civil Defence Committee referred to above, it was decided to consider the question of 'subversive' activities in more detail. On 5 March the Home Policy Committee discussed the activities of the PPU. The Home Secretary argued in favour of making it an offence to incite people to evade their duties under the National Service Act or to incite people to become conscientious objectors, but a decision on this specific issue was deferred pending the wider discussion of anti-war propaganda. [22] This wider discussion began the following day when the Civil Defence Committee considered a memorandum from the Minister of Information dealing with those organisations which were pursuing an anti-war line, and what action could be taken against them. [23] The most interesting part of this memo is a section subtitled 'Action - Present and Proposed'. Not only did it express a clear desire to control anti-war propaganda, it also gave specific examples of how a covert policy could work. Having argued that the impact of anti-war propaganda could be lessened by improving government propaganda and remedying grievances, the memo went on to say that there were more direct methods of control. It gave a number of examples of action that had already been taken, and these are worth quoting in full:

i) At the instigation of the Ministry, St. Andrew's Hall, which for a number of weeks had been retained by the Communists for meetings, attended sometimes by two or three thousand people, has been taken over by the 'Pleasant Sunday Evening' Group.

ii) Referring to a speaking tour in Lanarkshire by a prominent Communist the memo stated:
'on the suggestion of the Civil Defence Commissioner a number of selected people have agreed to attend anti-war meetings and ask pertinent questions'.

iii) In Kent, the memo said,
'the situation is being met by inviting the local press to publish short accounts of the arguments advanced by Conscientious Objectors at the tribunals and to undertake an intensive drive against the activities of the PPU and other bodies'. [24]

Regarding police action or active suppression, the memo warned that care must be taken not to make martyrs out of anti-war activists, and it was pointed out that:

> a Regional Information Officer has more than once intervened to induce the police not to break up Communist meetings and has instead suggested to the local socialist leaders that they should prevent their followers from attending. [25]

At the meeting of the Committee, Sir John Anderson, the chairman, said that there were two possible lines of attack on communist activity: the use of the criminal law, and the use of counter-propaganda. Regarding the use of the law, he said that 'it was contrary to our traditions to use this method against a purely political organisation'. [26] But it seems this view did not extend to the sort of tactics employed and advocated by the Ministry of Information. The meeting agreed the proposals and lines of action suggested in the memorandum. [27]

Discussion of 'subversive activities' was resumed at the 11th meeting of the Home Policy Committee [28] and it considered the Ministry of Information memo discussed above and a memo from the Home Secretary dealing with the preparation of a regulation to curb the activities of the Peace Pledge Union. [29] At the meeting, the Home Secretary described the terms of the new regulation but pointed out that careful observation suggested that the PPU were having very little effect and that it might therefore be better to leave the legal position as it stood rather than provoke adverse publicity by taking further powers and bringing proceedings against pacifists. The Minister of Labour apparently endorsed Anderson's view when he said that the percentage of people claiming a conscientious objection was falling, but he added that a careful watch should be maintained on the PPU. Agreeing, the Home Secretary said that it would be of great value if a close check could be kept on all forms of subversive propaganda. The meeting then moved on to discuss communist and fascist propaganda, and it was pointed out that both the coal owners and trade union leaders had expressed a desire to curb the activities of the Communist Party. In this connection the possibility of suppressing the 'Daily Worker' was mentioned. The Home Secretary said that he felt that fascist activity was the more dangerous of the two, but that a special inquiry was being carried out into the funding of the 'Daily Worker'. He argued that although the suppression of communist activities might be necessary if their influence grew in the future, for the time being other methods of control, such as counter-propaganda, should be used. The Lord Chancellor made it plain that he favoured the suppression of the 'Daily Worker' but the Home Secretary pointed out that special powers would be required to achieve this, and the subject was apparently dropped.

The meeting went on to consider the proposals of the memo from the Minister of Information and it appears that, as at the Civil Defence Committee meeting, the policy of covert control was approved. On the other hand, in line with Anderson's recommendation, the Home Policy Committee deferred the introduction of further powers to curb the Peace Pledge Union's activities around the question of conscientious objection. [30]

Taking the period from the beginning of the war to the end of March 1940, there were clearly a number of common features in the government's approach to anti-war activities and opposition propaganda. Firstly, on the level of public policy, the government maintained a liberal stance partly by avoiding the widespread use of the defence regulations and partly by their statements and actions which implied that government policy remained committed to the principle of freedom of expression even during wartime. Beyond the level of public policy, however, on what I have called the covert level, there was a clear and consistent desire to control anti-war propaganda and a general agreement that if it began to have any widespread success it should be suppressed. In terms of action on a covert level, the examples given in the Ministry of Information memo may illustrate methods that were in use for much of this period and, even if it is assumed that the police were independently responsible for the interference with anti-war activities, this nevertheless ties in with the general rationale behind government policy.

By mid-April 1940 the government were prepared to adopt a more aggressive stance in public. In a memo submitted to the Home Policy Committee on 23 April, the Home Secretary mentioned that, in conjunction with the Director of Public Prosecutions, he was thinking of proceeding against the PPU under regulation 39A. [31] Summonses against six officials of the PPU were issued on 2 May in respect of a two-year-old poster which said 'War will cease when men refuse to fight - What are YOU going to do about it?'. When the case came to court in June the six officials were convicted and bound over after giving an undertaking to withdraw the poster. [32] But the main thrust of policy in these last weeks of the Chamberlain government was to strengthen certain aspects of the defence regulations. The amendment of regulation 39A and the introduction of regulations 2C and 94A (see Chapter One) were specifically aimed at anti-war activities, but even then there was a degree of subtlety about the government's approach. Regulation 94A allowed the Secretary of State to close or seize any printing press which had been used to produce a document which had resulted in a conviction under regulations 39A, 39B or 2C. But this was not the main point of the regulation. A memo discussing the proposed changes in the regulations explained reg. 94A as follows:

> The object of this proposed new power is to provide an effective penalty to deter printers from allowing their plant to be used for the printing of mischievous propaganda, the distribution of which is prohibited by these Regulations [i.e. 39A, 39B and 2C]. It is thought that the production of this type of propaganda can be substantially checked by providing a really effective deterrent for the printers; and there is little doubt that the threat of sealing up their plant will deter printers far more effectively than the possibility of a fine or even a sentence of imprisonment. [33]

Since there was no way of telling what propaganda was illegal until a decision had been made by the courts, the regulation acted as a deterrent to printers of all forms of anti-war propaganda. It had an immediate effect, for Kidd notes that shortly after the regulation was made the regular printers of 'Peace News' refused to print the next issue. [34]

In explaining the changes in the regulations to Parliament, the Home Secretary tried to maintain a liberal stance while at the same time issuing a warning to anti-war organisations. He said that the government did not want to interfere unnecessarily with traditional liberties but believed that a distinction had to be drawn between the:

> mere expression of honest opinion and the deliberate and systematic advocacy of defeatist or anti-war policies with intent to weaken the national resolution to prosecute the war to a successful conclusion. [35]

Yet action the government had taken publicly was pallid when compared with what was to happen in the next few months.

THE COALITION GOVERNMENT AND THE INVASION CRISIS

In Chapters One and Three I have already discussed many of the public measures taken in the summer of 1940 which affected political opposition. In this section, therefore, I shall concentrate attention on the thinking that lay behind these measures, and the continuance of a covert policy to control anti-war propaganda.

During the invasion crisis the government's view of anti-war organisations acquired a new dimension. As well as seeing anti-war organisations as purveyors of subversive political propaganda, the government also looked at these organisations in terms of their potential military threat as a fifth column. This view is most clearly seen in the government discussions which took place between the 18 and 23 May. The memorandum, 'The Invasion of Great Britain and the Possible Cooperation of a Fifth Column' argued that there was no evidence to show that either the communists or fascists were likely to assist the enemy but that lists had been prepared and drastic action could be taken if this became necessary. [36]

I noted previously that Churchill said that he felt that the Cabinet as a whole wanted things tightened up, and the Prime Minister's personal view of what should be done was expressed in a memo to General Ismay dated 18 May. The memo, having mentioned the control of aliens, went on: 'Action should also be taken against Communists and Fascists, and very considerable numbers should be put in protective or preventive internment including their leaders.' [37] On 22 May, the Home Secretary again pointed out that there was no evidence linking the British Union with a fifth column. Nevertheless, the decision to 'cripple' that organisation seems to have been taken for military rather than political reasons. [38] In July 1940 this policy was taken to its logical conclusion.

On 25 June the Home Policy Committee considered a memo on the British Union from the Home Secretary. It argued that, since the leaders of the organisation had been interned, it had become possible to see the second line of leadership and that therefore the time was ripe to suppress the organisation altogether. The memo recommended that a new regulation - 18AA - should be made in order to give effect to that policy. The Home Policy Committee accepted these proposals [39] and, on 10 July, an Order under regulation 18AA was applied to the British Union. At about the same time it must have been decided to extend detentions of British Union members to a large proportion of the organisation for, as we saw in Chapter Three, by August 1940 about 750 people had been detained under regulation 18B on the basis of their connection with the British Union.

Although the maintenance of the ban on the British Union in the later years of the war must be seen in terms of political expediency, during the summer of 1940 the government were more worried about the organisation's possible role in a fifth column, rather than the effect of its propaganda. In this connection it is interesting that no similar public action was taken either against the communists or pacifists, even though Churchill had favoured the internment of communists. Although such action against these groups may have caused a good deal more opposition than was the case with the British Union, there is no evidence to indicate that the fear of opposition was a factor considered by the government. It seems more likely that there was far less concern about those organisations being involved in fifth column activities and that their propaganda could be controlled by other, more subtle, means.

Despite the government's worries about a fifth column, they remained concerned with controlling propaganda per se. This concern was shown on the level of public policy by the introduction of regulations 2D, 94B and 39BA during this period (see Chapter One). But these new powers were just the tip of an iceberg, for action against anti-war activists and their propaganda reached a new peak between May and July 1940, and seems to have been aimed at the pacifists and the left as much, if not more, than it was at the fascists.

As in October 1939, the activities of the police were of great importance but, in contrast to the earlier period, interference with propaganda activities resulted in numerous prosecutions, searches and interrogations. Ronald Kidd wrote, in a letter dated 24 July 1940, that:

> although the Communists are suffering under the heaviest attack in the way of searches and interrogation, the police action in this way is by no means confined to them. In some districts it would seem that any well-known co-operator or trade unionist or radical liberal can count upon search, interrogation or some kind of petty persecution. [40]

The NCCL archives contain a large quantity of correspondence which suggests that many of these searches were carried out without legal authority and that documents seized were only returned, if at all, after long periods of time and persistent complaints. [41]

Of particular interest is the use by the police of the charge of 'insulting words or behaviour likely to cause a breach of the peace' under Section Five of the Public Order Act. Many such cases are documented in the NCCL archives [42] and on 21 May Ronald Kidd wrote 'I have had an extraordinary number of these cases in this weekend, and I feel there must be some special instructions out to the police.' [43] Kidd had made a perceptive point. In a confidential memo from the Commissioner of the Metropolitan Police, on 14 May, it is stated:

> Of recent years our policy in connection with meetings has broadly speaking been to give considerable latitude to the speakers and confine action to cases where a breach of the peace appeared to be imminent or actually occurred or where the speaker clearly over-stepped the mark. In present circumstances we must, I feel, take rather a stronger line with a view to curbing activities of an anti-war character, especially in the vicinity of factories during the luncheon hour or in a locality where feelings, whether favourable or antagonistic to speakers, are likely to run high...Police Officers should therefore

not hesitate to make arrests if in their judgement a breach of the peace is being invited...A charge should be made under Section 5 of the Public Order Act...In all cases the CID should be notified... and Special Branch informed. [44]

Although this statement does refer to making charges where a breach of the peace is being invited, it is apparent that these instructions were intended to do rather more than simply uphold the law. It was hoped they would help to curb 'activities of an anti-war character'. Section Five of the Public Order Act was an ideal tool for the purpose. Not only was it a part of the ordinary criminal law, rather than a potentially controversial defence regulation, it also required a minimum of proof without reference to the political activities involved. Police officers simply had to convince a court that a defendent's actions or words were likely to cause a breach of the peace.

Should any doubt remain as to the objectives of police activity, further evidence is available in relation to a case Sir Walter Citrine raised with the Home Secretary. This concerned the prosecution of four men who had apparently been distributing trade union leaflets. It seems the Home Office requested the police to provide details of the case and two statements - from an Inspector and a Superintendent - are very revealing. The Inspector stated that on 28 May four persons were charged under Section Five of the Public Order Act 'the action which led to their arrest being distributing handbills of a communistic nature'. [45] The note from the Superintendent stated:

> Police have recently been paying attention to persons distributing handbills outside places of employment. As a result of such action four persons were arrested in this district for distributing communistic literature... All four persons were sentenced...to three months imprisonment. [46]

These statements say that the men were arrested for distributing 'communistic' literature - not because the distribution of such literature was felt likely to lead to breaches of the peace.

Once again it is difficult to say whether the Home Office or central government authorised or condoned such action, although it is perhaps significant that in the case cited above there is no indication that the Home Secretary reprimanded the police for their action. On the other hand, a Home Office circular to the police dated 14 June stated:

> The new Regulations, while giving very wide discretion to the police, do not of course justify anything in the

> nature of random searches, the police must have some good reason for pursuing a particular line of enquiry....For example, the fact that an individual is an alien, or is a conscientious objector, or a pacifist, or has been engaged in left wing political activities, is not in itself a reason for regarding him with suspicion. [47]

In one instance, however, there is clear evidence that central government instructed the police to stop an anti-government leaflet. On 4 and 5 July 1940 the Cabinet considered the question of communist propaganda and in particular a leaflet entitled 'The People Must Act'. [48] The Home Secretary stated that this widely distributed leaflet was clearly intended to discredit the government and foment opposition to the war, and that he was satisfied that it should be suppressed. He added that, to avoid the charge of inconsistency, the 'Daily Worker' should also be suppressed. 'A considerable measure of agreement was expressed with this proposal' [49] but a number of Ministers felt that such a move at that stage could be linked with the suppression of free speech in France and that country's subsequent collapse. It was decided, therefore, that the paper should be given a preliminary warning.But it was agreed that the communist leaflet should be suppressed and that proceedings should be instituted against distributors. A circular from the Home Office, dated 8 July, conveyed the War Cabinet's instructions to Chief Constables. It stated:

> while the police should not take any action to interfere with the distribution of the 'Daily Worker', vigorous steps should be taken immediately to prevent the dissemination of the pamphlet in question and all pamphlets of a similar nature...The police should seize and destroy any copies of the pamphlet which are in the process of distribution and wherever the facts and circumstances justify it they should consider the question of bringing proceedings against the distributors under Section 5 of the Public Order Act, 1936. [50]

It should be noted that this circular extended the Cabinet's instructions to cover 'all pamphlets of a similar nature', although whether this indicates that the Home Office were overstepping their instructions or were merely expressing the spirit of the Cabinet's decision is not clear. What is apparent though is that the policy was quickly implemented. In a statement dated 18 July, the legal department of the NCCL noted that the leaflet had been effectively banned and that distributors were being prosecuted. [51]

When Sir John Anderson was asked in Parliament why these leaflets were being suppressed he replied that action was being taken because the method of distributing the leaflets was likely to cause breaches of the peace. [52] This was clearly far from the truth. The Cabinet minutes make it clear that the main reason behind the government action was the political content of the leaflet, and that Section Five of the Public Order Act was again being used as a political weapon. It must be stressed that there was no basis, either in normal peace-time law, or under the defence regulations, for the actions authorised by the Cabinet. This was recognised in a memorandum from the Home Secretary in January 1941. It stated:

> The action of the police in England and Wales in seizing these leaflets was not challenged, but it must be recognised that the seizure by the police of leaflets in respect of which proceedings cannot be taken is a course which may at any time be open to question. [53]

In fact, according to the memo, the Scottish Office had refused to instruct the Scottish police to seize the leaflets 'since the Scottish Law Officers advised that they knew of no authority in Scottish Law or under the Defence Regulations which would enable the police to take such action'. [54]

I said earlier that it was difficult to say with any certainty whether the police action against anti-war propagandists between May and June 1940 was directed or condoned by central government, but there is a clear link between this action and the decision to suppress communist propaganda in July 1940. The common use of Section Five of the Public Order Act suggests that the strategy had been formulated at government level, probably by the Home Office, and such a strategy can be seen as part of a continuing policy of covert action designed to control anti-war and anti-government propaganda.

To sum up this section, we need to go back to the two aspects of the government's view of anti-war groups and their activities: the fear that such organisations could become involved in fifth column activities, and the government's attitude to anti-war propaganda. The action taken against the British Union under the defence regulations must, I think, be attributed to a belief that this organisation and its members might assist the Nazis in the event of invasion. Similar action was not taken against either the communists or the pacifists because, in terms of fifth column activities, they were not considered to be as dangerous as the British Union. There was, on the other hand, a consistent and continued desire to control and limit anti-war propaganda. Although this was given public expression by the extensions made to the defence regulations, on the whole the government tried to exercise control over these activities by more subtle and covert means. The use of such a policy does not seem to have been determined by any direct fear of the opposition which might have resulted from a stricter public policy, since the coalition government was at its strongest during the invasion crisis and drastic action against the communists and pacifists would have been welcomed in many circles. The use of a covert policy can perhaps better be seen in relation to dual desires, firstly of maintaining a democratic image, while at the same time having some effective control over opposition propaganda.

THE COMMUNIST PARTY IN THE BLITZ

One of the points that recurred in government documents in the first six months of the war was that action on the level of public policy could be avoided provided anti-war propaganda was having little effect. But it was agreed that, if such propaganda began to be successful, drastic action might be necessary. In the autumn and winter of 1940 there were several reasons why the government should have become even more concerned with the spread of opposition propaganda. The most obvious - the Blitz - began in September 1940 and was to continue until the spring of 1941. Pre-war forecasts had warned that civilian morale might collapse under air bombardment and, given that anti-war and anti-government propaganda was regarded as a threat to national morale, it would follow that a harder line against such activities might help to sustain it. Beyond the threat posed by the Blitz there were other reasons why the question of morale became a serious concern of the government during this period. Several writers have argued that some sections of public opinion were beginning to question the fundamental values underpinning British society by the autumn of 1940. Calder, for instance, citing from the Mass Observation archives, says that by November there was an increasing interest in politics but that 'It was not a matter of a conventional swing towards Labour, but a "trend towards uncertainty and questioning of the status quo," with a great increase in political talk.' [55] If this was the case, the government may have felt that public opinion had to be stabilised in support of the coalition government and its policies, and that one method of doing this would be to take action against propaganda which encouraged such questioning.

In November 1940, the Director of Public Prosecutions told the Peace Pledge Union that a new book of theirs, 'The Conquest of Violence', contained passages which made its possession an offence under the defence regulations and that unless all copies of the book were handed to the police they would be seized and those reponsible prosecuted. Consequently, the PPU gave an undertaking to the Home Office that no further copies would be distributed during the war. [56] This was not the only action taken against pacifist propaganda during the winter of 1940-41, [57] but during this period the government were far more concerned with the activities and propaganda of the Communist Party.

As I said earlier, the Communist Party was the most important political opposition to the government, and there are grounds for believing that support for their policies was growing towards the end of 1940 despite the tactics adopted by the government in previous months. From June, the Party had been closely involved with the formation of 'People's Vigilance Committees' around the slogan 'A People's Government for a People's Peace'. The culmination of these activities was the 'People's Convention', which met in London on 12 January 1941. The demands of the Convention can be briefly paraphrased as follows:

1. To raise the living standards of the people.

2. Adequate air-raid precautions, bomb-proof shelters and effective back-up services.

3. The restoration and safe-guarding of all trade union rights, democratic rights and civil liberties, including democratic rights for the armed forces.

4. Emergency powers to be used to take over the banks, land and large industries.

5. National independence for India and the right of self-determination for all colonial peoples.

6. Friendship with the Soviet Union.

7. A people's government truly representative of the working people.

8. A people's peace won by the working people of all countries and based on the right of all peoples to determine their own destiny.

Communist sources claim that a genuine mass social movement coalesced around these demands and that over one and a quarter million workers were represented by the delegates who attended the London convention. [58] Such claims are probably exaggerated, but there is no doubt that the People's Convention movement did obtain the support of many people who were not themselves communists.

Another important aspect of Communist Party policy during this period was their work around air-raid precautions. For many months the party had been calling for the construction of adequate shelters for workers and, with the onset of the Blitz, these demands evoked a positive response, particularly in the East End of London. The concrete public surface shelters had proved to be worse than useless, and the communists advocated the occupation of the London Underground as deep, bomb-proof shelters. The 'Daily Worker' politicised the issue by exposing the difference in shelter protection afforded to the rich and the poor, and party members were often at the forefront of the shelter committee organisations. In the large London shelters communists were able to put forward the party's policy as they had never done before.

Finally, it should be noted that the party seems to have been able to maintain its important industrial base during 1940. This factor is important because the government were making preparations for the introduction of extensive manpower controls and believed that a degree of popular support had to be maintained among the industrial workforce if these controls were to be accepted and successful. Communist opposition could threaten this support.

Until December 1940 the tactics described previously appear to have been considered sufficient to limit the spread of communist propaganda. Ernie Trory says that in September the police raided offices and bookshops suspected of having a communist leaflet on Tube shelters [59] and Tom Harrisson notes that, by the use of Port of London Authority by-laws, sales of the 'Daily Worker' were prohibited in the 'Tilbury' shelter in the East End of London. [60] The Civil Defence Report for the period 1 to 29 September noted 'Communist propaganda is now chiefly concerned with the need for deep shelters but generally speaking it still seems to be on a small scale.' [61] As late as 27 November, the Cabinet decided that no action should be taken against the 'Daily Worker' in respect of what were considered to be libellous remarks about Ernest Bevin. [62]

Things began to change during the first weeks of December. In a Ministry of Information file entitled 'Industrial Campaign to Counter Communist Propaganda in Scotland', an intelligence report of 2 December is quoted as mentioning signs of unrest in Scottish industry, and that 'A major factor in this is undoubtedly communist penetration.' [63] The file notes that the co-operation of the trade unions was being obtained unofficially to counter such propaganda and that small meetings were to be organised with a view to discrediting any rank-and-file communists who might attend. At a meeting of the Civil Defence Committee on 4 December, the Secretary of State for Scotland referred to increased communist activity in Clydeside and Edinburgh, and mention was made of the formation of ARP co-ordinating committees and the work of 'agitators' among shop stewards. The meeting asked the Secretary of State for Scotland to produce a memorandum on the subject. [64]

The memo, which was submitted to the Civil Defence Committee on 11 December, said that while communist propaganda had increased this was not the real problem. The main danger, it said, was communist agents in industry: the 'subversive work carried out surreptitiously'. The memo claimed that shop stewards had encouraged disputes, and that communists were using unscrupulous methods in an attempt to foster industrial unrest on a large scale. Tied to this was agitation around air-raid precautions and the gathering of support for the People's Convention. In conclusion, the memo pointed out that the civil defence services had been purged and that one way of curbing communist influence in industry was to try and ensure that shop stewards were elected by ballot rather than at general meetings. Finally, as a more general remedy, the memo suggested that perhaps the time was ripe to suppress the 'Daily Worker'. [65] At the meeting of the committee, Bevin said that he would be visiting Scotland shortly and would ask local trade union leaders whether they could deal with agitators or whether further legal powers were necessary. [66]

Despite the growing concern about communist activities, the Home Secretary seems to have remained sceptical about the ability of the Communist Party to have any significant effect on public opinion and the desirability of suppressing the 'Daily Worker'. On 27 December, Morrison submitted a memo to the Cabinet [67] which argued that, although the contents of the 'Daily Worker' had become as bad as they had been in July when the paper had been warned, neither the paper nor other forms of communist propaganda were having much effect except in a few factories and that, in terms of undermining national morale, their impact was negligible. The memo said, however, that there were sufficient grounds for proceeding against the paper under either regulation 2C or 2D but that the following points should be considered:

1. If regulation 2C were used it would allow the 'Daily Worker' to launch a propaganda campaign around the question of press freedom.

2. There had been little agitation in the press or elsewhere in favour of suppressing the 'Daily Worker' and that, since the press were sensitive about their liberties, suppression might result in unfavourable comment.

3. If the paper were suppressed those people who supported the war but were concerned about the loss of civil liberties might rally to the communist cause.

4. Account should be taken of international opinion, for instance the United States, where suppression would be seen as a break with tradition.

5. Whether, if the 'Daily Worker' were banned, other

> forms of communist propaganda ought to be dealt with similarly or the party itself banned and the leaders interned.

In relation to this latter point, the memo stated firmly that the proscription of the party should be avoided until it was absolutely necessary. It concluded that the government could suppress the 'Daily Worker' and 'The Week' (a duplicated newsheet edited by Claud Cockburn who was a regular contributor to the 'Daily Worker') but that the question of whether such action would bring positive benefit to the war effort and outweigh the disadvantages remained open. [68]

The reservations expressed in this memo do not appear to have been shared by the Cabinet as a whole for, according to Morrison, it was decided that the 'Daily Worker' should be suppressed. [69] But Ministers must have agreed not to implement their decision immediately for it was not until further Cabinet discussions had taken place that any action was taken.

On 12 January, the day that the People's Convention assembled in London, Churchill wrote to Morrison about a 'Communist circular, addressed to all active working men and women' which presumably called for support of the People's Convention. Churchill stated:

> This kind of propaganda ought not to be allowed, as it is directly contrary to the will of Parliament, and hampers the maintenance of resistence to the enemy. I do not see why if Mosley is confined subversives and Communists should not be equally confined. The law and the regulations ought to be enforced against those who hamper our war effort, whether from the extreme Right or extreme Left. That is the position which the Conservative Party adopt...I know it is your wish to enforce an even justice, and if you bring the matter before the Cabinet I am sure you will receive full support. [70]

There seems to be an indication here that Churchill was afraid that Labour Ministers were trying to protect the Communist Party, but all the Labour Ministers were virulently anti-communist, especially Morrison and Bevin, and the Home Secretary's reservations about taking such action appear to have been based purely on tactical grounds.

On 13 January the Cabinet returned to the question of the 'Daily Worker' and 'The Week', but the Home Secretary maintained his position. In a further memorandum [71] he argued that the suppression of the 'Daily Worker' should not be the first step in a campaign against communist propaganda, since it might prove more difficult to prevent the distribution of other material, and that such action was not at that stage necessary. The memo reiterated the point that 'any attempt to suppress the Party...would be undesirable at the present time,' but that, if it was decided to take such action and intern members of the Party:

> this should be done on the ground that they have, as individuals, been concerned in acts prejudicial to the public safety or the defence of the realm, such, for example, as slowing down production, and not on the ground that they are leaders or members of the Communist Party. [72]

At the Cabinet meeting Morrison said that the suppression of the 'Daily Worker' would probably result in a large scale distribution of leaflets, and that these would have to be dealt with, first by giving a warning (presumably under regulation 2C) and then by instituting court proceedings. [73] The minutes of the meeting also note that Duff Cooper, the Minister of Information, thought that many newspapers would oppose the suppression of the 'Daily Worker'. The Cabinet nevertheless agreed:

1. that the Home Secretary should suppress the 'Daily Worker' and 'The Week' under regulation 2D.

2. that the Home Secretary should take action against other communist publications where he felt there were sufficient grounds.

3. to set up a committee to consider what further action should be taken against the Communist Party. [74]

It is clear then that the Cabinet did not consider the question of the 'Daily Worker' in isolation, or in relation to the rest of the press. Rather it saw suppression as the first step in a public campaign to counter communist propaganda. The fact that these decisions were reached the day after the People's Convention met seems to be of significance, even though Morrison dismissed the gathering as irrelevant when he answered a question in the Commons. [75] Perhaps the Convention can best be seen as a catalyst which provoked the government into an open and immediate response.

On the morning of 21 January the Newspaper Proprietors Association were informed of the government's decision, and that afternoon the offices of the 'Daily Worker' and 'The Week' were raided by Special Branch Officers. The editors were told that their publications had been banned under regulation 2D and their presses closed under regulation 94B. The following day, Morrison told the House of Commons that the action had not been taken because of any specific change of line but because the 'Daily Worker' and 'The Week' had, continually:

> by every device of distortion and misrepresentation sought to make out that our people have nothing to gain by victory, that the hardships and sufferings of warfare are unnecessary and imposed upon them by a callous Government carrying on a selfish contest in the interests of a privileged class. [76]

The immediate opposition to the ban was not as great as had been anticipated. While 'Daily Worker Leagues' were set up and the NCCL organised a conference to oppose the ban, most of the national press approved of the government's action, and press criticism that did occur was limited to the suggestion that the papers should have been prosecuted through the courts rather than subjected to arbitrary suppression. When the issue was debated in the House of Commons, [77] Morrison made it plain that he would view it as a 'confidence debate'. Despite strong attacks on the government's policy from Aneurin Bevan, Sir Richard Acland and Willie Gallacher, the motion condemning the government's action was defeated by 297 votes to 11.

What few people knew at the time was that, even before Morrison announced the ban, the committee which the Cabinet had agreed to set up had begun consideration of what further action should be taken against the Communist Party, and one of the questions discussed was whether the Party itself should be suppressed.

The first meeting of the 'Committee on Communist Activities' took place on 20 January 1941, and Sir John Anderson, Morrison, Bevin, Duff Cooper and Sir Donald Somervell, the Attorney General, were all present. [78] Three memoranda were considered, one from Lord Swinton as head of the Home Defence (Security) Executive and two from the Home Secretary. Lord Swinton's memo [79] is worth considering in some detail, partly because it is one of the few documents relating to the activities of the Home Defence (Security) Executive which is publicly available, and partly because it articulates a view which seems to have been prevalent in government circles: that what would normally have been considered legitimate political activity - if it was undertaken by the government or the major political parties - amounted to subversion when undertaken by the Communist Party.

The memo noted that the party had organised the activities of its members in campaigns combining direct political action and propaganda with increasing representation on local councils and trade union bodies. The memo stated:

> the Executive have no doubt that the leaders of the Communist Party desire to destroy the authority of the government, of works' management and of the Trade Union leaders and to impede the war effort. [80]

The party, it was suggested, also had a covert influence on the policy of outwardly non-communist organisations such as the National Council for Civil Liberties and the Association of Architects, Surveyors and Technical Assistants. Serious concern was expressed about the effect of communist activity in industry for, it was claimed, the authority of trade union leaders was being undermined as communists won positions on district committees. The memo warned that 'If no action is taken, there is likely to be an early crisis in their affairs, and the help they can give the Government will correspondingly diminish.' [81] It was argued that, in industry as a whole, the communists' campaign was beginning to make itself felt as an influence aggravating trivial grievances, inducing strikes and opposing the settlement of disputes.

In terms of proposals, the Security Executive were divided but the memo noted that 'a strong section are convinced that further action is essential'. [82] The Executive had agreed that if further action was taken:

> it should be the proscription of the Party as an illegal organisation and the internment of a small number of the leaders.

on the basis that:

> if the Government's attitude towards the Communist Party is unequivocally declared, many of the rank and file will disassociate themselves from it. [83]

The Security Executive believed that, although some trade unions with communist majorities would cause trouble if the party was proscribed, it was unlikely that widespread strikes would follow, or that the country as a whole would be divided by such action. Thus, despite a few reservations, Swinton's memo argued that a tough public policy would be successful without provoking a great deal of opposition.

In contrast, the memos submitted by Morrison concentrated on the problems of controlling propaganda by means other than blanket suppression. [84] The Home Secretary pointed out that consideration had been given to the possibility of warning communist speakers under regulation 2C but that, on the whole, such action had been thought to be undesirable since it would probably be represented as an attack on freedom of speech. Similarly, regulation 18B had not been used against communist speakers since the detention of people simply for what they had said might be construed as an abuse of the regulation by the House of Commons. Morrison warned against the illegal seizure of leaflets, and argued that the crux of the matter was that there was no regulation in force which specifically dealt with opinions voiced in leaflets or speeches. He said that what was required was a new regulation which would be acceptable to the representatives of the House of Commons, while at the same time providing an effective control over propaganda. To this end, one of Morrison's memos made a detailed analysis of propaganda regulations made during the first world war. It was noted that a regulation had been made in December 1917 which required all leaflets to be submitted to a Press Bureau 72 hours prior to publication and allowed the police to seize those leaflets considered undesirable. [85]

At the meeting of the committee itself, Ministers appear to have been rather worried by the implications of the analysis and proposals made by the Security Executive. Morrison argued that:

> If the party was to be proscribed or individual members of it interned, such action could not be confined to the small circle of intellectuals and leaders of the Party, but must extend also to working class members. This might well lead to serious repercussions in industry...It would be most damaging if the Government, having committed themselves to strong action, were afterwards obliged to give way. [86]

Ernest Bevin pointed out that it was difficult to differentiate between subversive activities and genuine grievances and that there were many areas of industry in which conditions lent themselves to exploitation by agitators. Finally, Sir John Anderson, winding up the discussion, said that while the committee should take note of the recommendations of the Security Executive, in his view there was a clear distinction between fascists, who he said had been involved in secret activities, and communists who operated largely in the open. He added that he feared the ultimate effect the proscription of the Communist Party might have on the position of the constitutional leaders of the Labour Party. The meeting ended without endorsing any specific proposals but agreed to:

1. Continue discussions at the next meeting and invite Lord Swinton.

2. Invite the Home Secretary to circulate a memo outlining his suggestions for the control of anti-war leaflets.

3. Invite the Minister of Labour to circulate the views of the Production Executive on communist activities and the possible results of action taken against them. [87]

The 'Committee on Communist Activities' met again on 28

January, and discussion appears to have centred on proposals made by Morrison for a new regulation. In his memorandum, [88] the Home Secretary said that the government should stop communist leaflets and some of those issued by the Peace Pledge Union, but that in some cases, such as leaflets on shelter policy, regulation 2C was not wide enough. He therefore proposed a new regulation - 2DA - a draft copy of which was appended to the memo. Under paragraph 1(i) it would have become an offence to publish, or possess with intent to publish, any leaflet 'calculated to undermine or disrupt the unity of purpose necessary to ensure the maximum war effort from all classes of the community'. [89] Furthermore, the regulation required that all leaflets relating to the war or the making of peace would have to be submitted to a competent authority 72 hours before publication or distribution, and would have to carry the names of the author and printer. The memo explained the rationale behind the regulation. The Home Office, it was noted, would not be able to say whether any particular leaflet was illegal, as that would be a matter for the courts, but the inclusion of the 72 clause would mean that:

> In practice, if in the view of the Home Office the leaflet contravenes this Regulation, the Police will be told to warn the printers and publishers and to seize any stocks of the leaflet under the powers conferred by Defence Regulation 88A (2). If the owners of the leaflet object, it will open to them to take proceedings against the Police for exceeding their powers and to show a court, if they can, that the leaflet does not contravene the terms of the provision prohibiting anti-war propaganda. [90]

The proposed regulation was clearly modelled on the DORA regulation mentioned in Morrison's earlier memo, but it would also have been a continuation of the subtle approach to the control of propaganda. Communist activity would not be directly curtailed by executive action, for court proceedings would be involved. Opposition to the regulation might therefore be substantially reduced and the government could not be accused of arbitrary suppression. On the other hand, the distribution of leaflets could be prevented by police seizure, and it would be up to the publishers to engage in the time-consuming, expensive and possibly fruitless task of trying to show that the leaflet (which, over the time involved, may have become irrelevant) did not contravene the regulation. Morrison's memo warned that there might be some opposition to the regulation and it might therefore be necessary to limit its life to three months in the first instance.

Although Lord Swinton submitted a further memo to the

committee which still hinted at the possibility of suppressing the Communist Party, [91] the Committee:

1. Approved the draft of regulation 2DA subject to minor changes.
2. Noted that after approval by the War Cabinet the Home Secretary would enter into discussions on the subject with representatives of the House of Commons. [92]

It is interesting to note that Morrison's proposals were aimed at propaganda and bore little relation to the question of 'agitators' in industry, which had been one of the central points of Lord Swinton's first memorandum. Significantly, a memo from Bevin, submitted to the third meeting of the committee, argued that there was no definite evidence to show that communist activity was having a serious effect on production. [93]

Having approved the proposed regulation at their second meeting, the third and final meeting of the committee does not appear to have discussed any major issues and concluded that, apart from the introduction of regulation 2DA, no further action against the Communist Party was necessary. [94]

I have outlined the deliberations of the Committee on Communist Activities in some detail for it is one of the few full discussions of this subject for which the records are publicly available. But one of the most remarkable aspects of the committee's work was that its recommendation for a new regulation was never implemented. Indeed, as far as my researches have been able to ascertain, it vanished into thin air.

On 17 February, Sir John Anderson presented a memorandum to the Cabinet which summarised the committee's discussions and recommendations. [95] The Cabinet approved the introduction of regulation 2DA [96] but from that point on all reference to the new regulation disappears. A likely explanation is that representative members of the House of Commons opposed the regulation, but possibly by the end of February Ministers no longer felt that it was so necessary to curb communist propaganda because the suppression of the 'Daily Worker' was having a more serious effect on communist activities than had been anticipated. In any event, one would expect either the Cabinet or a Cabinet Committee to give the matter further consideration, yet I found no evidence of this. A new 'Committee on Communism' was set up in 1941 and perhaps this body discussed the question. Unfortunately, its records remain closed to public inspection. [97]

UNWELCOME ALLIES

Only five months after the ban on the 'Daily Worker',

Nazi forces invaded the Soviet Union and, as far as the British Communist Party was concerned, this changed the whole nature of the war. Although the party continued to campaign for the lifting of the ban of the 'Daily Worker' and quickly took up the call for a second front, they publicly pledged full support for the war and the coalition government, and communists became active and enthusiastic supporters of the government's industrial strategy, denouncing strikes and demanding greater efforts and sacrifices from workers.

Yet if on an international level the British government embraced their Soviet comrades, at home the communists were unwelcome allies. The government were prepared to forgo any material advantage and continued to obstruct communist propaganda and activities in order to prevent the Communist Party gaining any kudos either from their support of the war or the resistance of the Red Army. From June 1941, it was over a year before the government were prepared to lift the ban on the 'Daily Worker' and even then they did so under pressure and with obvious reluctance.

For the first month or so after the invasion of the Soviet Union it was 'harrassment as usual' as far as the Communist Party was concerned. In July, Willie Gallacher asked the Home Secretary whether he was aware that police had seized a Communist Party leaflet entitled 'Solidarity with the Soviet Union'. Morrison replied in the negative, [98] but in a letter to the Lord President dated 17 July 1941 it was noted that the new protected places by-laws could not be finalised (see Chapter Seven) because 'the Home Office are not yet ready to say how far action under the Control of Paper Order will suffice to check the distribution of communist news bulletins.' [99] It might be thought that the government had simply not had time to adjust their policy, but in July, when the War Cabinet did consider the Communist Party, they reaffirmed the ban on the 'Daily Worker', even though a memorandum from the Home Secretary had explained the party's change of line and had quoted an internal party circular which stated that 'In supporting the Churchill government we do it wholeheartedly and without any reservations.' [100]

The government now faced a new problem. While the communists were still regarded as subversives, government support for Soviet resistance had to be unqualified, in public at least. The Soviet connection, which in other periods of history has been emphasised in attempts to discredit the Communist Party, was in danger of backfiring. Through either a collective intellectual contortion or a cynical about-face, government advisors and Ministers suddenly discovered that the Soviet Union and international communism had little to do with each other. In a memo to the Prime Minister in August 1941, Major Morton, one of Churchill's personal advisors, explained that, since the German attack on Russia, the axis powers had 'fostered confusion' between the notions of the Russian people and international communism and that such confusion existed in Britain. The memo continued:

> This matter was raised at Lord Swinton's weekly Security Meeting and my view strongly upheld. Mr Wall pointed out that it would be disastrous if the enthusiasm of the people of England for the excellent Russian defence drifted into an enthusiasm for communism. Mr Wall stressed evidence in his possession that the Communist Party of Great Britain was alive to the possibilities and was using all means to increase this confusion of thought for the purpose of promoting communism, sympathy for which was, in his opinion, beginning to grow in an alarming fashion.
>
> Should not the Ministry of Information be invited to consider this with a view to counter-propaganda...obviously such counter-propaganda would have to be worked out with great care and subtlety but it should not prove impossible. [101]

Although hardly a subtle tactic, it was almost certainly this way of thinking which led to the government banning the playing of the 'Internationale' on the BBC, (see below Chapter Five). A greater degree of effectiveness was achieved in controlling communist propaganda in factories. A note to the Prime Minister explained that trade unionists had to obtain permits to visit protected places, and that no permits were issued until MI5 had checked on the applicant. The note added that 13 permits were being held up at that time because the applicants were thought to be communists. [102] In September 1941, the Lord President submitted a memorandum to the Cabinet [103] which pointed out that Harry Pollitt, the General Secretary of the Communist Party, was planning to hold a series of lunch-time meetings in government controlled factories in order to stress the need for increased production. The memo said that Pollitt had already spoken at some privately owned factories and had said nothing objectionable. But the Security Executive recommended that such meetings ought not to be allowed since the Communist Party had not abandoned their revolutionary aims and were exploiting their tactical support of the war to gain popularity and undermine the authority of the trade union leadership. The memo concluded 'If this rule is adopted, it will be important to avoid giving the impression that it is aimed solely at Mr Pollitt and the leaders of the Communist Party.' [104] But it clearly was. The Cabinet agreed that political meetings should not take place in government controlled factories, and that they would inform the Employers Federation and the TUC of their decision [105] hoping, presumably, that the government's lead would be followed in privately owned factories.

The reference to communist attempts to undermine trade union authority related to communist involvement in a national shop stewards organisation, for the two were linked in a further Cabinet discussion in October 1941. Another memorandum on the Communist Party was submitted to the Cabinet by the Security Executive but it has been closed to public inspection at the Public Record Office. [106] The Cabinet minutes indicate that discussion centred on whether Ministers should receive shop stewards' delegations and it was concluded that they should not, on the grounds that such direct contact would tend to weaken the official trade union structure. The Ministry of Information were instructed to ensure that no undue publicity was given to meetings and conferences organised by the Shop Stewards National Council. [107]

One of the most interesting aspects of this continuing strategy of controlling communist propaganda is that, from 1941, the government's fundamental home front policy was to maximise production. As we shall see in Chapters Six and Seven, they were prepared to go to great lengths to achieve this end. Given that this was also one of the Communist Party's central policies from July 1941, we must assume that the continuing obstruction of communist activities, including the ban on the 'Daily Worker', resulted from a deep rooted belief that the Communist Party should not be allowed the normal freedoms of liberal democracy - presumably because its ultimate aim was to change the fundamental structure of society. It was not until the government's policy threatened to damage relations with the government and the rank and file of the labour and trade union movements (thus endangering industrial relations and industrial production) that they were prepared to make a concession. Significantly, this occured on the level of public policy. The fact was that, in spite of government action, the Communist Party enjoyed a growing popularity during these years. Furthermore, they were able to argue convincingly to an increasingly attentive audience that the continued ban on the 'Daily Worker' was unnecessary, unjust and an affront to press freedom. In May 1942 the Labour Party Conference disobeyed the advice of their Executive and voted in favour of lifting the ban, and many important and moderate trade unions adopted similar resolutions.

Although the government were coming under increasing pressure to modify their public policy, Lord Swinton still favoured tough anti-communist measures. In what can only be described as an alarmist memo to Churchill in April 1942, Major Morton reported that Lord Swinton had pointed out that the Communist Party had reorganised into factory branches, of which nearly one thousand had been established. The memo claimed that members of these branches were 'receiving intensive training in the techniques of revolution'. [108] It seemed to imply that a revolution was imminent, for it continued:

> Apart from the considerable expansion of support this move indicates, the big point is that up until now...the CP has not been able to establish...the organisation laid down by the official text-books of the Third International as ideal for staging a revolution. Where a successful rising has occurred in foreign countries, it has been preceded by the establishment of these Factory Units, trained to seize the centres of production. [109]

It is difficult to believe that Lord Swinton or Morton really felt that a communist revolution was just around the corner and it seems more likely that the memo was an attempt to convince Churchill of the need to continue the campaign against the communists in the face of the increasing pressure to lift the ban on the 'Daily Worker'.

If this was the case the memo had little impact. On 1 June 1942, the Home Secretary submitted a memo to the Cabinet which noted that pressure was mounting in favour of the 'Daily Worker' and that the respectable press and many MPs believed the continuance of the ban to be an unjustifiable infringement of press freedom. [110] At the meeting, Morrison reminded Ministers of the Labour Party Conference resolution and said that, if the TUC passed a similar resolution, the government could be embarrassed. He added that, as long as the Communist Party maintained their pro-war stance and refrained from pursuing their revolutionary aims, it would be difficult for the government to hold its position. The Cabinet did not feel the ban should be lifted but agreed that such action could be given further consideration. [111] In August 1942, Morrison submitted a further memo to the Cabinet which suggested that the time was ripe to lift the ban on both the 'Daily Worker' and 'The Week'. [112] The Cabinet felt that the ban should not be lifted at once, but in view of the fact that the TUC might complicate matters later, they authorised the Home Secretary to lift the ban at his discretion. [113] On 26 August the editorial board of the 'Daily Worker' were informed that the Order under 2D had been revoked, and on 7 September the 'Daily Worker' reappeared.

The government then, albeit reluctantly, had made a public retreat in the face of pressure from the labour and trade union movements, but there is no evidence to suggest that they had changed their fundamental attitude to the Communist Party. It was simply that by mid-1942 the image of political and industrial unity was beginning to look shaky and the government could not afford to exacerbate this by publicly maintaining a hard line against the Communist Party. As for the more covert activities mentioned in this and previous sections, there is no evidence to suggest that these ceased. Indeed, the fact that the secret 'Committee on Communism', set up in 1941, continued to meet until 1945 rather suggests the opposite.

TOWARDS D-DAY AND PEACE

With the Communist Party supporting the war, the British Union still banned, and the Peace Pledge Union having failed to win any mass support for their policies, the potential for any organised political opposition to the government or the war had been greatly diminished. Whereas until 1942 the activities of what were seen as subversive organisations had been discussed at the highest levels of government, from mid-1942 until the end of 1943 (with the exception of the 'Committee on Communism' mentioned above) virtually no such discussions took place. [114] But in the last eighteen months of the war central government again became concerned with actual or potential opposition in the form of trotskyists, communist journalists and an anarchist paper called 'War Commentary'. Since they were distinct issues I shall discuss them separately, beginning with what was seen at the time as 'the trotskyist menace'.

In Chapter Seven I deal with industrial disputes in some detail, so let it suffice here to say that, from 1942, there was a steady increase in the number of strikes that occured in wartime Britain. What is more remarkable is that few, if any, of these strikes received the official backing of the trade unions and they were consistently opposed by a united front consisting of management, the government, the TUC and Trade Union Executives and last, but not least, the Communist Party. Had this latter body still been opposing the war it is likely that much of the industrial unrest would have been laid at the door of 'communist agitators', as indeed had been the case in earlier years. As it was, attention was directed elsewhere and, in the autumn of 1943 and spring of 1944, it became focussed on the target of British trotskyists.

As early as April 1942 a Tory MP asked the Home Secretary whether he intended to suppress the trotskyist paper 'Socialist Appeal', given its 'subversive nature'. When the question was raised again in a debate in July 1942, Morrison pointed out that 'Socialist Appeal' was a little paper produced by a small organisation of not more than 500 members. [115] He added that the people involved in that organisation did not start strikes among miners, an indication that trotskyists were already being seen as agitators by some people. On the other hand, the Home Secretary's disinclination to take action under the defence regulations is in line with the position discussed in previous sections: that there was no point in taking action against propaganda which was having no effect.

The issue lay dormant for over a year but, in October 1943, Morrison was asked about evidence that recent strikes had been the result of subversive propaganda. He replied that a close watch was being kept on such activities but that there were so few people involved, 'it would be misleading to suggest that strikes have been the result of their propaganda'. [116] But Ernest Bevin and some of his Ministry of Labour officials agreed with the press that agitators were at work and, in speeches in September 1943, he attacked subversive political elements and threatened to take action. In October the paper supplies to 'Socialist Appeal' were cut. [117]

One of the strikes in which it had been intimated that trotskyist agitators had been involved was the Barrow Engineering strike, but a Ministry of Labour report of that dispute hardly suggests that trotskyists had kept the workers on strike. The report pointed out that when two prominent trotskyists, Ray Tearse and Jock Haston, had been in touch with the strike committee, the committee had then recommended a return to work! [118] But other Ministry of Labour files do indicate a general concern with trotskyist activities. In relation to a strike at Rolls Royce in 1943, the Industrial Relations Department in Glasgow wrote to the London Headquarters 'It cannot be doubted that certain very strong influences of an insidious kind played no small part in stirring up the dissatisfactions which resulted in this withdrawal of labour.' [119]

Interestingly, in view of Bevin's strong connection with the trade unions, it seems that the Ministry was just as concerned with bolstering up the authority of the trade union leadership as with ensuring the continuity of production. In a memo prepared for the Lord President's Committee it was stated:

> In recent months there have been signs of unofficial action by workers which if persisted in would undermine authority of the Trade Unions and the constitutional machinery. It is known, for example, that in Clydeside certain militant organisations are attempting to build up a rank and file organisation outside the Trade Union movement...These organisations take advantage of what may be legitimate grievances to foment unrest and to encourage unconstitutional action. [120]

On 3 April 1944, Bevin, reporting to the Cabinet on industrial relations, said that apart from the mines things were fairly steady, but that the apprentices' strike in Newcastle (over the Coal Mining Ballot) was clearly political and instigated by a group who had broken away from the Communist Party when Russia became Britain's ally. (sic) He said that he was checking with the Director of Public Prosecutions to see whether any action could be taken under the 1927 Trade Disputes Act but that he was thinking of bringing in a new regulation. The Cabinet endorsed his action. [121] On 5 April, Bevin presented a memo to the Lord President's Committee which argued in favour of new powers to deal with unofficial strikes. The use of regulation 18B and the Trades Disputes Act were possible but, the memo argued, 'existing powers are not adequate to deal with certain militant organisations who were at present engaged in fomenting unrest'. [122] The Home Secretary said he was in agreement with the need for a new regulation but that 'Socialist Appeal' should not be suppressed under regulation 2D, since it would give the organisation a first class advertisement. The Lord President's Committee agreed that a new regulation should be introduced but that no action should be taken against 'Socialist Appeal'. [123] The same day, Bevin reported to the Cabinet that he had obtained TUC support for a new regulation aimed at the instigators of strikes. He added that there was definite evidence that a political organisation was at work in the Sheffield area and that he was considering the use of 18B and the Trades Disputes Act. The Home Secretary said that he too was examining what action might be taken. [124] On 14 April, Bevin presented a draft copy of the new regulation - 1AA - to the Lord President's Committee. On the 17th it was approved by the Home Policy Committee and became law that day. [125]

Under regulation 1AA it became an offence, punishable by up to five years penal servitude, to 'declare, instigate or incite any other person to take part in, or otherwise act in furtherance of any strike or lockout likely to interfere with essential services', except by reason of either simply ceasing work or refusing to continue to work, or by any act done at a duly constituted and authorised meeting of a trade union to which a person belonged. As we shall see in Chapter Seven, the terms of this regulation could be applied to the leaders or activists of any unofficial strike, and it was suggested at the time that the claims regarding trotskyist agitators were simply a cover by which the government could justify the introduction of a regulation to control the spate of unofficial strikes that were occuring throughout industry.

There is no doubt that Bevin and other Ministers were aware of the scope of the regulation and that this came into their calculations. But the evidence above does suggest that the regulation was introduced primarily to stifle trotskyist activities. This specific concern is further illustrated by the decision to make the first ever use of the 1927 Trades Disputes Act. Towards the end of April 1944, four members of the Revolutionary Communist Party were charged under the Act in connection with the Tyneside Apprentices' strike. They were all convicted and given prison sentences, although later in the year the Court of Criminal Appeal quashed their convictions on a technical point. [126]

Yet although Bevin and at least some Ministry of Labour officials saw trotskyist activities as a problem to be eradicated, other government departments appear to have questioned this view. A memo from the Ministry of Supply referred to all the talk about agitators but pointed out that when hard evidence was obtained from MI5 it transpired that, in the Barrow Engineering strike, trotskyists did not appear on the scene until after the strike had begun, and that the Rolls Royce strike had been a dispute over a specific industrial grievance. [127] On 19 April, the Home Secretary submitted a memorandum to the Cabinet which dealt with trotskyist activities in some detail. The memo argued that their propaganda was intended to stir up class feeling among workers but that, as an organisation, they were 'too small and scattered to be able to start trouble on any considerable scale'. [128] It was stated that the evidence of trotskyist involvement in strikes was slight and that where there was such evidence, their activities had largely consisted of advising and encouraging strikers rather than provoking disputes. [129]

How can these events be summed up in terms of the influences on and development of government policy? Both Parker in his study of Manpower and Bullock in his biography of Bevin say that there was little evidence to indicate that trotskyists played a significant role in the development of industrial unrest. But they agree that Bevin believed that political agitation was an important factor. [130] Parker suggests that Bevin was obsessed with the idea of agitators, [131] and certainly he was the prime advocate both of regulation 1AA and of use of the Trades Disputes Act. But perhaps this point should not be stretched too far. Morrison, who never appears to have accepted that trotskyists were having much influence, also agreed that the new regulation was necessary, and Bevin's plans were endorsed by the Cabinet and two major Cabinet Committees. There is no doubt that the government were deeply worried by the rise of industrial unrest, and any measure likely to assist in the control of disputes must have appeared an attractive proposition in the few months prior to D-Day. Finally, there is the point that 'agitators' in industry were always seen as something that should be curtailed. The notion of the political agitator in industry is a familiar but suspect concept, for the activities of so-called agitators often amount to no more than the expression of their opinions and views: an activity which in the abstract is held to be a fundamental right in a democratic society. In the case we have just considered, there is no indication that trotskyist activities ever exceeded these boundaries.

In the case of trotskyists, government policy was at least partly a response to their activities. In the case of communist journalists, it was a preventive measure - a continuation of government attempts to minimise the impact and popularity of the Communist Party and its policies.

As the war progressed and the allies went onto the

offensive, accredited war correspondents allowed the national press to present up-to-the minute news and stories from the battle front. Any daily newspaper which did not have such correspondents was therefore at a disadvantage and might lose out in terms of its popularity and circulation. It appears that the War Office were responsible for arranging the system of war correspondents, but in January 1944 the matter was brought before the Cabinet to obtain an authoritative decision in the case of the 'Daily Worker'.

A memo to the Cabinet from the Secretary of State for War [132] stated that, in 1943, the editor of the 'Daily Worker' had put forward the names of four people to be accredited as war correspondents, but that all four had been rejected by the Security Services on an individual basis. It was noted that war correspondents were entitled to treatment as officers and were privy to information not normally available to the press or the public. The War Office view, therefore, was that no nominee of the 'Daily Worker' would be acceptable, since any sensitive information obtained by such correspondents would at least be given to the leadership of the Communist Party and that there was a danger that such information might not only be transmitted to the Russians but also to the Nazis. The Cabinet agreed that no nominees of the 'Daily Worker' should be accredited as war correspondents. [133]

The records of this discussion suggest that the decision had been reached solely on the grounds of military security and this explanation recurs in a number of government documents. For instance, in a minute to the First Lord of the Admiralty dated 29 May 1944, Churchill wrote:

> The reason why this Communist newspaper has not been allowed to send war correspondents to operational theatres or to occasions where security has to be maintained is because Communists do not hesitate to betray any British and American secrets they may find to the Communist Party, no doubt for transmission to Russia. [134]

The government's public explanation was also couched in terms of security considerations, [135] yet there is evidence to suggest that there was rather more to it than that. In a letter to the Prime Minister, dated 23 June 1944, Sir James Grigg, the Secretary of State for War, said that:

> The decision in the case of the 'Daily Worker' was attributed to the danger of military security...No doubt other factors entered into the decision but all the same the published reason still holds good. [136]

A clue to what these other factors were is found in a letter, written by Churchill to Macmillan, who was in Italy at the time. In the absence of war correspondents, the 'Daily Worker' tried to get members of the Italian Communist Party to send them articles about the state of the war. Macmillan had apparently been instructed to prevent such articles being sent to London but had pointed out that there was no political censorship in Italy, and that it was difficult to suggest any reasons which could justify action by the allied censorship. In a terse reply Churchill wrote:

> You surely ought to be able to stop this sort of thing going on in one way or another. The reason why we are not allowing the 'Daily Worker' to have war correspondents and presumably foreign correspondents like other papers, is because they are the organ of the particular Communist sect in this island which did all they could to pull us down during the time we were alone and only came whinnying back when Russia was attacked. Therefore we have no trust in them at all. [137]

After making the point that British communists were always ready to betray their country the letter continued:

> I shall be greatly disappointed in your vigour and skill if you cannot manage to prevent this advertisement for a venomous anti-British rag. [138]

There was no suggestion that the articles written by Italians would threaten security. Churchill's letter is simply based on his view of British communists and the fact that these articles would be an advertisement for the 'Daily Worker'. This position was not simply a Churchillian idiosyncrasy for, at a Cabinet meeting on 9 August, the Home Secretary said that he did not like the idea of the 'Daily Worker' receiving articles from Italy and had asked the Italian Premier to stop messages being sent to the 'Daily Worker'. The Cabinet approved his action. [139]

These points suggest that there were reasons beyond the security considerations for preventing the 'Daily Worker' from obtaining news from the battle front. Other evidence undermines the security argument itself.

In October 1944, the Trades Union Congress passed a resolution protesting about the ban and, in March 1945, a TUC deputation on the issue was received by Churchill, Eden and the Secretary of State for War. Churchill's notes of the meeting [140] indicate that Ministers concentrated on the threat to security but that these arguments were by-passed by Sir Walter Citrine who asked whether non-communist men of integrity would be acceptable as 'Daily Worker' war correspondents. Churchill apparently said that he was prepared to consider this possibility but, when it was discussed by the Cabinet, it was rejected since it might be construed as a sign of weakness. [141] At about the same time the government were embarrassed by the fact that the Soviet 'Tass' News Agency had asked that a British communist, Andrew Rothstein, should be accredited as one of their war correspondents. A memo from the Secretary of State for War [142] said that both the War Office and the Home Office felt that the accreditation of Rothstein would prejudice the government's case against the 'Daily Worker', but that the Foreign Office had said he had been granted security clearance, was reliable, and would be preferred to an unknown Russian. The Cabinet felt that the 'Tass' application could hardly be refused, but asked for a report on how they could be consistent in allowing a British communist to act as a war correspondent for 'Tass' while retaining the ban on the 'Daily Worker'. [143] Eventually it was agreed that Rothstein could go to the battle front, but only as a civilian correspondent. [144]

Even after hostilities in Europe had ended, further applications by the 'Daily Worker' were rejected. A memo to Churchill from the Secretary of State for War at the beginning of June 1945 noted that the security argument no longer applied, but argued that 'the 'Daily Worker' will be an unmitigated nuisance in Germany, and I should like to keep them out'. [145] It was not until September 1945 that the new government agreed to lift the ban. [146]

Although it is likely that security considerations were an important factor in the continued ban on 'Daily Worker' war correspondents, a number of other factors were clearly involved. There is little doubt that both Labour and Conservative Ministers were alarmed by what they saw as the growth of communist popularity. In February 1944, Attlee had written to Churchill saying that, in a General Election, both the communists and Commonwealth were likely to gain important representation in the House of Commons. [147] This perceived danger combined with the deep hostility towards the Communist Party may well have been a motivating factor in the adoption of a policy which might lessen the appeal and popularity of the 'Daily Worker'. Beyond this, there is the point that on many battle fronts the western allies were manoeuvering to prevent communist partisans forming governments in liberated countries, and reports from 'Daily Worker' war correspondents would be likely to expose western foreign policy. So I would suggest that the ban was not simply motivated by security considerations but also by political considerations, both domestic and foreign.

The last incident I wish to discuss in this section is rather curious, for it involved the use of regulation 39A - the incitement to disaffection regulation - at a very late stage of the war. In August 1944 one of Churchill's personal advisors submitted a memorandum to the Prime Minister [148] concerning a pamphlet which, among other things, advised soldiers to hold on to their weapons and called on civilian workers to sabotage production in preparation for the coming revolution. The memo said that inquiries had revealed that the author and distributor was a member of the editorial staff of the anarchist paper 'War Commentary', and noted that the police and Director of Public Prosecutions proposed to bring a prosecution but had wondered whether there were any objections on grounds of policy. They had been informed that there were not. [149]

In December 1944 Special Branch raided the offices of Freedom Press and private houses (using their powers under regulation 88A) and large quantities of documents were seized. [150] In February, four anarchists were charged with a number of offences including conspiracy to contravene regulation 39A and contravening regulation 39A by the dissemination of three seperate issues of 'War Commentary'. When the case came to court the three male defendents were sentenced to nine months imprisonment but the other defendent, a woman, was found not guilty.

Coming as it did at the very end of the war, the use of regulation 39A caused something of a storm and a number of prominent individuals made their protests public. [151] But there is no indication that central government were seriously worried about anarchist propaganda and, in fact, it appears that the initiative for the prosecutions came from the police rather than central government. Nevertheless it remains difficult to understand why proceedings against the Freedom Press Group should be instituted at that stage given that 'War Commentary' had been published regularly throughout the war.

COMMENTARY

In democratic theory it is axiomatic that in a democratic society there should be free and unfettered political competition - that individuals or groups should be at liberty to try to convince the rest of the population of the validity of their views. Yet in Britain during the war this was manifestly not so. Both the Chamberlain and Churchill governments employed a variety of methods to discriminate against and control the activities of political organisations which expressed dissident views. Even after the Communist Party gave full political support to the coalition it was not immune from such discrimination and control. The activities of government in this sphere can best be analysed if a distinction is drawn between what I have called the level of public policy and what can be seen as a level of covert or quasi-covert policies.

On the level of public policy - which includes actions as the promulgation of defence regulations such as 39B, 2D, 2C and 18AA, the banning of the British Union and the suppression of the Daily Worker - government policies were explicit in the sense that it was admitted that such actions were designed to limit the activities and propaganda of political organisations. In attempts to justify these policies, government spokesmen usually stressed a general commitment to liberal democracy but argued that, in wartime, the government could reasonably curtail activities and propaganda which they claimed were an abuse of democratic freedoms. The case of the British Union is distinct because its members were also seen as a potential fifth column but, in general, it is apparent that what the government saw as an abuse of democratic freedoms often amounted to little more than the expression of opinions and views which were opposed either to the war itself or to various aspects of government policy. The impossibility of defining an abuse of democratic freedoms in such wide terms, while at the same time preserving a democratic image, is highlighted by the problems encountered by the government in trying to draft a regulation to control and limit propaganda. I shall come back to this point in the next chapter. It should be stressed, however, that the desire to maintain a democratic image was an influence in setting limits to the government's public policy. In this context, both domestic and international opinion were of importance, especially since government spokesmen had frequently argued that the war was being fought to maintain democratic values. This would explain why the government were somewhat wary of taking their public policy too far - to the extent, for instance, of banning the Communist Party and interning sections of its membership. As it was, the public measures that were taken caused little immediate trouble, either in Parliament, in the country, or in terms of international opinion - a testimony perhaps to the shrewdness of the government's policy.

Despite the importance of maintaining a democratic image, a significant feature of the evidence available is that there is little indication that Ministers or their advisors had any principled commitment to the values of liberal democracy, a point which is strongly reinforced by the evidence of covert or quasi-covert actions by the government to impede the activities of certain political groups.

What I have called the covert or quasi-covert policies of government in this sphere cover a range of activities - the secretive manoeuvres outlined in the memo from the Minister of Information in March 1940, the decision by the Cabinet to suppress the leaflet 'The People must Act', the ban on 'Daily Worker' war correspondents and the use of controls over paper supplies to check the distribution of communist leaflets.

Some of these actions did become matters for public debate but what unites them all, and distinguishes them from the level of public policy, is that the government would not acknowledge that such actions were deliberate attempts to impede political activities. Of course those activities which remained secret did not have to be explained but, for instance, in the case of the 'Daily Worker' war correspondents, the government's policy was explained in terms of security, and in the case of the leaflet 'The People Must Act' it was claimed that the leaflet was only being restricted because the method of its distribution was likely to cause breaches of the peace. Another important point is that such activities did not involve the use of emergency powers, rather they relied on the ordinary law or other, often informal, methods. In this way there was no clear evidence that anything out of the ordinary was going on - which may be true, since peacetime governments could clearly employ similar tactics.

In discussing this form of government action I have limited my comments so far to those activities which the available evidence indicates were carried out by, or at the behest of, central government. But it may be that such activities are only the visible parts of a wider and more systematic policy of covert activities. I pointed out that there was no conclusive evidence to show that the police harrassment of pacifists, communists and other activitists in 1939 and the spring of 1940 was centrally directed, but the question remains open. Then there was the Home Defence (Security) Executive - the committee responsible for MI5. What policies and activities did this committee organise or authorise? The Committee's chairman until 1942, Lord Swinton, appears to have consistently argued for tough public measures against the Communist Party. It seems likely, therefore, that his committee may have been responsible for a wide range of covert activities which at present we know nothing about. Finally, the very nature of covert activities may ensure that other activities remain concealed from historical research.

Whatever the scope of covert or quasi-covert policies they cannot be justified. For the state to use its enormous power and influence to control and limit the activities of political groups by such methods is a complete negation of any form of democratic process.

It seems to me that two arguments might be advanced in attempts to justify both the public and covert policies of the wartime governments in relation to the control of political action. Firstly, it could be suggested that those organisations discriminated against did not confine their work to open political propaganda but were involved in more sinister activities. This was an argument levelled at all organisations which had ever opposed the war and government policies. But even if these organisations were involved in sinister activities, which for the most part seems unlikely, these could have been dealt with by the ordinary criminal law and would not themselves justify actions designed to curtail open and perfectly normal political activities.

The second argument might claim that, in times of war,

even a democratic regime is entitled to take whatever measures necessary to suppress anti-war propaganda. There is an empirical problem with this view since, in respect of action taken against the Communist Party after June 1941, the government sought to curtail propaganda that supported both the war effort and the coalition government. More philosophically, there does not appear to be any prima facie reason why a democratic regime should be entitled to suppress anti-war propaganda. Indeed, I would argue that if a regime claims to engage in war for and on behalf of the people, then, in a democratic society, people must be allowed to hear any opposition to the war which any individual or group wishes to express.

This brings us to the crux of the matter, for although the wartime governments never claimed an absolute right to suppress anti-war or any other form of propaganda, their policies were clearly aimed at limiting what people should hear or read, either by directly curtailing propaganda or by impairing the capacity of the organisations involved to present their case. Essentially then, government policy was directed towards manipulating public opinion and ensuring its own ideological hegemony - either in the short term or, in the case of the Communist Party in the later stages of the war, in the long term. This point is well made in government documents where the success of anti-war propaganda was taken as the criterion of whether action should be taken.

The 1978 BBC Television documentary series 'Propaganda with Facts' [152] examined the operation of the governments own propaganda machine during the 1940s. In the first episode of that series, the point was made that the wartime governments tried to control the overall perceptions of the general public. Attempts to limit and curtail political action can be seen as another aspect of that process - a process with which I shall continue to deal in the next chapter.

CHAPTER FOUR: NOTES

1. R. Benewick, The Fascist Movement in Britain, (Allen Lane, 1972) p.286.
2. 'The Times', 2 and 4 September 1939 and 'Peace News' 8 December 1939.
3. Benewick, The Fascist Movement in Britain, p.286.
4. NCCL Archives, Filing Case No. 4, 'Wartime', Section 6, 'Emergency Powers (Defence) Regulations. Filing Case No. 7, 'Police', Section 4, 'Police - General Correspondence 1937-40', Filing Case No. 16, Section 2, 'Peace Pledge Union 1939-40'.
5. NCCL Archives, Filing Case No. 16, Section 2, 'Peace Pledge Union 1939-40'.
6. R. Kidd, British Liberty in Danger, (Lawrence and

Wishart, 1940) p. 218.

7. 'News Chronicle', 12 October 1939, 'Daily Herald' 13 October 1939: and 'Manchester Guardian' 7 October 1939.

8. NCCL Archives, Filing Case No. 4, 'Wartime', Section 6, 'Emergency Powers (Defence) Regulations'.

9. PRO CAB 67/1, WP(G)(39)36.

10. Ibid.

11. Ibid.

12. PRO CAB 65/1, WM 49, 16 October 1939.

13. PRO HO 158/31, Circular No. 827733/2 to Chief Constables dated 28 September 1939.

14. See v.352 H.C.DEB 5s cols. 1833-4 & 1873.

15. Letter from Kidd to Gerald Bailey dated 8 January 1940. NCCL Archives, Filing Case No. 4 'Wartime', Section 6 'Emergency Powers (Defence) Regulations'.

16. Ibid.

17. v.357 H.C.DEB 5s cols. 1505-6.

18. v.358 H.C.DEB 5s cols. 2106-7.

19. PRO INF 1/375, 'Fascist, Communist and Pacifist Propaganda'.

20. PRO CAB 68/5, WP(R)(40)88, 14th Civil Defence Report dated 8 March 1940.

21. PRO CAB 73/2, CDC(40) 7th Meeting.

22. PRO CAB 75/4, HPC(40) 9th Meeting.

23. PRO CAB 73/2, CDC(40) 8th Meeting, 6 March 1940 and Memo PRO CAB 73/3, CDC(40)8.

24. PRO CAB 73/3, CDC(40)8.

25. Ibid.

26. PRO CAB 73/2, CDC(40)8th Meeting, 6 March 1940.

27. Ibid.

28. PRO CAB 75/4, HPC(40)11th Meeting.

29. PRO CAB 75/6, HPC(40)45.

30. PRO CAB 75/4, HPC(40)11th Meeting.

31. PRO CAB 75/7, HPC(40)87.

32. For more details of this case see S. Morrison, _I Renounce War - The Story of The Peace Pledge Union_, (Sheppard Press, 1962) pp.45-49. Interestingly, 'The Times' reported the judge as saying that the poster read 'War will cease when soldiers refuse to fight' see 'The Times' 7 June 1940

33. PRO CAB 75/7, HPC(40)94, Memo from the Home Secretary to the Home Policy Committee, considered by the HPC on 30 April 1940.

34. Kidd, _British Liberty in Danger_, pp.226-7.

35. v.360 H.C.DEB 5s col.1387.

36. PRO CAB 67/6, WP(G)(40)131, Memo submitted to the Cabinet 18 May 1940.

37. W. Churchill, _The Second World War_ Vol.II, (Cassell, 1949) p.49.

38. PRO CAB 65/7, WM 133, 22 May 1940.

39. PRO CAB 75/8, HPC(40)174.

40. NCCL Archives, Filing Case No. 7, 'Police', Section

5, 'Searches carried out 1940'.

41. Ibid.

42. NCCL Archives, Filing Case No.9, Section 7, 'Cases of Insulting Words and Behaviour 1940-1'.

43. Ibid. Letter from R. Kidd to S. Murray dated 21 May 1940.

44. PRO MEPOL 2/6260, confidential memo from the Commissioner dated 14 May 1940.

45. PRO MEPOL 2/6029, Minute by an Inspector from Walthamstow dated 12 June 1940.

46. Ibid, Note by a Superintendent dated 13 June 1940.

47. PRO MEPO 2/6325, Circular from Home Office to Chief Constables dated 14th June 1940, Number 700378/100.

48. PRO CAB 65/8, WM 193 and WM 194, and see memo PRO CAB 67/7, WP(G)(40)171.

49. PRO CAB 65/8, WM 193.

50. PRO HO 158/32, Circular to Chief Constables, No. 832463/105.

51. NCCL Archives, Filing Case No.9, Section 7, 'Cases of Insulting Words and Behaviour 1940-41'.

52. v.363 H.C.DEB 5s col.969.

53. PRO CAB 98/18, Memo CA(41)4 from the Home Secretary to the 'Committee on Communist Activities'.

54. Ibid.

55. A. Calder, The People's War, (Panther, 1971), p.160.

56. Peace Pledge Union, Minutes of Executive Committee Meetings 19 November and 3 December 1940.

57. In January 1941, for instance a PPU speaker was arrested after speaking at a group meeting and charged under regulations 39B and 39BA: Peace Pledge Union, Minutes of Executive Committee Meeting 18 February 1941.

58. see for instance W. Rust, The Story of the Daily Worker, (Peoples Press Printing Society, 1949) p.81

59. E. Trory, Imperialist War - Further Recollections of a Communist Organiser (Crabtree Press, Brighton, 1977) p.133.

60. T. Harrison, Living Through the Blitz, (Collins, 1976) p.119.

61. PRO CAB 68/7, WP(R)(40)196, 22nd Civil Defence Report.

62. PRO CAB 65/10, WM 295, 25 November 1940 and WM 297, 27 November 1940. The Daily Worker had apparently suggested that Bevin was taking bribes from capitalist organisations. The Cabinet considered taking legal proceedings and suppressing the Daily Worker but these proposals were later dropped.

63. PRO INF 1/673, Intelligence Report dated 2 December 1940.

64. PRO CAB 73/2, CDC(40)45th Meeting.

65. PRO CAB 73/3, CDC(40)67.

66. PRO CAB 73/2, CDC(40)46th Meeting, 11 December 1940.

67. PRO CAB 66/14, WP(40)482.

68. Ibid.

69. see PRO CAB 66/14, WP(41)7, Memo from Morrison on Daily Worker.

70. Churchill, Second World War Vol. III, p.640.

71. PRO CAB 66/14, WP(41)7.

72. Ibid.

73. Discussion minuted in Secretary's Standard File, PRO CAB 65/21, WM5.

74. Conclusions minuted in Secretary's Standard File, PRO CAB 65/21, WM5.

75. v.368 H.C.DEB 5s cols.310-311.

76. v.368 H.C.DEB 5s cols.186.

77. v.368 H.C.DEB 5s col.463-534.

78. PRO CAB 98/18, CA(41)1st Meeting.

79. PRO CAB 98/18, CA(41)2, Memo from Lord Swinton, Head of the Home Defence (Security) Executive, to the Lord President, entitled 'The Communist Party of Great Britain - An estimate of the effect of its present campaign and recommendations for action by the government.'

80. Ibid.

81. Ibid.

82. Ibid.

83. Ibid.

84. PRO CAB 98/18, CA(41)4, Memo from the Home Secretary on the Communist Party and CA(41)5, Memo from the Home Secretary on the control of propaganda.

85. PRO CAB 98/18, CA(41)5.

86. PRO CAB 98/18, CA(41)1st Meeting.

87. Ibid.

88. PRO CAB 98/18, CA(41)6, Memo from the Home Secretary on proposed regulation 2DA.

89. Ibid. Paragraph 1(i) of draft regulation 2DA

90. Ibid.

91. PRO CAB 98/18, CA(41)7.

92. PRO CAB 98/18, CA(41)2nd Meeting.

93. PRO CAB 98/18, CA(41)8, Note from the Minister of Labour regarding the views of the Production Executive.

94. PRO CAB 98/18, CA(41) 3rd Meeting.

95. PRO CAB 66/14, WP(41)27.

96. PRO CAB 65/17, WM 18.

97. The 'Committee on Communism' is referenced at the Public Record Office in the CAB 93 series.

98. v.373 H.C.DEB 5s col.296.

99. PRO CAB 123/93, Letter to the Lord President dated 17 July 1941.

100. PRO CAB 65/19, WM 72, 21 July 1941 and PRO CAB 66/17, WP(41)169.

101. PRO PREM 4, 64/5.

102. PRO PREM 4, 37/9A.

103. PRO CAB 66/19,WP(41)229, submitted to the Cabinet 29 September 1941.

104. Ibid.

105. PRO CAB 65/19, WM 98, 29 September 1941.

106. PRO CAB 66/19, WP(41)244, marked 'closed for fifty years', submitted to the Cabinet 20 October 1941.

107. PRO CAB 65/19, WM 104, 20th October 1941.

108. PRO PREM 4, 64/5, Memo to Prime Minister dated 22 April 1942.

109. Ibid.

110. PRO CAB 66/25, WP(42)230.

111. The discussion and decisions of the meeting were minuted in the Secretary's Standard File, PRO CAB 65/30, WM 70.

112. PRO CAB 66/27, WP(42)323.

113. The discussion and conclusions of this item were minuted in the Secretary's Standard File, PRO CAB 65/31, WM 101. It was also agreed that the ban on 'The Week' could be lifted at the Home Secretary's discretion.

114. One exception was a general discussion of communists and fascists in April 1943 which considered publishing pamphlets on the activities of those groups. The Cabinet decided against such a move. see PRO CAB 65/34, WM 60.

115. v. 379 H.C.DEB 5s cols. 1065-6.

116. v.392 H.C.DEB 5s col.1063.

117. It seems that the cut in paper supplies was a result of the growth in governmental interest in trotskyist activities, but Calder says that Haston had been able to persuade the Paper Controller that 'Socialist Appeal' had a pre-war circulation of 20,000 and paper supplies during the war were based on such figures. Haston's claim was a gross exaggeration and it appears to have been the discovery of this fact that led to the cut in supplies. See Calder, People's War, pp.509-10 and a memo from the Home Secretary to the Cabinet on trotskyism, PRO CAB 66/49, WP(44)202.

118. PRO LAB 10/262, Report on the Barrow Engineering Strike

119. PRO LAB 10/281, Report from the Industrial Relations Department in Glasgow on a strike at Rolls Royce, dated 9 November 1943.

120. Ibid. Memo for Lord President's Committee dated 3 March 1944.

121. PRO CAB 65/42, WM 43.

122. PRO CAB 71/16. LP(44)64.

123. PRO CAB 71/15, LP(44) 16th Meeting, 5 April 1944.

124. PRO CAB 65/42, WM 45, 5 April 1944.

125. PRO CAB 75/18, HPC(44) 10th Meeting, 17 April 1944.

126. see H.M.D. Parker, Manpower, History of the Second World War, (UK Civil Series) (HMSO, 1957) p.466.

127. PRO LAB 10/281, Memo from Ministry of Supply on Reg.1AA.

128. PRO CAB 66/49, WP(44)202.

129. Ibid.

130. Parker, Manpower, p.471 and A. Bullock, The Life and Times of Ernest Bevin Vol. II 'Minister of Labour' (Heinemann, 1967) pp.269-70.

131. Parker, Manpower, p.471.

132. PRO CAB 66/45, WP(44)7.

133. PRO CAB 65/41, WM 4.

134. Churchill, Second World War, Vol V, p.630.

135. see for instance the Adjournment Debate in the House of Commons on 3 August 1944, v.402 H.C.DEB 5s cols.1722-42.

136. PRO PREM 4, 13/1, pp.486-7, letter from Sir J.Grigg dated 23 June 1944.

137. Ibid, pp. 477-8, Prime Minister to Macmillan, 6 August 1944.

138. Ibid. pp. 477-8.

139. PRO CAB 65/43, WM 104, 9 August 1944.

140. PRO PREM 4, 13/1, Notes on proceedings of deputation, 16 March 1945.

141. PRO CAB 65/49, WM 33, 19 March 1945.

142. see PRO PREM 4, 13/1, Memo from the Secretary of State for War to the War Cabinet.

143. PRO CAB 65/49, WM 33, 19 March 1945.

144. See PRO CAB 65/50, WM 49 and CAB 66/64, WP(45)238.

145. PRO PREM 4, 13/1, p.317-20, Memo to Prime Minister dated 7 June 1945.

146. PRO CAB 128/1, CM 29, 6 September 1945.

147. PRO PREM 4, 65/1, Memo from Attlee to Churchill on the possibilities of keeping Labour in the coalition, dated 4 February 1944.

148. PRO PREM 4, 37/14A, Memo to Prime Minister dated 9 August 1944.

149. Ibid.

150. see 'New Statesman and the Nation' 3 March 1945 and v.408 H.C.DEB 5s cols.1561-2.

151. A letter condemning the raid, published in the 'New Statesman' of 3 March 1945, included the signatures of T.S. Eliot, E.M. Forster and Stephen Spender. On 31 March the 'New Statesman' published a further letter which announced that a Defence Committee had been set up. The Officers of the Committee included Herbert Read and Fenner Brockway.

152. This series was originally screened in six weekly parts on BBC2 Television begining on 10 January 1978.

Chapter Five

CENSORSHIP AND THE MEDIA

Throughout the war it was universally accepted that the government should operate some form of censorship in order to prevent the leakage of military information which would be of value to the enemy. No regime involved in a total war could afford to let an enemy gather details of shipping or troop movements simply by reference to the press or radio, or by receiving or intercepting postal and similar communications. Thus the censorship of such material was a direct attempt to restrict enemy intelligence gathering. But the systems of British censorship during the war went a good way beyond this particular need, not only by having an extended view of what information might be useful to an enemy, but also by becoming involved with the censorship of views and opinions. In this chapter therefore, I shall examine the various forms of censorship and control that were used by the government, and the extent to which attempts were made to prevent or curtail the expression of opinion.

POSTAL AND TELEGRAPHIC CENSORSHIP

Postal and telegraphic communication was the area in which the most systematic and publicly acknowledged censorship was established. It involved setting up a network of censorship offices around the country and the employment of thousands of civil servants. Unfortunately, a number of files related to this topic remain closed at the Public Record Office, including one which contains a selection of documents to illustrate the work of the Postal and Telegraphic Censorship! [1] One is left, therefore, with the problem of assembling the few available pieces of information to form a general picture. This formal censorship can be usefully divided into two types: external censorship relating to material being sent out of the country, and internal censorship - relating to material circulating within. Whereas internal censorship was mostly concerned with letters, parcels, telegrams etc., the external censorship was also responsible for examining newspapers, news agency reports and books being sent out of the country. I shall firstly consider external censorship, which included Northern Ireland because its common border with Eire was seen as a security threat.

On 1 September 1939, the government announced that all postal and telegraphic services to addresses outside Britain were to be subject to censorship. In a statement published the next day the Home Office advised people of what sort of material should be omitted from letters, etc., to avoid censorship delays. [2] This statement implied that the censorship was to be used solely to prevent information of military value reaching the enemy, but from the outset it had at least one other important function which both the external and internal censorship were to retain throughout the war - the gathering of information 'of military or intelligence value'. [3]

I found no evidence to indicate that censorship of opinion occurred during 1939 in relation to external communications, but criticisms of such activity began to emerge in the first few months of 1940. In February a left-wing news agency complained to the NCCL that political statements and cartoons were being censored prior to dispatch overseas. The NCCL wrote to the Head of the Press and Censorship Bureau about the case, and he replied saying that he would personally take up such complaints. [4] This would suggest either that there was no official policy to censor opinions or that such a policy was not to be publicly acknowledged. The March edition of 'Civil Liberty' reported that the publishers Lawrence and Wishart had been refused a permit to export their publications. [5] The Minister of Information confirmed this in an answer to a Parliamentary question in April 1940, but when he was asked whether this ban had been imposed because Lawrence and Wishart published socialist books, he replied 'I prefer not to answer more specifically.' [6]

There was a significant tightening of external censorship in respect of opinions and views from the time of the invasion crisis in 1940. On 7 May, the Home Policy Committee instructed the Ministry of Information to prohibit the export of the 'Daily Worker' and the British Union paper 'Action' and to consider similar action in respect of other publications. [7] According to a government spokesman, this ban had been extended to cover nine newspapers and periodicals by November 1940, and most of these had a left-wing or communist orientation. [8]

In a letter from the Chief Censor to the NCCL in November 1941, it was pointed out that censorship was guided by an Order made in 1940. This Order, which was probably made during the invasion crisis, specified that the following three categories of material were liable to censorship:

i) information valuable to an enemy.
ii) matter which endangers or brings into disrepute the war effort of this country or its allies.
iii) false statements defamatory to the allied cause or laudatory to the German cause. [9]

The correspondence between the Chief Censor and the NCCL concerned cuts made to reports dispatched by the General News Service Agency and the Censor stated that these cuts had been made under (ii) above. His letter added that, in this category, officials had been given three examples of material which should be censored. These were:

a) that there was a large 'peace party' in the Cabinet who wished to capitulate to Hitler
b) statements that the war was imperialist, fought by the allies for the sake of the bosses or international finance
c) that the French Army consisted largely of reluctant communists. [10]

The letter from the Chief Censor shows that censorship of opinion was taking place between 1940 and November 1941, but statements made in the spring of 1942 contradict this. A Ministerial Committee set up to consider action against the 'Daily Mirror' (see below p.148) also examined the question of outgoing press messages which might cause ill-will among the allies. [11] The committee's report to the Cabinet recommended that previous assurances that there would be no censorship of opinion should be withdrawn. [12] The Cabinet agreed [13] and on 26 March 1942 the Minister of Information announced that, while previously, outgoing press messages had only been subjected to censorship on security grounds, in future a stricter control was to be exercised to prevent the outside world getting a distorted picture. [14] The most likely explanation for this apparent contradication is that although most of the material leaving the country was censored as indicated by the Chief Censor, some arrangement had been made whereby the 'respectable press' were allowed to send out uncensored reports. It would then follow that the Minister's announcement meant that, in future, even opinions in such reports would be liable to censorship. The only alternative explanation would be that Ministers were unaware that censorship of opinion was already taking place.

The censorship of opinion in material leaving the country was maintained for most of the war, and it provoked occasional rows in Parliament. In November 1942, for instance, Emmanuel Shinwell suggested that reports of the proceedings of the House of Commons were being censored and that criticism of the government was being cut out. A government spokesman said that messages correctly reporting proceedings were not censored and that it would be a grave matter if this occurred. Shinwell retorted that he had information to the contrary. [15] A relaxation that was considered in 1943 was the lifting of the export ban on the 'Daily Worker' but, after this paper had said that the exiled Polish government was composed of fascists, the Cabinet agreed that the ban should remain. [16]

So far I have said little about the censorship of private mail to external destinations and the reason for this is that specific information in this area is more or less unavailable. One example though can be found in files of the Ministry of Labour. In April 1944, the General Secretary of the Amalgamated Society of Woodworkers wrote to a Branch Secretary in Northern Ireland suggesting that the Executive Council would call a strike if an employer did not recognise the latest pay award. The letter was seized by the Postal and Telegraphic Censorship, and copies sent to the Home Secretary, the Minister of Labour and the Home Defence (Security) Executive. [17] Because the letter was being sent to Northern Ireland it was automatically examined, but it illustrates the political and intelligence gathering role of the censorship. What is perhaps more interesting is how far such activities also occurred in relation to internal censorship. Again it is difficult to say, because information in this area is even more scarce than that in respect of external censorship.

There does not appear to have been any general censorship of internal postal and telegraphic communications between September 1939 and April 1940, although there was some examination of mail entering Britain [18] and Calder says that all internal telephone trunk lines were tapped from the beginning of the war. [19] On 29 May 1940, a memorandum considered by the Civil Defence Committee suggested that a regional organisation ought to be established for the censorship of internal mail and that snap checks ought to be made on telegrams and telephone calls. But the memo added that there was little point in imposing restrictions on the use of telephones, one of the reasons being 'that MI5 are able to make arrangements for the observation of such circuits as they desire at any time'. [20] At the meeting of the Civil Defence Committee the Chairman said that, to give effect to these proposals, the Home Secretary would have to sign a general warrant and that the only safeguards would be purely administrative. He pointed out that the action proposed was quite unprecedented and that he wished the Committee to be aware of this point in case it was questioned later. The Committee nevertheless agreed to the proposals [21] and on 25 June the Home Secretary signed a general warrant for the censorship of internal communications. [22]

Although the powers for full internal censorship had thus been made available it is difficult to assess the extent to which censorship was imposed. In a memo to the Standing Interdepartmental Committee on Censorship in May 1942, it was suggested that, up until then, a more general censorship had only been introduced on one or two occasions, and then in specific areas and only on the grounds of military security. The memo proposed that snap checks on these grounds should continue but, at a meeting of the committee on 22 June, it was noted that this kind of censorship would inevitably grow with the growth of combined operations. [23] The phrase used in public in relation to internal censorship was 'operational security'. In May 1942, for example, the Minister of Information stated that there was no internal censorship except occasionally for reasons of operational security. [24] As the war progressed and southern England became, as Churchill put it, 'a vast military camp', censorship was inevitably tightened and such developments were again justified on the basis of operational security. [25] Unfortunately, it is by no means clear what 'operational security' meant. No doubt it was intended to prevent the leakage of information of military value, but it was also probably used to keep tabs on communists, trotskyists and other dissidents who criticised the government's policy. One allegation that was raised on a number of occasions was that letters to MPs were particularly prone to examination by the censor. This allegation was consistently denied. [26]

With the exception of letters to and from detainees it is probable that the internal censorship only cut out material likely to be of military value. But in terms of intelligence gathering the scope of the censorship was much wider. In reply to a Parliamentary question in February 1944 the Minister of Information said that information from civilian letters was only copied and circulated to other departments if to do so was in the interest of the 'efficient prosecution of the war or the defence of the realm' [27] - a phrase which, as we have seen, had an almost unlimited application.

THE NATIONAL PRESS

As I noted in Chapter One, the defence regulations introduced at the beginning of the war gave the government wide powers to control the press. Yet in the first weeks of the war, as with anti-war propaganda, the press were not subjected to a series of prosecutions, nor did the Secretary of State attempt to use his powers under regulation 39B. The main problem the press faced at that time was the way in which the government censored their own information output.

After only five days of war the National Executive of the National Union of Journalists passed a resolution expressing grave concern at the failure of the Ministry of Information to provide the public with adequate news of the war and asked that immediate steps should be taken to prevent the unnecessary and arbitrary suppression of news which conveyed no information of military value. [28] It seems that censors of government information not only had a distorted view of what might be of use to the enemy, but also witheld information which had already been broadcast or published in other countries. This created a good deal of antagonism and produced some bizarre results. On 10 September 1939, the Ministry of Information released the news that the British Expeditionary Force had been despatched to France. This news had already been published in France and cabled to the USA, but the War Office then had second thoughts about releasing the story. The Ministry of Information therefore reversed its previous decision, although by then many early editions of newspapers had been printed and were in the process of distribution. Sir Samuel Hoare, who at the time was Lord Privy Seal, recalled that:

> There followed several hours of complete confusion, in the midst of which an official of the War Office, without any authority, instructed Scotland Yard to seize any papers which contained the news. Upon the strength of this instruction, the police visited the newspaper offices and waylaid early morning travellers in order to obtain possession of the newspapers. [29]

Whether or not an anonymous War Office official was to blame, the government were clearly embarrassed by this incident and, on 3 October, the Prime Minister announced that the pre-war system of distributing government information was to be restored and that the responsibility for the release of official news would rest with the department concerned.

Beyond the vagaries of their internal arrangements, the government relied on a system of voluntary censorship throughout the phoney war period, although the possibilities of proceedings being taken under the defence regulations, or compulsory censorship being introduced, no doubt encouraged participation in such a scheme. As in peace time, the press were asked not to publish matter covered by Defence or D-Notices and editors could also submit articles to a Press and Censorship Bureau, who would examine them and suggest cuts if they were felt to be necessary. The Press were asked not to indicate in their papers where cuts had been made by the censors. It is difficult to say to what extent D-Notices or other guidelines covered matters not related to military security, or how far voluntary censorship was extended to cover the expression of opinions. But there is no doubt that the government did make attempts to stifle criticism in the press. James Margarch, who shows in his book 'The Abuse of Power' that attempts to control the press are not confined to wartime, notes that in November 1939 the Cabinet agreed that the Prime Minister should 'consider the best method of approaching the newspaper proprietors with a view to securing a cessation of the present Press campaign against the Government'. [30] A more specific example was given by Hoare-Belisha (who up until January 1940 was Secretary of State for War) in an interview with W.P. Crozier in March 1940. [31] Hoare-Belisha had written an article on Finland which was to be published in the 'News of the World' but the Foreign Secretary contacted the editor of the paper, and then the writer, saying that some changes in the article were necessary. It was agreed that a Foreign Office official would make the necessary amendments but, according to Hoare-Belisha, when the article was returned a piece of it was missing and half the article had been re-written to support the government's position - arguing directly contrary to the original article. Hoare-Belisha refused to accept the edited version and eventually the article was published in its original form although with certain passages omitted.

Despite the government's concern with critical opinion, the combination of voluntary censorship, the government's own internal system and the apparent desire of many newspapers to support the government without qualification, was sufficient to give the impression that most newspapers were little more than mouthpieces for government policy in the first few months of the war. On 13 September the Conservative MP Captain Cazalet claimed that uniformity had been created among the press, and that it was difficult to know whether one was reading 'The Times' the 'Daily Express' or the 'Daily Herald'. [32] Aneurin Bevan put the point more colourfully. In respect of both the national press and the BBC, he wrote:

> Immediately on the outbreak of war England was given over to the mental level of the 'Boy's Own Paper' and the 'Magnet'. The Children's Hour has been extended to cover the whole of British broadcasting and the editors of the national dailies use treacle instead of ink. If one can speak of a general mind in Britain at all just now, it is sodden and limp with the ceaseless drip of adolescent propaganda. [33]

After the debate in the House of Commons on 31 October 1939 the formidable powers under regulation 39B were significantly curtailed. So between November 1939 and May 1940 the government relied more heavily on the voluntary system of censorship. It was to be an enduring feature of government-press relations throughout the war. Since the national press as a whole supported the war the voluntary system was largely successful in preventing the publication of information of military value. But the new government formed in May 1940 utilised a variety of tactics in attempts to control the expression of opinion in the national press, particularly that which was critical of government policy or the military command.

One of the last acts of the Chamberlain government was the introduction of regulations 2C and 94A and they were supplemented only three weeks later by regulations 2D and 94B. As I have already mentioned, both regulations 2D and 2C related to the systematic publication of matter which, in the opinion of the Secretary of State, was calculated to foment opposition to the war. Under 2C the people or organisation involved had to be first warned and then prosecuted through the courts. But under 2D a newspaper could be summarily suppressed. Regulations 94A and 94B provided powers to close or seize printing presses. There is no doubt that these regulations could be applied to national newspapers and they restored legal sanctions over the expression of opinion. But, when they were made, 2C and 94A were aimed at anti-war propaganda and 2D and 94B were specifically discussed in relation to the 'Daily Worker' and 'Action'. During the invasion crisis from May to July 1940 the government considered other methods of controlling the national press.

On 14 June, the Cabinet decided to set up a committee to consider how compulsory censorship might be introduced [34] and Cabinet minutes for 16 and 17 June express the view that, while the national press were often helpful and probably doing their best to support the government, 'stunts' and 'inquests' tended to undermine national morale and that even the most reputable newspapers treated the 'guidance given' in a cavalier sprit. [35] Ministers felt that eventually prosecutions would have to be brought, but that such a course of action was undesirable at that time. [36] The Committee on Compulsory Censorship, chaired by Chamberlain, only met once, but agreed to investigate the possibility of setting up a Censorship Board which would tell the press which sources of information they could use. [37] According to Barry Cox, Duff Cooper warned newspaper editors that - in his opinion - voluntary censorship had broken down and a compulsory system would have to be introduced. [38] On 3 July, Attlee told the House of Commons that government policy was to interfere as little as possible with the liberties of the press, but that it had to be recognised that statements could be put out in the guise of opinion which either gave information of value to the enemy or were calculated to impede the war effort by weakening the resolution of the public. He stated 'The government are not prepared to give any assurance that the publication of such statements will not be interfered with.' [39] On 18 July the Cabinet returned to the question of the press. The Minister of Information reported that the Newspaper Proprietors Association had rejected the proposals for a Censorship Board. The Cabinet agreed to drop this scheme in favour of tightening up the D-Notice system and preparing a Bill which would enforce compulsory censorship in the event of invasion. [40]

Thus, during the invasion crisis, there were no changes

made to the formal structure of the censorship system, and the national press united to oppose the proposals that were made. Unfortunately, no information is publicly available in respect of changes in the D-Notice system, but clearly the government had imposed further restrictions and issued a warning to the press to toe the line. The desired effect was probably obtained for it was to be several months before the Cabinet returned to the question and, when they did, they were concerned with the activities of one or two newspapers rather than the press as a whole.

On 2 October 1940 the Cabinet discussed the 'News Chronicle'. The Cabinet minutes of this item remain closed to public inspection, [41] but the 'Index to Cabinet Minutes' note that the meeting considered 'mischevious articles' on Spain and that the Secretary of State for Air, Sir Archibald Sinclair, was asked 'to use his influence with the proprietors'. [42] On 5 October Churchill sent a minute to Sinclair which stated:

> I really must ask you to exert your influence to prevent these reckless and mischievious articles being written in the 'News Chronicle', which so greatly endanger this country in a situation already serious enough... Reluctant as I should be to do so, I should not hesitate, if I thought the safety of this country was imperiled by irresponsible action, to ask Parliament for further powers. [43]

Whether Churchill had been responsible for bringing this topic before the Cabinet is not clear, but there is no doubt that in the autumn and winter of 1940 he took a particular interest in the activities of two papers published by the 'Mirror' group - the 'Daily Mirror' and the 'Sunday Pictorial'.

At a Cabinet meeting on 7 October 1940, [44] Churchill argued that the two papers appeared to be trying to disrupt discipline in the army and make trouble between the government and organised labour. He felt there must be an ulterior motive behind these activities, and Ministers agreed with Churchill's view. The possibility of prosecuting the papers under regulation 39A was discussed, but the Attorney General said that such prosecutions were not really possible. Beaverbrook reminded the Cabinet that the Newspaper Proprietors Association had some disciplinary powers and that it might be better to make an approach to that body. [45] The meeting adjourned without any decision being taken but two days later the Home Secretary presented a memorandum to the Cabinet entitled 'Subversive Newspaper Propaganda'. The memo questioned whether the 'Daily Mirror' or the 'Sunday Pictorial' intended to impede the war effort since, while the papers had attacked some government ministers and the military command, they had also made a number of patriotic comments too. It pointed out that it would be difficult to suppress those particular papers without suppressing the 'Daily Worker' and other newspapers, and that suppression would allow comparisons to be drawn between the blanket censorship imposed in France and that country's subsequent collapse. The memo argued that, although drastic action might be necessary if these papers continued their criticisms, at that stage there was no clear case for proceeding against the 'Mirror' or the 'Pictorial'. It recommended that the Cabinet should accept Beaverbrook's suggestion of an approach to the Newspaper Proprietors Association and that this approach should be made on a friendly basis rather than in the form of a threat, as the latter course might be interpreted as an attack on the freedom of the press. [46]

The Cabinet minutes for the meeting on 9 October, indicate that both Churchill and Attlee felt Morrison's proposals to be too soft. Churchill argued that members of the War Cabinet should not ask favours from the press, and Attlee wanted strong action to be taken. General agreement was reached that 'a continuance of such articles could not be tolerated', but Morrison said that many newspapers had acted as badly as the 'Mirror' and the 'Pictorial' and that the government should avoid a debate in the House of Commons which might split down party lines. The Cabinet finally agreed that Beaverbrook and Attlee should summon representatives of the Newspaper Proprietors Association and warn them that the government would not tolerate such criticism from the press. In addition Morrison was instructed to check who owned and controlled the 'Mirror' newspapers. [47]

Attlee and Beaverbrook saw representatives of the Newspaper Proprietors Association on 11 October and, according to Cecil King's diary, warned them that if the irresponsible criticism in the 'Mirror' and the 'Pictorial' continued, the government would introduce compulsory censorship of both news and views. [48] The following day Cecil King and Guy Bartholomew visited Attlee and were told that both the 'Mirror' and the 'Pictorial' showed a subversive influence. [49]

A meeting of the Cabinet on 16 October was told that the Newspaper Proprietors Association and representatives of the newspapers had appeared 'somewhat chastened' and had said that they would take more care. Beaverbrook expressed the view that the newspapers would behave better in the future. [50] This particular episode was finally closed on 4 November 1940, when the Cabinet considered a memo from Morrison on the ownership and control of the 'Mirror' newspapers. The memo itself remains closed to public inspection [51] but the Cabinet minutes record that there was no one controlling interest in the paper, and Morrison pointed out that, since the warning, the papers had been much better. [52]

Although the Cabinet did not return to the question of the 'Mirror' newspapers until the autumn of 1941, Churchill himself kept up the pressure in correspondence and a meeting with Cecil King in the first few months of 1941. This correspondence has been reproduced in full elsewhere, [53] but a few of the central points should be noted. At the beginning of January, Churchill's private secretary wrote to King on the Prime Minister's behalf, castigating him for two articles which had appeared in the 'Daily Mirror'. One suggested that Churchill had criticised Eden and the other attacked four members of the government. In reply, King stressed the 'Mirror's' loyalty to Churchill but said that an unflattering view was taken of some of his colleagues. Churchill then wrote to King personally and suggested not only that the 'Mirror' newspapers expressed a spirit of malice and hatred towards the government but also that the 'Mirror' was conducting a campaign which would be ideally suited to a fifth column movement. King then suggested that the two men should meet to discuss the matter. His letter concluded 'if you consider we have gone beyond what should be permissable in wartime, we should, of course, meet your wishes in so far as we conscientiously can'. [54]

King and Churchill met at Downing Street at the end of January, and King's record of the meeting notes that the Prime Minister maintained that the 'Mirror' newspapers showed malignancy towards the government and great 'artistry' in undermining the morale of the nation. After the meeting the interchange of letters continued. In a final letter to Churchill on 11 February, King wrote:

> As I cannot emphasise too strongly, all of us here wish to give you personally all the support possible and it has come as a great shock to learn that you have been so distressed at the line these papers have been pursuing. I am afraid I had assumed that if anything published by us should cause you serious annoyance you would send a message through one of your secretaries asking us to be more moderate.
>
> However, thanks to your very full and frank letters and the talk we had, we now have your point of view clearly before us. The staff have had their instructions and you may have already noticed a marked change of tone. If in the future you have any fault to find with our contribution to the nation's war effort, I hope you will let us know at once. [55]

King's conciliatory attitude must be placed in the context of the warning given the previous autumn and the fact that the 'Daily Worker' had just been suppressed. But that Churchill could exact a promise to toe the line from the executive director of the most radical of Britain's big national newspapers is in itself symptomatic of the relations between press and government in general. As it was, although the 'Mirror' may have moderated its criticism, by the autumn of 1941 it was in trouble again.

At a Cabinet meeting on 9 October 1941, Churchill resurrected the question of the 'Daily Mirror' in relation to an article which had attacked Franco's dictatorship in Spain. He said that there was already a danger of Spain joining the Axis and that, if newspapers could not refrain from publishing such articles, the government would have to take further powers. The Cabinet therefore instructed the Foreign Secretary, the Minister of Information and the Home Secretary to report on the possibilities for action. [56] On 27 October the Cabinet also asked the Home Secretary to report on an article in the 'Sunday Pictorial' which had ridiculed members of Parliament: to consider whether it constituted either a breach of Parliamentary Privilege or an offence under any of the defence regulations, and, in conjunction with Sir John Anderson, consider whether any further powers were necessary. [57]

Morrison's memo on this latter case was the first to be considered and was presented to the Cabinet on 10 November. It said that the article probably did infringe upon Parliamentary Privilege but according to the Director of Public Prosecutions it neither contravened any of the defence regulations nor did it amount to sedition in common law. Regarding the possibility of taking further powers the memo stated:

> However limited may be the use which the government would make of such powers in practice, any Regulation which would be effective for dealing with such an article as that in the 'Sunday Pictorial' would have to be so framed as to cover a wide field and would be open to attack on the ground that it would empower a Government to exercise a much more extensive control over expression of opinion than the present Government would in fact exercise or would think it right to exercise. [58]

From the Cabinet instruction it would seem that this statement represented the views of both Morrison and Anderson, and at the Cabinet meeting discussion concentrated on whether the question of Parliamentary Privilege should be taken up. Even this possibility was apparently discounted after the Attorney General pointed out that, if the question of privilege was raised, the government might have to answer a number of difficult questions. [59]

A week later the Cabinet discussed the 'Mirror's' article on Spain and another memorandum from Morrison on the possibility of taking further powers. Morrison's theme was the same as before - that any new regulation would have to be wide and was therefore likely to be strenuously opposed. The memo stated:

> Any defence regulation which was wide enough to check such expressions of opinion as appeared in the article in the 'Sunday Pictorial' would not only be open to attack from the defenders of civil liberties in the House of Commons, but would unite the Press in opposition to the Government... and would drive them into alliance with the worst on the issue of freedom of expressions of opinion. [60]

In a similar vein, a joint memorandum from the Foreign Secretary, the Minister of Information and the Home Secretary discounted the possibility of extending censorship to cover opinions, since such an extension would be opposed by the press and provoke a good deal of opposition in Parliament. The memo could only suggest that the Prime Minister might make a statement in the House of Commons condemning irresponsible journalism. [61] The Cabinet agreed that no further action should be taken, [62] and thus the issue rested until the spring of 1942.

In their biography of Herbert Morrison, Donohugue & Jones refer to these discussions in the autumn of 1941 and state that 'Morrison had again... in the secret confines of the Cabinet, defended freedom of the press against Churchill.' [63] suggesting not only that Morrison and Churchill were the chief protagonists but that Morrison's views were based on a deep seated belief in freedom of expression. The Cabinet minutes reveal neither Churchill's views on the taking of further powers nor whether there was a major division of opinion within the Cabinet. But it is clear that Morrison was not the only Minister to reject such a course of action. Sir John Anderson, Anthony Eden and Brendan Bracken, (by now Minister of Information) were all involved in the preparation of memos on the subject and presumably agreed with the line adopted in them. That Morrison should have such allies, if indeed he needed them, is not suprising when the rationale behind the rejection of further controls is examined. These measures were not precluded on the grounds that freedom of expression should be maintained, but on pragmatic grounds: that the disadvantages involved with taking further powers outweighed the advantages. As far as any new regulation to control the press was concerned, it was the potential scope of any useful measure which was seen as the main problem. Had it been possible to devise a more specific regulation, which might therefore have provoked less opposition, it seems likely that it would have been made.

This point is supported in an historical appendix to Morrison's memorandum presented to the Cabinet on 17 November. But this document is also important because it relates the problem of devising a specific regulation not only to the type of material the government desired to control, but also to the principles of democratic government and the extent to which freedom of expression should be allowed. The appendix, referring to the deliberations concerning the control of the press and communist propaganda in the autumn of 1940, stated:

> The Home Office... after considering various forms of words...came to the conclusion that it would be impossible to devise a Regulation covering propaganda conducted with a subversive intent or covering reckless attacks on authority, such as would be generally condemned by responsible opinion, without at the same time covering expressions of opinion for which the traditions of this country suggest that liberty ought to be allowed. It was recognised that the traditional doctrine of liberty for expressions of opinion gives great and, indeed, dangerous liberty to agitators who may do harm to the war effort, but no way could be found of reducing this danger without at the same time rendering liable to prosecution critics for whose expressions of opinion liberty ought to be allowed if the principles of democratic government are to be maintained. The democratic principle of freedom for expressions of opinion means taking the risk that harmful opinions may be propagated. [64]

Donohugue and Jones, apparently referring to this historical appendix, say that Morrison's memo 'concluded with the classic liberal position, which he and his departmental advisors firmly held'. [65] Now while the last sentence in the above passage may be construed as such, in the passage as a whole the concept of freedom for expressions of opinion is of a limited nature. A distinction is drawn between criticism which is seen as subversive and harmful, and criticism which is considered responsible. It is inferred that freedom of expression should only apply to responsible criticism and that subversive or harmful criticism could therefore be suppressed without detracting from the democratic principle of freedom of expression. The above passage does not tackle the problem of who defines what is harmful, subversive or responsible, but it seems to be assumed that this is the function of government. In the context of this historical appendix, certain articles in the 'Daily Mirror', as well as communist propaganda, are certainly seen as harmful or subversive. The appendix implies that had it been possible to draft a specific regulation, such views could have been suppressed without infringing on the principle of freedom of expression. If we now turn to the government's discussion of the 'Daily Mirror' in the spring of 1942, we can see that the views put forward in this historical appendix were assumed from the outset and that, once again, discussion centred on the question of expediency.

In the first few months of 1942 the government were going through a particularly traumatic period. Military disasters in North Africa and the Far East had combined with the growing rigours of domestic survival to precipitate considerable political and public unrest. From the beginning of the year commentators at home and abroad were asking whether the Churchill government could survive. In January 1942, Churchill called for a vote of confidence and, with the whips on, the House of Commons voted 464-1 in favour of the government. But if this appeared to be an overwhelming victory, the critics were not silenced. Churchill himself wrote that he could feel the tension in political circles growing. [66] In February, Cecil King wrote in his diary that, within a fortnight, public support for the Prime Minister might collapse altogether and that of all the national newspapers only the 'Telegraph' and the 'Express' remained behind the coalition. [67] The same month Churchill made a number of changes in the government. These changes were generally welcomed in the press, but many felt they did not go far enough and Churchill's personal image began to slip. In March 1942, Mass-Observation noted a startling drop in the Prime Minister's popularity [68] and in the next few months the government were to suffer a number of embarrassing by-election defeats.

The 'Daily Mirror' was amongst the government's severest critics: attacking the incompetence of the military command, the inefficiency of the civil service and the continued importance of class and privilege in wartime Britain. Perhaps typical of their critical style was an article published on 20 February concerning the Parliamentary system - a subject that had already got them into trouble. The article included the following passage:

> If this war lasts another three years this bankrupt Parliament will have lasted a decade. Everything in Britain has changed since 1935 except the management. The same old faces talking the same old bluff. The same old raddled intellects unalterably engraved with the same old prejudices and stupidities. Where is the new broom to sweep out this dusty mausoleum of dead minds? [69]

Was this irresponsible criticism or fair comment? Morrison and the Home Office were in no doubt, for it was to be cited as an example of the newspaper undermining public morale. [70] Yet according to popular belief it was not articles such as this which caused the Cabinet to return to the question of the 'Daily Mirror', it was a cartoon by 'Zec' published on 6 March 1942.

The cartoon depicted a sailor clinging to a raft in the middle of the ocean, and the caption read, 'The price of petrol has been increased by one penny - Official.'.

According to Hugh Cudlipp, the theme of the cartoon was directed against black market activities which were hampering the war effort [71] and other people took it as a tribute to the courage of merchant seamen and an enjoinder to petrol users not to complain about petrol price increases. But Ministers apparently interpreted the cartoon as suggesting that excess profits were being made by petrol companies while courageous seamen suffered.

On 9 March the Cabinet discussed the press and the minutes note that the view was 'strongly expressed' that certain organs of the press were undermining national morale. [72] It has often been said that Churchill demanded that the 'Daily Mirror' should be instantly suppressed, and although this seems likely in view of the Prime Minister's earlier clashes with the paper, the Cabinet minutes neither confirm nor refute this view. The Cabinet agreed in principle that effective control must be exercised to stop the publication of material which undermined national morale, but rather than taking immediate action they decided to set up a Ministerial Committee, under the Chairmanship of Sir John Anderson, to consider in detail what methods should be employed in achieving their goal [73].

Anderson's 'Committee on Press Censorship', as it was called, met twice, on 14 and 16 March. Churchill did not attend, but three other members of the War Cabinet did - Attlee, Eden and Bevin. Also present were the Home Secretary, the Minister of Information and the Attorney General. [74]

The first meeting of the committee considered two memoranda, one from the Home Secretary and one from the Minister of Information. Both these documents dealt with the subject on a general level. Morrison's memo asked whether journalists were to be allowed to say that the government and military authorities were incompetent, and argued that while constructive criticism should not be hindered, action should be taken against irresponsible criticism. The memo pointed out, however, that it was difficult to prove that criticisms were working against the public interest and that, since regulation 39B had been withdrawn in its original form, it had proved impossible to draft an effective regulation which would allow legitimate but not irresponsible criticism. It was stated that regulation 2C was of little use because a vigorous defence could be mounted in court, and that there were many objections to compulsory censorship of opinions. The memo made no specific recommendations. [75]

The memo from the Minister of Information warned that the introduction of compulsory censorship would 'strike at the foundation of press freedom itself' and would force a cleavage between government and Fleet Street. It was suggested that, rather than taking universal action, it would be better to deal with specific offences as they arose and that, in regulations such as 2C, 2D, 39B and 39BA, there was sufficient scope to deal with any newspapers who published matter likely to undermine public morale. [76]

In discussion, the committee agreed that the censorship of opinion was an impractical proposition, and concentrated their attention on the possible suppression of the 'Daily Mirror' under regulation 2D. In adjourning their discussion the committee agreed that:

1. the Attorney General should check whether the 'Daily Mirror' could be suppressed under regulation 2D,

2. the Home Secretary, in the light of the Attorney General's judgement, should consider
   a) whether the 'Daily Mirror' had been systematically fomenting opposition to the war
   or
   b) what further regulation was necessary,

3. Ministers ought to react strongly against irresponsible articles in the press. [77]

Prior to 16 March, the Attorney General must have circulated the view that the 'Daily Mirror' could be suppressed under regulation 2D, for discussion at the second meeting of the committee centred around a memorandum from Morrison entitled 'The Question of Action under 2D Against the Daily Mirror'. [78]

Regulation 2D stated that the Secretary of State had to be satisfied that a newspaper was systematically fomenting opposition to the war before he could suppress it. The first part of Morrison's memo addressed itself to this question. It said that an examination of the paper's files showed that, while there were a number of articles supporting the war, there were many that were starkly critical. The memo continued:

> They would no doubt contend that the articles which throw contempt on the authorities...are intended to awaken the public mind to a realisation that changes of outlook and changes in the political, social and economic system of the country are necessary in order that victory may be secured...It is, however, plain that in the conduct of this paper there is a reckless disregard of the question of whether its articles may create a sense of discouragement and doubts as to victory...Its 'line' is so systematic as to have the cumulative effect of spreading a spirit of defeatism among certain types of people. [79]

Thus Morrison confirmed that, in his view, the newspaper was systematically fomenting opposition to the war. But the memo then went on to discuss some of the problems that might arise if the newspaper were suppressed, and this section highlights the tensions inherent in the desire to suppress critical opinion, while at the same time maintaining a liberal and democratic image. It was suggested that many people did not realise the scope of the powers under regulations 2D and that if the 'Mirror' were suppressed 'it will be obvious that the Home Secretary is himself the judge of what is and what is not legitimate criticism of the authorities.' [80] In such circumstances, the memo pointed out, the press as a whole might rally to the support of the 'Mirror' and clamour for an amendment to the regulation so as to render it impotent. There was also the problem of explaining the government's action to the general public which, the memo said, would be necessary in view of the paper's wide circulation. It warned:

> the reasons for its suppression will not be generally understood, and it is possible that a very large number of people would resent the suppression of a popular newspaper which has posed as a champion of the general public as distinct from the 'privileged classes'. [81]

Similarly, an explanation would have to be given to Parliament and the memo suggested that a White Paper might have to be produced giving extracts from the paper which were considered irresponsible or damaging to national morale. It would then be necessary:

> to consider what effect the quotation of these extracts would have on the minds of Members in the light of their wording and of their relation to the events to which the extracts refer. Some Members of Parliament might urge that there is some considerable truth in each of them. [82]

In its conclusion, the memo did not make any specific recommendation but offered the following four alternatives:

1) suppress the 'Daily Mirror' under regulation 2D without any warning.
2) warn the newspaper under regulation 2C.
3) see the editor and warn him that the newspaper faced imminent suppression under 2D.
4) that the Prime Minister could make an outspoken attack on the newspaper in the House of Commons. [83]

In the committee's report to the Cabinet, the point is reiterated that many people were probably not aware of the scope of regulation 2D and that material such as that published in the 'Daily Mirror' could result in suppression. The report went on 'If only for this reason, we do not think it would be expedient to take immediate action to suppress the 'Daily Mirror' under Regulation 2D without previous warning.' [84] On the other hand, the report said, the government should make a strong attack on irresponsible journalism and that 'Above all, it would be helpful if an example could be made of one of the newspapers which has been a flagrant offender in this respect.' [85] The report therefore recommended that the Home Secretary should make a strong attack on the 'Daily Mirror' in the House of Commons, and should warn the paper that it faced immediate suppression under regulation 2D if it did not moderate its criticism.

On 18 March the War Cabinet endorsed the committee's report and also agreed that immediate action should be taken against the 'Daily Mirror' if it published further 'unwarranted and malignant criticism'. [86] The following day Morrison duly warned a director and the editor of the 'Daily Mirror' and, in response to a set question in the House of Commons about the 'Zec' cartoon, announced that the 'Mirror' had been warned. He launched a vigorous attack on the paper, which he said had 'repeatedly published scurrilous misrepresentations, distorted and exaggerated statements and irresponsible generalisations'. [87]

For the first time, then, the government had made a clear public attack on a major national newspaper. Although the powers under the defence regulations were not used, the threat to suppress the 'Daily Mirror' under 2D was specific enough to constitute a clear break with previous policy. Many writers have mentioned this particular incident in biographies and various other works, but there has been a tendency to personalise and trivialise - to reduce the episode to a clash between Churchill and Morrison over the 'Zec' cartoon. [88] What is necessary is to explain the decision to warn the 'Daily Mirror' in terms of previous policy and prevailing circumstances.

As we have seen, attempts to limit the expression of opinion in the press by informal methods had been going on since the beginning of the war, and the 'Daily Mirror' had been specifically discussed in the Cabinet as early as the autumn of 1940. Thus the decision to switch to a public policy - the threat of suppression - can be seen as part of a cumulative process: a response to the fact that the informal contacts and pressure had not had a lasting effect and that further action was felt necessary. That such action should be taken in the spring of 1942 may also be related to the political and military crisis facing the government at the time: a point inferred by Morrison in his autobiography. [89] In this context it is significant that the warning to the 'Daily Mirror' was not the only attempt to limit critical opinion at that time. As we saw earlier, it was also decided in the spring of 1942 that a stricter control should be enforced in respect of press messages being sent abroad. Furthermore, on 26 March, the Home Secretary made a thinly veiled threat to the pacifist newspaper 'Peace News'. [90] Unfortunately, it is not possible to prove the exact nature of the relationship between the government's actions and the political crisis, but two explanations are plausible. These measures could have been a deliberate attempt to diffuse the political crisis, on the basis that newspapers such as the 'Mirror' formed, rather than articulated, popular opinion. If critical opinion in the media was effectively curtailed, public opinion might swing back in the government's favour. Although stricter control of outgoing press messages can be linked to such a motive (since the British press could report views expressed in foreign papers without committing themselves to an opinion) there would seem to have been little need to threaten 'Peace News', which only had a small circulation largely among committed pacifists. On the face of it, it is more likely that the political crisis had made Ministers highly sensitive to criticism, and that the measures taken reflected this increased sensitivity. Michael Foot makes this point in his biography of Aneurin Bevan. Describing the 'Daily Mirror' affair he says 'It revealed into what a hypersensitive state Britain's war leaders had got themselves; they were living in a "cocoon" of their own.' [91]

Yet if this explanation is correct it only serves to illustrate the falsity of Morrison's differentiation between harmful and responsible criticism as criteria that could be objectively determined and points to the dangers of Ministers believing that they were capable of such judgements. The Zec cartoon was interpreted by many people as a patriotic enjoinder rather than evil and mischevious, and Cudlipp points out that a leading article quoted by Morrison in the House of Commons was actually concerned with an Army Council instruction which the Mirror approved of. [92] The 'News Chronicle' noted that, while this article was open to evil interpretation, 'no one who has followed the Mirror's policy over the war period will doubt that it has been designed...to aid and not hinder the war effort'. [93]

The government's warning to the 'Daily Mirror' provoked an outcry in defence of press freedom. A stormy debate took place in the House of Commons [94] and, in contrast to their reaction when the 'Daily Worker' had been suppressed, most national newspapers condemned the government's actions. But the decision of the Ministerial Committee proved to be sound: the government rode out the storm without difficulty and, more significantly, their object seems to have been acheived. As Morrison put it in his autobiography, 'We had no further cause for complaint about the 'Mirror'.' [95] Morrison added that the paper managed to continue its forthright outlook but Foot challenges this view, saying not only that the Mirror softened its criticisms but also that other newspapers may have been encouraged to do likewise. [96]

An interesting postscript to the 'Daily Mirror' episode occurred in 1942. One or two leading critical journalists, including 'Cassandra' from the 'Daily Mirror' and Frank Owen, editor of the 'Evening Standard', were called up for the armed forces. Although I have found no documentary evidence to show that their call-up was linked to the policy of curtailing critical opinion, a number of writers have implied that these journalists were conscripted into the forces to get them out of the way. [97] In 1942 correspondence between the Prime Minister and Bevin shows that Churchill had considered the possibility of calling up Cecil King, an executive director of the 'Mirror' newspapers, after the 'Sunday Pictorial' had published an article calling for the establishment of a second front. [98]

In 1943 the government suppressed a Gaullist newspaper published in London by the simple method of witholding paper supplies [99] but, in general, the government returned to the policy of informal pressure and contacts and no further public action was taken against any of the major national newspapers. In July 1942 the Cabinet considered an article in the 'Daily Mirror' regarding the appointment of a supreme commander of the allied forces. It was agreed that the Minister of Information should explain to the editors in confidence that speculation on such matters should be discouraged. [100] Similarly, in August 1942, the Cabinet agreed that the tone of an article in 'The Times' was ill-judged and that 'further guidance' should be given to that paper in respect of their attitude to changes in the Middle East command. [101] As a final example, Churchill wrote to Roosevelt in February 1943 saying 'I am having quite a lot of trouble in persuading some of the newspapers not to criticise the American handling of the North African campaign.' [102] Although he may have been having some trouble, the task of persuading the press not to publish critical opinion was clearly continuing, but not on the level of public policy.

THE BBC

Prior to the war, according to Asa Briggs, the BBC had been proud of its independence from central government, and he says that even at the beginning of the war there had been 'a deep seated reluctance' even to contemplate the 'deliberate perversion of the truth in order to maintain national morale'.[103] Yet, in terms of the corporation's attitude towards political dissidents and critical opinion, its structural independence masked more subtle and pervasive links with government in terms of ideology and social class. In other words, those responsible for BBC policy shared the values and beliefs prevalent in Whitehall and during a national emergency could be expected not only to follow any guidance given by central government, but also, when working from their own initiative, take a stance which in general would be compatible with government policy.

Even so, during the war the BBC had close links with the Ministry of Information and although Briggs says that the exact degree of control exercised by the Ministry cannot be established, he cites a phrase of Sir Allan Powell's that 'silken cords' could sometimes feel like 'chains of iron'. [104] In October 1941, the Under Secretary of State at the Ministry of Information stated in reply to a Parliamentary question that 'The BBC accepts the direction of the Ministry of Information in all matters affecting the national effort...Political speakers do not broadcast except with the approval of the Ministry of Information.' [105] This statement caused some political embarrassment and brought protests from the BBC, [106] but as we shall see it was true of at least certain areas of the BBCs activities. A full analysis of the BBCs approach to politics during the war would be an immense task and would go far beyond the scope of this book. I propose therefore to confine myself to those examples which have a direct relevance to other issues which I have already discussed.

At the end of August 1940, an internal BBC note entitled 'Broadcasting in Wartime' stated that:

> No one who is shown to belong to an organisation the policy of which is inconsistent with the national effort... or who is shown to have expressed views which are inconsistent with the national effort, may be invited to broadcast in any programme or to contribute material for broadcasting. [107]

This position was adopted by the BBC on its own initiative for, in a meeting of the Civil Defence Committee in March 1941, it was stated that the Ministry of Information had not been consulted when the original ruling had been introduced. [108] A prohibition of this sort probably existed for most of the war in respect of participation in current affairs programmes or political discussions. But, in the autumn of 1940, it was extended to cover all areas of BBC programmes. In December 1940, Sir Hugh Robertson was due to conduct the Glasgow Orpheus Choir in a programme to be broadcast before Christmas. The broadcast was cancelled on the grounds that Robertson, a pacifist, had expressed views inconsistent with the national effort. On 11 December the Minister of Information was asked whether he had instructed the BBC to impose such a ban. He replied in the negative, but when asked whether he would approach the BBC with a view to getting the ban lifted he said he tried not to interfere with the BBCs entertainment policy. [109] On 19 December, Mr Strauss tried to raise the issue on the Adjournment of the House, but was ruled out of order on the grounds that the government were not directly responsible for the activities of the BBC. [110]

The ability of the government to control the BBC on such matters was, however, amply demonstrated in March 1941 when, what Barry Cox describes as a 'furious protest' [111] developed over a news series of bannings. The 'News Chronicle' broke the story on 4 March under a front page headline 'BBC Gives Stars an Ultimatum'. The BBC had informed a number of people who had supported the 'People's Convention', including musicians, actors, playwrights and producers, that they would not be allowed to contribute to broadcasts unless they withdrew their support of the convention. The 'News Chronicle' described the ban as outrageous, and forty MPs tabled a motion against the ban. [112] Although the BBCs action followed the spirit of the government's recent ban on the 'Daily Worker', its effect ran directly counter to the government's general policy of having the maximum effect with the minimum of publicity. Musicians, actors etc. were not likely to get a chance to make their views known on the air, but the effect of the ban had stirred up a good deal of publicity. On 12 March, Duff Cooper, the Minister of Information, said that he would ask the BBC to reconsider the cases of supporters of the 'People's Convention' since, as he put it, many of the had supported it without any 'reprehensible motive' being involved. [113] About a week later Churchill himself announced that the ban on the supporters of the 'People's Convention' was to be lifted and that, furthermore, the BBCs policy of banning musicians or actors on the basis of their political opinions was to be revoked. [114] An ironic postscript to this affair is that from the beginning of the war the BBC had adopted a policy of sacking conscientious objectors, even though such people had often been registered on the condition that they continued to work for the BBC. This policy was still in force in November 1941, for it was stated in reply to a Parliamentary question that no conscientious objectors were employed by the BBC. [115]

These political bannings were almost certainly an example of the BBC's own policy which the government asked them to amend to avoid political embarrassment. The next example - the banning of the Internationale - was a clear case of a government initiative which, as I suggested in the previous chapter, was probably a result of a widespread fear that enthusiasm for Russia would become enthusiasm for communism. At the time of the Nazi invasion of the Soviet Union, the BBC was broadcasting a popular programme, the 'National Anthems of the Allies', before the 9 o'clock news on Sunday evenings. A Foreign Office minute quoted by Addison states that Churchill had instructed 'that the Internationale is on no account to be played by the BBC'. [116] According to Briggs the BBC looked for an alternative piece of music to play but then dropped the 'Anthems' programme altogether. [117] When questions were asked in Parliament the Ministry of Information at first denied government involvement but eventually admitted that the government, and not the BBC, were responsible for the decision. [118] This ban was not lifted until the beginning of 1942 after the Foreign Secretary, Anthony Eden, had pointed out that it was becoming embarrassing because the Russians played 'God Save the King'. Even then, the BBC were asked not to overdo it, and only to play the Internationale when the occasion really called for it. [119]

The final episode I wish to deal with is of particular interest, because it is an example of a government Minister interfering with criticism of the government's handling of an important civil liberties issue. In Chapter Three I discussed the debate on regulation 18B which took place in the House of Commons in November 1941, during the course of which there was a good deal of criticism of the government's policy. As a result of the debate an article discussing regulation 18B appeared in 'The Economist' and the BBC contacted the author asking him to prepare a broadcast on the regulation. This broadcast was subsequently cancelled at the request of the Ministry of Information. When the matter was raised in Parliament, government spokesmen said that there had been some doubts as to the impartiality of the script and the Home Secretary had been consulted. He had felt that the script was not impartial and contained a factual innaccuracy. Therefore the broadcast had been cancelled. [120] When the issue was raised again, on the Adjournment of the House, [121] the script of the broadcast was read out in full. It was pointed out that scripts can be altered quickly and that the script was little more than a description of the House of Commons debate. More fundamentally, MPs asked how the Home Secretary, who was responsible for the operation of 18B, could judge what was impartial. In relation to this point Sir Archibald Southeby claimed that the BBC news reports of the House of Commons debate were a travesty of what had actually taken place. Aneurin Bevan remarked that 'No document can ever be produced for the BBC which does not butter up the Government.' [122]

COMMENTARY

There is no doubt that one of the primary purposes of censorship was to prevent the leakage of information of military value, but I have focussed attention on the more questionable aspects of censorship - especially attempts by the government to control the expression of opinion. As I have shown, the output of the BBC could be directly controlled by the government and the Postal and Telegraphic Censorship was used as a system of information gathering in areas not related to military security. In many ways the issues arising out of this area parallel those discussed in Chapter Four, because it is again possible to distinguish a level of public and a level of covert policy, particularly in relation to the government's approach towards the national press.

On the level of public policy it appeared, with the exception of the warning to the 'Daily Mirror', that the national press could express itself freely. But on the level of covert policy the government were consistently active. The D-Notice system remained shrouded in secrecy throughout the war and it is still not clear to what extent it covered the expression of opinion. Beyond this semi-formal system, the government pursued an informal policy based on direct contact with the owners and editors of the national press. Every major national newspaper supported the war effort and this - combined with social, political and economic links between Ministers, owners and editors - ensured that guidance would often be given and accepted in a spirit of patriotism and common interest. As we have seen, the press in general, and the 'Mirror' newspapers in particular, were not always compliant. At such times the government - still using their informal channels - would cajole, threaten or bully offenders back into line. The switch from the informal level to the level of public policy was only used as a last resort and even then never extended beyond an explicit threat.

It appears that, in terms of public policy, the government were rather more concerned with potential opposition than in many of the other areas I discuss in this book. I would suggest two reasons for this: firstly the government's desire to maintain a liberal democratic image and secondly the potential power of the press.

Although the government could get away with suppressing the 'Daily Worker', it would have been far more difficult to explain why the introduction of compulsory censorship or the suppression of a mass circulation national daily was not a direct and fundamental attack on press freedom. If one adds to this the political weight of the owners and editors of the national press and their ability to put this point of view across, the government's circumspection can be understood. Having said this, it should not be assumed that the public measures taken, or the threat of them, were of no consequence. As I pointed out, it seems that the threat to establish compulsory censorship had a salutory effect and similarly with the warning to the 'Daily Mirror'.

A peculiarity of censorship in respect of the expression of opinion was that material which circulated in Britain became liable to censorship if it was sent abroad. The 'Daily Worker', for example, had an export ban imposed upon it many months before it was suppressed in Britain and it seems that outgoing press messages were more strictly controlled than opinions and views expressed in British press. The existence of a formal censorship system for all outgoing material might have encouraged firmer controls, but the most likely explanation is that, once out of the country, critical opinion could have been represented as 'the British view' or 'the views of the British people'. It might have proved difficult for the government to counter such interpretations. In Britain, on the other hand, the government always had a ready platform for any statement they might wish to make: the national press and the BBC.

Chapter Five: Notes

1. The memoranda submitted to the 'Standing Interdepartmental Committee on Censorship' are mostly closed to public inspection at the Public Record Office. This makes the minutes of the meetings of this committee difficult to interpret. See PRO CAB 76/9. The files illustrating the work of the Postal and Telegraphic Censorship are referenced PRO DEFE 1 and are closed for fifty years.

2. 'The Times', 2 September 1939.

3. This point was made at the first meeting of the 'Standing Interdepartmental Committee on Censorship' in 1940. PRO CAB 76/9, SCC(40)1st Meeting.

4. NCCL Archives, Filing Case No. 4, 'Wartime', Section 7, 'Press (Censorship of Dispatches of General News Service)'. Letter from Walter Monckton, Head of the Press and Censorship Bureau, to NCCL dated 16 February 1940.

5. NCCL Archives, Filing Case No. 4, 'Wartime', Section 5, 'Wartime Regulations, Cuttings from 'Civil Liberty'', 'Civil Liberty', March 1940.

6. v.359 H.C.DEB 5s col.1127.

7. PRO CAB 75/5, HPC(40)15th Meeting.

8. v.367 H.C.DEB 5s col.200. The other papers and periodicals banned were: 'The Week', 'Russia Today', 'Russia Today Newsletter', 'Challenge', Inside the Empire', 'The New Propellor', 'Labour Monthly' and 'Kypriaka Nea'.

9. NCCL Archives, Filing Case No. 4, 'Wartime', Section 7, 'Press (Censorship of Dispatches of General News Service)'. Letter from Chief Censor to NCCL dated 29 November 1941.

10. Ibid.

11. PRO CAB 76/12, 'Committee on Press Censorship'.

12. PRO CAB 66/23, WP(42)124, submitted to the War Cabinet on 18 March 1942.

13. PRO CAB 65/25, WM 35, 18 March 1942.

14. v.378 H.C.DEB 5s cols.2156-9.

15. v.385 H.C.DEB 5s cols.332-3, 18 November 1942.

16. PRO CAB 65/34, WM 67, 10 May 1943.

17. PRO LAB 10/281, Notice from Postal and Telegraphic

Censorship P.C.72.

18. PRO CAB 76/9, SCC(40)1st Meeting.

19. A. Calder, The People's War, (Panther, 1971) p.76.

20. PRO CAB 73/3, CDC(40)29.

21. PRO CAB 73/2, CDC(40)19th Meeting, 29 May 1940.

22. Apparently such a warrant could be signed by Royal Prerogative and did not require special authority under emergency legislation. see v.397 H.C.DEB 5s col.43. The fact that such a warrant was signed is recorded in a memo to the 'Standing Interdepartmental Committee on Censorship', PRO CAB 76/11, SCC(42)4, May 1942.

23. For the memo see PRO CAB 76/11, SCC(42)4 and the meeting PRO CAB 76/11, SCC(42) 1st Meeting, 22 June 1942.

24. v.380 H.C.DEB 5s col.210.

25. see for instance v.383 H.C.DEB 5s cols.529-30 and v.390 H.C.DEB 5s cols.865-6.

26. see for example v.380 H.C.DEB 5s col.210.

27. v.396 H.C.DEB 5s col.1760, 9 February 1944.

28. Resolution passed by the NEC of the National Union of Journalists, 8 September 1939, NUJ documents held at the Modern Records Centre, Warwick University.

29. quoted in J.A. Cross, Sir Samuel Hoare, A Political Biography, (J. Cape, 1977) pp.304-5.

30. quoted in J.Margarch, The Abuse of Power (W.H.Allen, 1978) p.62.

31. W.P. Crozier, Off the Record - Political Interviews 1933-1943, ed. A.J.P. Taylor, (Hutchinson, 1973) pp.148-50.

32. v.351 H.C.DEB 5s col. 693.

33. M. Foot, Aneurin Bevan Vol. I, (MacGibbon and Kee, 1962)p.307.

34. According to notes on the Committee on Compulsory Censorship. PRO CAB 76/13.

35. PRO CAB 65/7, WM 168, 16 June 1940 and WM 170, 17 June 1940.

36. PRO CAB 65/7, WM 170.

37. PRO CAB 76/13, CC(40) 1st Meeting.

38. B. Cox, Civil Liberties in Britain, (Penguin, 1975) pp.85-6.

39. v.362 H.C.DEB 5s col.835-6.

40. PRO CAB 65/8, WM 207.

41. PRO CAB 65/9, WM 264, 2 October 1940, closed at the PRO.

42. Public Record Office, 'Index to Cabinet Minutes', Sept-Dec 1940, 'Press'.

43. PRO PREM 4, 66/2, p.381, Minute from Churchill to Sinclair dated 5 October 1940.

44. PRO CAB 65/9, WM 267.

45. Ibid.

46. PRO CAB 66/12, WP(40) 402.

47. PRO CAB 65/9, WM 268. Morrison became worried that the investigations into the ownership and control of the

Mirror might be publicised. He wrote to Churchill that the police would make enquiries using the powers available under regulation 80A but that, although banks would not give publicity to such action, holding companies might do so. See PRO PREM 4, 66/1, Memo from Morrison to Churchill dated 11 October 1940.

48. Cecil King, With Malice Towards None, ed. W. Armstrong, (Sidgwick and Jackson, 1970) p.81.

49. H. Cudlipp, Publish and be Damned, (Andrew Dakers, 1953) p. 152.

50. PRO CAB 65/9, WM 272.

51. PRO CAB 66/13, WP(40) 430, closed to public inspection.

52. PRO CAB 65/9, WM 282.

53. see King, Malice Towards None, p.94-112 and Cudlipp, Published and be Damned, p.160-8.

54. quoted in Cudlipp, Publish and be Damned, p.164

55. Ibid, p.167.

56. PRO CAB 65/19, WM 101.

57. According to the Home Secretary's memo submitted to the Cabinet on 10 November 1941. see PRO CAB 66/19, WP(41) 262.

58. PRO CAB 66/19, WP (41) 262.

59. PRO CAB 65/20, WM 110, 10 November 1941.

60. PRO CAB 66/19, WP(41) 268.

61. PRO CAB 66/19, WP(41) 269.

62. PRO CAB 65/20, WM 115.

63. B. Donohugue, and G.W. Jones, Herbert Morrison - Portrait of a Politician (Weidenfeld and Nicolson, 1973) p.299.

64. PRO CAB 66/19, WP(41) 268, Historical Appendix.

65. In their biography of Morrison, Donohugue and Jones, p.299 & 616 (footnote 14) cite WP(41)269 as Morrison's memo. In fact this was the Joint memo prepared by Morrison, Eden and the Minister of Information. WP(41) 268 was Morrison's memo.

66. W. Churchill, The Second World War, Vol IV, (Reprint Society, 1953) p.74.

67. King, Malice Towards None, p.159

68. cited in L. Mosley Backs to the Wall, (Weidenfeld and Nicolson, 1971) p.240.

69. PRO CAB 76/12, P(42)5.

70. Ibid.

71. Cudlipp, Publish and be Damned, pp.175-6.

72. PRO CAB 65/25, WM 32.

73. Ibid.

74. PRO CAB 76/12, Committee on Press Censorship.

75. PRO CAB 76/12, P(42)2.

76. PRO CAB 76/12, P(42)3.

77. PRO CAB 76/12, P(42) 1st Meeting.

78. PRO CAB 76/12, P(42)5.

79. Ibid.

80. Ibid.
81. Ibid.
82. Ibid.
83. PRO CAB 76/12, P(42) 2nd Meeting.
84. PRO CAB 66/23, WP(42) 124.
85. Ibid.
86. PRO CAB 65/25, WM 35, 18 March 1942.
87. v. 378 H.C.DEB 5s col.1665.
88. see for instance, Donohugue and Jones, Herbert Morrison, pp.297-300.
89. Morrison notes that the warning was given at a time when the question of morale was very important. Lord Morrison of Lambeth, Herbert Morrison - An Autobiography, (Odhams, 1960) p.223.
90. In response to a set question in the Commons suggesting that the paper should be suppressed, Morrison replied that the newspaper had recently gone beyond the straight forward expression of pacifist opinion, see v.378 H.C.DEB 5s cols. 2137-8.
91. Foot, Aneurin Bevan, p.355.
92. see Cudlipp, Publish and be Damned, p.184 and 186-7.
93. Ibid. p.189
94. for the debate see v.378 H.C.DEB 5s cols.2233-2308.
95. Morrison, Autobiography, p.224.
96. Foot, Aneurin Bevan, p.356.
97. see for instance, Foot, Aneurin Bevan, p.356 and Calder, People's War, p.333.
98. In November 1943, Bevin wrote to Churchill: 'You mentioned to me the case of Cecil Harmsworth King, Editorial Director and Vice-Chairman of the Sunday Pictorial. Mr. King has already been examined for military service and was placed in the lowest medical category. There is therefore no question of calling him up for military service...' PRO PREM 4, 66/4.
99. M. Panter-Downes, (ed.) W. Shawn, London War Notes, 1939-45, p.285.
100. PRO CAB 65/27, WM 97, 28 July 1942.
101. Discussion and conclusions minuted in the Secretary's Standard File, PRO CAB 65/31, WM 116, 22 August 1942.
102. W. Churchill, The Second World War, Vol. IV, (Cassell, 1951) p.649
103. A. Briggs, The History of Broadcasting in the United Kingdom, Vol.III The War of Words, (Oxford 1970), p.6.
104. Ibid, pp.33-4.
105. v.374 H.C.DEB 5s cols.583-4.
106. Briggs, War of Words, p.340 appears to be referring to this statement.
107. quoted by Briggs, War of Words, p.205.
108. PRO CAB 73/4, CDC(41)10th Meeting, 5th March 1941.
109. v.367 H.C.DEB 5s cols.899-900.
110. v.367 H.C.DEB 5s cols.1455-60.

111. Cox, Civil Liberties in Britain, p.84.

112. The motion was never debated, see v.369 H.C.DEB 5s cols.1148-50.

113. v.369 H.C.DEB 5s cols.1269-71.

114. v.370 H.C.DEB 5s cols.283-5.

115. v.376 H.C.DEB 5s cols.189-90.

116. quoted in P.Addison, The Road to 1945, (J. Cape, 1975) p.134-5.

117. Briggs, War of Words, pp.389-90.

118. see v.373 H.C.DEB 5s cols.583-4 and Adjournment Debate, v.373 H.C.DEB 5s cols.1160-8.

119. Briggs, War of Words, p.394.

120. v.376 H.C.DEB 5s cols.2068-70.

121. Adjournment Debate v.376 H.C.DEB 5s col.2189-2224, 18 December 1941.

122. v.376 H.C.DEB 5s cols.2206.

Chapter Six

MOBILISATION FOR THE TOTAL WAR ECONOMY

From the mid 1930s, when the government began detailed planning of the measures that would be necessary in the event of a major war, the questions of manpower control and industrial conscription were given serious consideration. Between 1941 and 1945 they were at the forefront of the government's domestic strategy. One of the most remarkable features of the second world war was the extent to which Britain took powers to mobilise and relocate labour: powers greater, it has been suggested, than those taken by any other belligerent nation. [1] Yet despite this, the term industrial conscription has rarely been used to describe the processes involved. Rather it has been argued that the government's strategy was accepted voluntarily by the vast majority of workers affected. Now while it is no doubt true that considerable numbers of people were willing to aid the war effort, the notion of voluntary mass participation in the government's manpower strategy has been grossly exaggerated, and serves only to obscure the rationale behind the government's policies. We have already looked at the government's use of covert and indirect methods in other contexts and, as I shall show, this form of action was of great importance in this area too.

As to the powers to control and direct labour, certain preconditions were necessary to ensure that their introduction would not provoke industrial confrontation. Of these the most important was undoubtedly the co-operation and support of the trade union leadership. In the period of the Chamberlain government this support was not forthcoming but, after the formation of the coalition government, the trade union leadership not only co-operated with the government: they came to act as an additional arm of the state. The fact that a General Secretary of the Transport and General Workers Union should become the Minister responsible for taking powers over the workforce of Britain is both symptomatic of that process and of great significance to it.

But before describing in detail the measures taken by the

coalition government it is worth considering the government's attitude to manpower controls prior to the formation of the coalition.

EARLY CONCEPTS OF MANPOWER POLICY AND THE NEED FOR CONSENSUS

As we saw in Chapter One, the report of the 'Ad-Hoc Interdepartmental Committee' in April 1937 had argued that a clause should be included in an Emergency Powers Bill prohibiting the introduction of industrial conscription by means of defence regulations, and that 'restrictions on the freedom of civilian workers to take or leave employment should not be imposed except by legislation directed to that specific purpose.' [2] Although there is no documentary evidence to show why such recommendations were made, it seems likely that one of the major factors taken into account was that an Emergency Bill which allowed for industrial conscription might encounter strong opposition in Parliament. The line proposed by the Committee was adopted and the 'Emergency Powers (Defence) Act 1939' specifically excluded any form of industrial conscription. But this did not mean that no consideration had been given to the question of controlling civilian labour.

From at least the mid 1930s, a manpower sub-committee had been attached to the Committee for Imperial Defence and, in 1937, they produced a report dealing with the possibilities for labour controls. Rather than proposing powers which would allow the government to direct people to specific jobs, the report argued that it might be possible to exercise effective control by introducing legislation requiring jobs to be filled through the National Service Offices, that is, the Labour Exchanges. It explained that:

> If a workman leaves his employment and then unreasonably declines alternative employment offered through the National Service Office, he will be ineligible for unemployment benefit, and will be condemning himself to privation. [3]

Thus, by using loss of benefit as an economic sanction, it was felt workers could be forced into jobs that were considered to be important. The report stated 'In all ordinary circumstances these measures should serve to maintain essential services and necessary civilian production.' [4]

It seems government advisors felt that such indirect control, which would not be spelt out in the legislation itself, could be introduced without arousing widespread opposition from the labour and trade union movement, but in this belief they were proved wrong.

Although the Parliamentary Labour Party and the TUC had accepted the need for the Emergency Powers (Defence) Act, when the government introduced a Control of Employment Bill on 5 September 1939 it met with stiff opposition both from Labour MPs and from the TUC. The Bill incorporated the rationale of the 1937 proposals, empowering the Minister of Labour to make Orders prohibiting advertisements for classes of employment, and requiring such jobs to be obtained from the Labour Exchanges. Despite the fact that the Ministry of Labour and the TUC had discussed wartime controls at several meetings earlier in 1939, the TUC opposed the specific terms of the Bill and on 9 September sent a deputation to discuss the issue with Ministers. A note in the Ministry of Labour files indicates that, following further discussions, the TUC approved a final draft of the Bill on 13 September. [5] The Minister of Labour appears to have felt that the main aim of the Bill had been preserved, for on the same day he wrote 'it is very desirable indeed to get the Bill on the statute book before they have a weekend in which to have second thoughts, and perhaps make further proposals which we shall be unable to accept.' [6] As it was, the TUC did have second thoughts and the government accepted a number of amendments to the Bill proposed by Labour MPs. The final Act was much milder than the original proposals. Hancock and Gowing point out that the Minister of Labour gave an assurance to Parliament that the Act would only be used in special circumstances on a clear demonstration of need and that, after a stormy debate, clauses were added setting up a 'cumbersome mechanism of joint consultation' which could lay a report before Parliament alongside any Order the Minister might make under the Act. Furthermore, if the Ministry refused to engage a worker they were obliged to find him suitable alternative work or else compensation was payable. [7] Thus the basic concept of the original proposals - to give the Ministry control over labour by the threat of privation - became unworkable.

A number of writers have pointed out that, from the outbreak of war until well into 1940, the main problem faced by the government in relation to production was not a shortage of labour but a lack of industrial capacity. [8] This would suggest a straightforward explanation of why the first wartime government did not introduce extensive controls over civilian labour and were prepared to curtail the effective scope of the Control of Employment Act. Yet while this factor is no doubt of importance, it is significant that one of the first acts of the coalition government was to take the powers necessary to exert full control over civilian labour. As I have already indicated, the Chamberlain government were aware of the possible repercussions of trying to introduce industrial conscription, and the opposition to the Control of Employment Bill was a clear warning that, while the Labour Party remained in opposition, they were likely to oppose any extension of control over civilian labour. Thus not only was it unlikely that a political consensus could be established over the issue: any attempt to extend control might also damage the fragile consensus that had been achieved in other areas. Furthermore, in the absence of a political consensus, any industrial unrest that might be provoked by the introduction of industrial conscription would be more difficult to control or condemn, since it might receive the support of the trade union leadership and the Parliamentary Labour Party. In fact Hancock and Gowing argue that the reason why firm labour controls were not introduced in the first period of the war was that the Ministry of Labour was terrified of the possibility of industrial unrest. [9]

I would argue then, that one of the principal reasons why the Chamberlain government did not introduce extensive controls over the civilian labour force was that they could not create a consensus among Britain's political elite on the need and desirability of such measures. Once the political consensus was structurally based these objections were no longer relevant. The inclusion of a number of senior Labour politicians in the government was sufficient to ensure an overwhelming parliamentary majority for any proposals which might be made, but another important factor was the attitude and role of the trade union leadership. For this reason the appointment of Ernest Bevin as Minister of Labour and National Service was both obvious and yet a move of great political acumen. With Bevin in charge of manpower policy and Labour in the coalition, the trade union leadership's critical support for the war was transformed into active support for the government. Thus, not only was the leadership of the potential opposition to industrial conscription drawn into the government process, it could also add its weight and power to that of the government in trying to damp any unrest or dissension that might be caused by the introduction of labour controls.

In other words, the formation of the coalition government provided for the establishment of a broad-based consensus which effectively incorporated the leadership of the labour and trade union movements into the government.

THE MACHINERY OF COMPULSION

Within a fortnight of the formation of the coalition government, the principal Act and regulation which provided for the mobilisation and control of civilian labour had been made. On 22 May 1940 a new 'Emergency Powers (Defence) Act' passed through Parliament with little discussion, and a new regulation - 58A - was made under the Act the same day. Regulation 58A allowed the Minister of Labour to 'direct any person in Great Britain to perform such services...as may be specified' [10] and it was under this regulation that the most far-reaching controls were to be introduced in later years. During 1940, however, little use was made of these powers except in an attempt to prevent employers 'poaching' each others' skilled workers. In June 1940, an 'Undertakings (Restriction on Engagement) Order' specified that all future engagements in the building, engineering and civil engineering industries must be made through labour exchanges or other approved bodies. Employers were forbidden to advertise such posts. This form of Order effectively supplanted the Control of Employment Act and, later in the war, was extended to cover many essential industries. In August 1940 an 'Industrial Registration Order' required that, in a number of engineering occupations, every worker who was not already employed wholly on government work had to register with the Ministry of Labour, and that any worker who had one year's experience in the occupation specified at any time in the previous twelve years also had to register. It was not until 1941 that this Order was extended to cover all occupations in industries such as shipbuilding and coalmining.

To explain why the government used their vast powers so sparingly in 1940 there seems little need to look for political explanations, or ones relating to the personality of the Minister of Labour. [11] The continued reliance on free market allocation (with the exceptions mentioned above) was simply because there was no general shortage of labour at the time. Indeed Hancock and Gowing state that there was very little unfulfilled demand for unskilled labour until the spring of 1941. [12] It should also be mentioned that, until the summer of 1940, there had been little effort to assess future manpower requirements and so there would have been little rational basis for the wide use of powers under regulation 58A.

From the mid 1930s it was appreciated on a general level that, in a long war, great strain would be placed on Britain's productive potential by the call up of men for the forces, and that demand for labour in industry would inevitably exceed the normal supply. In the summer and autumn of 1940 the government began to make detailed calculations about the extent of this problem. It was the results of this first serious manpower survey which led the government to make a far more extensive use of the powers under regulation 58A in the spring of 1941.

In November 1940, the 'Manpower Requirements Committee' circulated a report which attempted to project the needs of the armed forces and industry to the end of 1941. The report concluded that there would be, as Parker put it, 'a famine...of male labour for industry and a dearth of recruits for the Forces'. [13] The main conclusions of the report were accepted and, on 20 January 1941, Bevin submitted plans to the War Cabinet. The next day they were announced to the House of

Commons and, following an amendment to regulation 58A, the 'Essential Work (General Provisions) Order' was introduced on the 5 March, followed ten days later by the 'Registration for Employment Order'. In essence the proposals were very simple but, in terms of the numbers of people that were to be affected by them, they were the main statutory tools in the government's plan to mobilise and control civilian labour.

Under the original Essential Works Order, and subsequent Orders made for specific industries and undertakings (all Essential Works Orders, or EWOs for short), the Minister of Labour was able to schedule an undertaking engaged on essential work and, once an undertaking was so designated, no employee was allowed to leave their job without the permission of a National Service Officer (NSO), an official of the Ministry. Similarly no employer could dismiss any employee without the permission of an NSO except on the grounds of 'serious misconduct'. If either the employer or employee was dissatisfied with the decision of an NSO they could appeal to a local board constituted on a tripartite basis with representatives of the Ministry, employers and trade unions. Such boards, however, could only make recommendations which an NSO was not bound to accept. [14] A further provision of the EWO allowed the employer in any scheduled undertaking to report any worker who was persistently late or absent from work without permission. If the NSO felt that the complaint was justified, he could issue directions instructing the worker to report for work at a certain time and to work for a specific number of hours. Contravention of such directions was an offence. An appeal to the local boards was allowed in such cases, but again the board's findings were simply recommendations.

When he announced the introduction of the EWO, Bevin had argued that obligations had to be placed on both sides of industry. To this end the EWO included provision for the Minister to set a guaranteed wage in scheduled undertakings, and stated that, prior to scheduling an undertaking, the Minister should be satisfied that working conditions were reasonable. A detailed discussion of this complex area is beyond the scope of this book, but a number of writers have suggested that these provisions did offset the use of compulsory powers. [15] It seems, though, that with the exception of compelling employers to provide canteen facilities the Ministry did little to improve wage rates or working conditions.

The Registration for Employment Order (RfEO) allowed the Minister of Labour to order men and women to register at local labour exchanges at which time they would be required to give details of their present employment if any and, in the case of women, their marital status, household responsibilities and whether they had children under the age of fourteen. This was the specific extent of the order, but it had far wider implications. Having registered, those people whom local officials felt could be transferred to essential work would be interviewed and 'advised' of jobs they could take to aid the war effort. If an individual refused to take such work, formal directions could then be issued under regulation 58A. Registrants were to be called up by age groups, unemployed and part-time workers being registered before those in full time employment. Since men up to the age of forty-one had already been registered under the National Service Act, the objective of the RfEO was to draw women and older men into the essential war industries.

By July 1941, the War Cabinet felt it necessary to approve a further survey of manpower requirements and, when the study was completed in the autumn, it indicated that there was likely to be further acute shortages in relation to both the demands of industry and the forces. The report was considered by the Lord President's Committee, and Parker states that, after long discussions, the committee concluded that to try to meet the requirements of the forces by withdrawals from industry would create too great a strain in that sector and that the ages for call-up to the forces would therefore have to be extended, and women would have to be conscripted to the auxiliary forces. [16] Anderson submitted the Committee's proposals to the Cabinet, which discussed manpower on 10 and 28 November. It seems that the proposal to conscript women to the auxiliary forces generated a good deal of controversy and Churchill initially opposed the plan. This is rather odd given that at the same time, in relation to directing women into industry, he argued that 'the existing powers should be used with greater intensity'. [17]

The 'National Service (No. 2) Act' which resulted from these discussions declared that all persons in Great Britain were liable to perform some form of national service either under the terms of the National Service Acts or the defence regulations. The Act's specific provisions amended previous National Service Acts to allow women to be conscripted to the auxiliary forces, with the exceptions that no married women or women with children under the age of fourteen were to be called up, and that the use of lethal weapons by women was to be on a voluntary basis. [18] By including them under the terms of the original National Service Act, women were automatically granted the same entitlement as men to claim exemption from military service on the grounds of conscientious objection. Although the Act provided for the conscription of certain groups of women, the Cabinet had already agreed that, in practice, women called up under the Act should be given the alternatives of serving in the auxiliary forces, in civil defence, or in a limited number of jobs in industry. [19] In fact it appears that the Act was as useful as a means of getting women to work in unpleasant industrial jobs as it was in gathering recruits for the auxiliary forces.

Another power taken by the government in December 1941, was regulation 29BA, under which civilians could be directed to serve in the civil defence and allied services. Men and women could be directed to undertake either full or part-time service and, once directed, could not leave without permission. The only ground for exemption was exceptional personal hardship and, as the the Ministry of Labour and National Service Report for the years 1939-46 put it, 'Under this power it was possible to direct persons to the Civil Defence Services in much the same way as they were directed to industry.' [20]

The final two Orders which completed what I have called the machinery of compulsion were made in January 1942. Firstly, an Order was made empowering the Minister of Labour to direct men to serve in the Home Guard. Secondly, on 22 January, an 'Employment of Women (Control of Engagement) Order' allowed the Minister of Labour to specify groups of women by age and other criteria who were required to obtain employment through a labour exchange or other approved body. The Order was designed to plug a loophole whereby women, unless they worked in an undertaking scheduled under the EWOs, could leave a job they had taken voluntarily and then find other work as they desired. By forcing women to obtain work though the labour exchanges the distribution of the female work force could be more easily regulated and women kept in essential work. The Order was initially applied to women between the ages of 20-30, other than those with children under the age of fourteen, but as we shall see this Order was eventually extended to cover most of the female population.

The measures described above, together with the 'Industrial Registration Order' and the 'Undertakings (Restrictions on Engagement) Order', were the principal legislative tools by which the government was to mobilise and control the civilian labour force during the course of the war. Taken individually, these measures look comparatively innocuous and no one Order made from 1941 to the end of the war can be isolated as THE measure which introduced industrial conscription into wartime Britain. This is perhaps one reason why writers and commentators have avoided using this term. Yet, taken as a whole, these measures gave the government formidable powers both to draw people into productive labour and to determine where individuals should work. They were the practical application of the view expressed in the 'Emergency Powers (Defence) Act 1940' and defence regulation 58A, that the government should have full powers to direct any person to do whatever the government saw as being in the interests of the efficient prosecution of the war or the defence of the realm. As we have seen in previous chapters, a discussion of the powers available to the government is only one aspect of any given issue and we also need to consider how such powers were used. The rest of this chapter concentrates on this question.

THE APPLICATION OF CONTROLS IN GENERAL

In looking at the general application of the controls discussed above, two distinct phases can be isolated. The first phase, covering the period from 1941 to about the summer of 1942, can be distinguished by the widespread use of the 'Registration for Employment Order' and the 'Essential Work Orders'. During this phase the government were chiefly concerned with expanding the labour force and keeping those people who worked in essential industries in their jobs. The second phase, from mid-1942 to the end of the war, can be seen as something of a 'mopping up' operation in respect of expanding the labour force and applying the EWOs. Most of the government's efforts during this period were directed towards transferring workers to where they were considered most useful, both geographically and in relation to specific industries or projects. These phases are not only of importance in relation to the general application of controls, but also appear to have been tied to the government's attitudes towards directions and prosecutions which I shall discuss in the next section.

The Process of Expansion

The government began registering men and women under the RfEO only a month after its introduction and, by December 1941, men between the ages of 41 and 46 had been registered, as had some 3.5 million women between the ages of 20 and 31. In April 1942 it was decided to register nineteen-year-old women and by June of that year women up to the age of 41 had been registered, making a total of about 7.5 million. This figure constituted a substantial proportion of the 10.5 million women who were to be registered under the RfEO during the course of the war. [21] From December 1941, women registered under the RfEO, whose particulars fulfilled the requirements laid down by the National Service (No. 2) Act, had their registration transferred to one under the Act. In March 1942, those people engaged in full-time work in civil defence (mostly men) were ordered to register. This was an attempt to transfer some of them into industry or the forces.

The call for various groups to register under the RfEO was made by issuing notices through the press and such notices could of course be ignored. But this did not mean that an individual could easily avoid registration. It was an offence under regulation 58A not to register and, in December 1941, a new regulation - 80B - gave the Minister of Labour power to call people for interview or medical examination, the maximum penalty for failing to attend being, on summary conviction, three months imprisonment, a one hundred pound fine, or both. In January 1942 a Ministry of Labour memorandum to Regional Controllers pointed out that 'many women have failed to register on account of a conscientious objection to war work', [22] but it seems few women refused to register on grounds other than conscientious objection.

After registration, the local offices of the Ministry selected those people who appeared eligible for redeployment and called them to interview. Large numbers of those registered were not interviewed for a variety of reasons: perhaps because they were already engaged in essential work or, in the case of many women, because they had household reponsibilities or had children under the age of fourteen. For those who were called to an interview the standard letter asking people to attend carried a warning of the penalties that could be incurred under regulation 80B. [23] Some people may have divined from this alone that they would have little choice when it came to taking jobs offered them by the Labour Exchanges.

Turning to the call-up of women under the National Service (No. 2) Act, I noted in the previous section that the Act was used not only to draw women into the auxiliary forces but also to get them to take certain jobs in industry. The first proclamation under the Act was issued in December 1941 and covered women between the ages of 20 and 31. In January 1943 women aged 19 were made liable to call-up. It seems that in practice, however, only single women aged 19-24 were called up. Although the Cabinet had agreed that conscripted women should be given the choice between service in the auxiliary forces, civil defence or industry, the option for civil defence was withdrawn in July 1942 and, in January 1944, so too was the option to serve in the auxiliary forces. [24] Unfortunately, it is not clear how many of the women called up under the Act were in fact placed in industry, although the Ministry of Labour and National Service Report states that while women had a choice between the auxiliary forces and civilian employment, one third of those called up opted for the auxiliary forces, one third opted for civilian employment and one third expressed no preference. [25] Since about 125,000 conscripts joined the auxiliary forces up until 1944 it seems likely that a similar number were posted to industry up to that time. [26]

I noted that in March 1942 it was decided to register those people employed in the civil defence services under the RfEO, and that, in July 1942, the civil defence option for those women called up under the National Service (No. 2) Act was withdrawn. The government had decided that many of the men employed in civil defence and the potential recruits to the service from young single women could be used to better advantage elsewhere, and that the service could be staffed by less mobile women. Under regulation 29BA, men and women could be directed to serve in the civil defence services and, up until September 1944, some 273,000 directions were issued under this regulation, 212,340 of them to women. [27] Since the number of women serving in civil defence reached its peak in 1942 it is likely that many of these directions were issued during the course of that year. [28]

By the summer of 1942 the supply of new recruits had been more or less exhausted yet there were still acute shortages of men for the armed forces and of 'mobile' workers who could be transferred to work away from their home areas. As we have seen, there had been a number of restrictions placed on the operation of the measures so far discussed. As well as age limits, women married to men serving in the armed forces or with children under the age of fourteen had not been requested or directed to transfer to war work, and women who satisfied officials that they had significant household responsibilities had also been exempted. Similarly, the Control of Engagement Order had not been applied to women with children under the age of fourteen. It was to these groups of previously exempted women that the government turned in the latter half of 1942 and in 1943 in an attempt to increase the overall mobility of female labour force. It was not expected that these women themselves would either be mobile or generally available for full time employment. The scheme was rather that, if older women or part-time workers could be brought into the war industries near their homes, younger and more mobile women could be transferred to priority areas to alleviate shortages or allow for the release of men to serve in the forces.

In the second half of 1942, therefore, women aged 41-46 were registered under the RfEO and at the same time 'sterner standards were applied in the interviewing of women with household responsibilities'. [29] In January 1943 Bevin announced that the Control of Engagement Order was to be extended to cover women up to the age of forty and that regulation 58A was to be used more freely and was to include directions to part-time work. [30] Finally, in July 1943, it was announced that women up to the age of 51 were to be registered under the RfEO and this measure was quickly dubbed the 'conscription of grannies'. The effect of these measures was not dramatic but nevertheless added a significant number to the total work force. This is probably best judged in relation to the number of women in part-time employment. In June 1942 approximately 380,000 women were in part-time work but within a year this figure had more than doubled to approximately 750,000. It was to rise to about 900,000 by June 1944. [31]

These measures were the climax of the government's attempts to expand the total labour force, and it may therefore be useful to summarise the numerical results that were achieved, since this will serve as a useful background to the discussion of the use of directions and sanctions which follows in the next section.

By the autumn of 1943, when the peak of mobilisation was reached, just over 15 million of the 15.9 million men of working age were employed either in forces, industry or commerce. In 1939 about five million women were employed in the forces, industry or commerce out of about 16 million women of working age. By 1943 a further 2.25 million women had been drawn into employment. Moreover, 90 per cent of single women aged 18-40 were so engaged as were 80 per cent of or married or widowed women who had no children. [32]

As well as the total increase in the work force, account must also be taken of the redistribution of labour that took place during the course of the war. By June 1943 almost 5 million people were serving in the forces, civil defence and fire services and at the same date the numbers employed in the metal and chemical industries stood at about 5.2 million, an increase of over two million since 1939. In the less essential industries the work force was reduced by some 3.25 million between June 1939 and June 1943. [33] It should be stressed that these figures only indicate the net changes in the numbers employed in the various sectors between fixed points in time, and therefore underestimate, possibly by a significant degree, the actual numbers of people changing their employment.

The Essential Work Order

As with the RfEO, the government lost no time in utilising their powers under the EWOs. As early as December 1941 almost 30,000 undertakings employing some 5.8 million workers had been scheduled and, by the end of 1942, over 55,000 undertakings employing more than 8 million workers had been covered by the Orders. Although the figures for the number of scheduled undertakings was to rise to about 67,000 in the later years of the war, the number of workers affected by the Orders never rose much beyond 8.5 million. [34] Thus, as with the RfEO, extensive use of the EWOs occurred in 1941 and 1942.

As I said earlier, some writers have pointed to the provisions relating to reasonable working conditions and a guaranteed wage to argue, as Bevin did at the time, that the basic principle behind the EWOs was equality of sacrifice, and that the orders did not operate to the disadvantage of workers. [35] But in relation to the primary objectives of the Orders - to keep workers in jobs where they were needed and to keep them working - many Labour MPs, the NCCL and many trade unionists felt there was considerable evidence to suggest that the EWOs operated in favour of employers.

It will be recalled that under the terms of the EWOs an employee could not leave work nor be dismissed from it (except for serious misconduct - see below) without the permission of an NSO. In the Ministry of Labour and National Service Report for 1939-46 figures are given for the number of applications made by workers to leave their jobs and by employers to discharge their employees. These are shown in Table 6.1.

Table 6.1: Essential Works Orders, permissions to leave and discharge. Numbers of applications made and numbers granted 1941-45.

Permission to leave	Number of Applications	Number Granted
1941	495,020	371,650
1942	1,389,766	1,072,882
1943	1,595,359	1,225,377
1944	1,563,891	1,235,783
Jan-June 1945	855,276	687,251
July-Dec 1945	1,021,125	869,859
Permission to discharge		
1941	146,600	140,442
1942	580,017	565,122
1943	674,598	653,533
1944	707,770	685,817
Jan-June 1945	408,907	398,547
July-Dec 1945	726,613	719,712

Source: Ministry of Labour and National Service, Report for Years 1939-46, Cmd. 7225, Appendix V.

It is clear that the majority of applications by both employers and employees were accepted, but there is a significant difference between the two sets of figures. If, in each case, the number of applications refused (i.e. the number of applications minus those granted) is expressed as a percentage of the number of applications made, the results shown in Table 6.2 are obtained. While applications by employers were almost invariably accepted, a significantly higher percentage of applications by employees were consistently rejected. It could be argued that, in general, employers only applied to an NSO when they had a reasonable case and that many applications from workers could not be justified. But such a view begs the question of what was 'reasonable' and what constituted justification.

Table 6.2 Essential Works Orders, permissions to leave and discharge. Percentage of applications refused 1941-45.

<u>Percentage of Applications Refused</u>

		Permission to leave	Permission to Discharge
1941		24.9	4.2
1942		22.8	2.6
1943		23.2	3.1
1944		21.0	3.1
1945	Jan-June	19.6	2.5
1945	July-Dec	14.8	0.9

Figures derived from Table 6.1 above.

In many instances, the relationship between employers and Ministry officials was likely to have been close, either because of similar class or social backgrounds, regular contact, or simply because Ministry officials and employers were predominantly concerned with similar basic problems - controlling a work force and maintaining or increasing production. It is not therefore surprising to find that views of Ministry officials and employers were more likely to coincide than the view of local officials and individual workers. While it is unlikely that there was any conscious attempt to discriminate against workers, the operation of the EWOs in this field did result in a degree of differential treatment. If we now turn to examine the general application of the sanctions available under the EWOs a similar pattern can be discerned.

In cases where a worker left his job or an employer discharged a worker without permission, the Ministry could not only bring proceedings against the person or company concerned but, where a prosecution was successful, could order that the worker returned to his job or that the employer reinstated him. Two main criticisms emerged. The first was that while workers were regularly prosecuted for breaches of the EWOs, employers who committed comparable offences were allowed to get away with it. To the embarrassment of many trade union leaders who supported EWOs, the Trades Union Congress passed a resolution in September 1943 which stated that:

> Congress expresses alarm at the fact that it appears that practically the only persons prosecuted for breaches of the Order are work people, while continual breaches by employers are left practically unchallenged. Congress therefore demands that the Order shall be administered on the basis of equality as between employers and workpeople. [36]

The second main criticism was that, on the odd occasion when employers were prosecuted, they tended to be fined lightly in relation to their assets and were rarely forced to reinstate workers. Workers were often fined heavily or sentenced to imprisonment and then ordered to return to their jobs. A number of questions in the House of Commons attempted to draw attention to such discrepancies and even an internal Ministry of Labour memorandum accepted that 'The penalties which have been imposed tend to support the complaint that employers get off more lightly than workers.' [37] The memo went on to say, however, that whereas cases against workers were usually clear-cut, in cases against firms which involved possible reinstatement, there was usually an element of doubt involved. [38]

Such an explanation highlights an important anomaly built into the terms of the EWO which could only operate to the disadvantage of workers. Although there were no circumstances in which a worker could leave his job without permission (and thus cases were 'clear-cut') it will be recalled that employers could dismiss a worker for 'serious misconduct' without reference to a National Service Officer. Only if a worker appealed against such dismissal could an NSO investigate the case. In many cases where workers were dismissed without reference to an NSO, employers claimed that serious misconduct was involved. But serious misconduct was not defined in the EWOs. Thus employers were given the dual advantage of being able to dismiss workers and also, by maintaining that serious misconduct was involved, ensure that an element of doubt could be introduced in any case in which workers were prepared to go through the legal proceedings necessary to obtain reinstatement.

Even in cases where the courts decided against a firm it was possible for employers to make nonsense of the court's ruling. The Mass Observation report, 'People in Production', gives details of a case in which 170 workers at a factory had asked for one and a half hours off work to do Christmas shopping. The management refused and the workers walked out. They were all dismissed for 'serious misconduct'. The courts ruled against the firm and ordered that the workers be reinstated. All the firm did was disperse their machinery, pay the workers a further weeks wages, and then make them redundant. [39]

Another important provision of the EWO dealt with the question of absenteeism and lateness for work, an area of industrial relations which caused considerable political controversy. Originally, the procedure regarding absenteeism or persistent lateness was that an employer had to report a worker to an NSO who could then issue directions that it was an offence to contravene. But in March 1942 the general provisions of the EWO were amended to make absenteeism and persistent lateness a direct offence and thus, in cases where a worker was reported, proceedings could be instituted immediately. Whether this amendment came about as a response to an increase in absenteeism or was a result of Tory pressure is not clear but, as with other offences against the industrial regulations, the number of prosecutions for absenteeism was small between March 1941 and June 1942, but rose steeply in later years, as we shall see shortly.

One final point which needs to be raised is the role of the trade unions and the joint production committees in attempts to control absenteeism. In September 1941, Bevin stated that instructions had been issued to the effect that, wherever possible, NSOs should enlist the assistance of trade union officials or works committees in dealing with cases of absenteeism and lateness. [40] It seems to have become the general rule that proceedings against absentees only occured after consultation between some form of 'workers representative' and Ministry officials. Such consultations were claimed to be a significant safeguard of workers interests, yet it may be more accurate to see them as a subtle system of social control. As I have already suggested and will show in more detail in the next chapter, trade union officials became largely divorced from their rank and file in the later years of the war, and with the trade union leadership committed to support of the coalition government, trade union officials often appeared to be carrying out tasks more akin to those of the civil service than of workers' representatives.

The Coal Mining Ballot Scheme

By and large, the transfer of workers into priority areas was achieved by the use of the various powers already discussed. But in one industry - coal mining - a novel procedure was adopted which achieved a good deal of notoriety. As early as 1941 the government had felt that the labour force in the coal mining industry should be built up, when it realised that the earlier policy of allowing miners to join the armed forces had denuded the industry of many experienced men. Young men were therefore given an option to work in the coal industry when they had been called up under the National Service Acts. This scheme did not solve the problem and as the demand for coal grew the government explored other voluntary methods of recruitment. Firstly, the age limit in the above option scheme was dropped and then, in the summer of 1943, a publicity campaign was begun to get suitable men, not engaged in other key jobs, to volunteer for jobs in coal mining. This recruitment drive can perhaps best be seen as a public relations exercise designed to prepare the ground for compulsion, for it was never anticipated that this scheme would solve the labour shortage. As early as July 1943 Bevin warned that some form of compulsory direction to coal mining might be necessary.

Rather than dealing with the underlying problems of poor wage rates in this unpleasant and dangerous industry (which ensured the failure of voluntary schemes) the government chose instead to introduce compulsory recruitment. In November 1943 Bevin stated in a memo to the Lord President's Committee that, as predicted, the voluntary schemes had not produced sufficient recruits and that it would be necessary to introduce compulsory direction. The memo pointed out that any compulsory scheme must not only be fair but be seen to be so. Therefore service in the boys training corps should not provide a basis for exemption as this would exempt almost all public-school boys. [41] The system which the Cabinet approved was a lottery based on the National Service registration number. After each registration and medical examination of young men called up under the National Service Acts, a number or numbers were to be drawn. Those considered fit and whose registration number ended in the figure or figures drawn were to be directed to training centres and then to the mines. The only classes not included in the ballot were those who had been accepted either for flying duties in the RAF or Fleet Air Arm, as artificers in submarines, or were included on a short list of specially skilled occupations. Once selected, ballotees could appeal to the local boards established under the EWOs, but the only grounds for exemption were exceptional personal hardship or medical reasons. Since ballotees had already been medically examined, and should have also claimed exemption on the grounds of personal hardship, this appeal procedure was clearly designed to be of a very limited nature.

The Minister of Fuel and Power announced the introduction of the coal mining ballot on 2 December 1943. From then until the end of the war with Germany, when the scheme was ended, some 21,800 young men were directed to coal mining. [42] Although Parker says that conscripts mostly settled down with reasonable contentment and efficiency, there is little doubt that the ballot was extremely unpopular among the age group likely to be affected by it. Almost forty per cent of those selected lodged appeals with the local boards [43] and, in March 1944, nearly twelve thousand apprentices in the shipbuilding industry struck in support of a demand that all apprentices should be exempted from the ballot. Parker states that the main grounds given for appeals were preference for service in the armed forces or medical reasons but that, in the case of the former, appeals were consistently rejected and, in the case of the latter, a further medical examination was ordered. Out of 8,619 appeals dealt with by May 1945, no less than 8,153 were rejected. [44] Having lost his appeal the reluctant Bevin Boy either had to accept his fate or face prosecution. I shall deal with this aspect of the issue in the following section.

DEGREES OF COERCION - PRESSURE, DIRECTIONS AND PROSECUTIONS

In discussing the application of the controls over the civilian labour force, Parker and Bullock, who deal with the subject in most detail, have argued (in line with the Ministry of Labour Report for 1939-46) that the government used their powers judiciously and sympathetically, and that the vast majority of the people affected were prepared to accept restrictions and changes of employment in order to win the war. [45] In support of this view it has been pointed out that only about one million directions were issued under regulation 58A and that, in comparison with the number of people covered by various industrial regulations and controls, the proportion of prosecutions was small. [46] I shall question the interpretation of such figures later in this section. But even if it is correct I would argue that it misses a crucial point. Because directions and prosecutions occurred on a limited scale it cannot be assumed that people accepted their lot happily and willingly and that the Ministry of Labour did little more than act as a benevolent adviser. Such assumptions only serve to obscure rather than clarify the rationale behind government policy. They ignore the dynamic effect of statutory powers to act either as a deterrent or as a form of indirect pressure. Bevin described the government's manpower strategy as 'voluntaryism', stressing that the government wished to obtain people's consent rather than to use compulsion or legal sanctions. [47] What needs to be examined is what constituted consent and the methods by which it was obtained.

The concept of law as a deterrent is familiar enough and as we have seen, many wartime regulations were designed to act in that way. The concept of statutory powers being used to pressurise people to take certain courses of action is rather more unusual, but its importance within the framework of compulsory powers over civilian labour has been mentioned by both Parker and the Ministry of Labour and National Service Report 1939-46. The report states:

> The number of directions that were in fact given to secure compulsory transfer is no criterion of the effect of the Regulation which provided the sanction behind the large scale movement of labour [48]

Parker, discussing the number of directions that were issued, concludes that 'The chief value of the powers of direction was in the indirect pressure it could bring to bear.' [49] Significantly, neither Parker nor the Ministry Report see this point as central to their analysis of labour controls, adhering in general to the view that the government's policy for the control of civilian labour was achieved voluntarily. It is of course impossible to quantify the effects of indirect pressure, and this is perhaps one reason why this question has been largely ignored. But there is evidence to show that such pressure was applied quite deliberately and as a matter of policy. Much of the evidence available relates to women, but no doubt similar (if not greater) pressures were brought to bear on men who attended the labour exchanges.

As I noted in the previous section, those people who were registered under the RfEO or the Industrial Registration Orders and considered suitable for transfer to war work were called to interview at the local labour exchanges. Similarly, people who were covered by the Control of Engagement Order were obliged to seek work through the labour exchanges. For many ordinary men and women who had little previous contact with bureaucratic structures (and this applied particularly to women who had no experience of work outside the home) the interview procedure may often have been a harrowing experience. Faced with civil servants explaining, albeit politely, that it was one's duty to take the jobs being offered and that refusal might result in compulsory direction to a more unpleasant job, it is not perhaps surprising that the majority of people agreed to take the jobs offered.

Initially women, if not men, were given a relatively wide choice of work, and during the first few months of registrations under the RfEO they were also given the opportunity of not making a decision until a second interview had taken place. In August 1941, however, a list of vital war work was issued which was restricted to jobs in the manufacture of aircraft, tanks etc., work in the Royal Ordnance Factories, Nursing and the Land Army. Women interviewed after this list was published were expected to take jobs in these areas. [50]

Towards the end of 1941, the Ministry of Labour issued a circular to local offices directing them to intensify the firmness of decisions requiring women to transfer, and to speed the pace at which women were being moved into vital war work. The circular suggested that the practice of allowing women a second interview should cease and that where women were not prepared to join the auxiliary forces or to take work or training in industry, directions to industry should be issued forthwith. Furthermore, a woman should be considered mobile (i.e. she could be transferred to a different part of the country) unless she was the wife of a man serving in the armed forces or was married with household responsiblities. [51] These uncompromising instructions, which were shown to the Cabinet in 1941, leave little room for doubt that the Ministry's view was that women should be pressed into taking work in the areas the government deemed suitable. As early as November 1941 such practices had been questioned in the House of Commons and it was stated that:

> in some cases...National Service Officers are claiming that the Ministry have delegated to them complete

arbitrary powers to order these girls to go to any part of the country to serve, and...it is not generally known these girls have any rights of appeal. [52]

The Ministry spokesman denied the allegation but further evidence of the use of indirect pressure is available in relation to what was termed 'voluntary recruitment' to the women's auxiliary forces. In a memorandum to the Cabinet dated 10 November 1941 (that is, before the introduction of the National Service (No. 2) Act) it was stated that women were being encouraged to join the auxiliary forces by threats of unpleasant jobs in munitions factories. [53] Bevin warned the Cabinet that this policy was being pushed to the limit and that further pressure would result in articulated complaints of pressure and discrimination. [54]

For women called up under the National Service (No. 2) Act the possibilities of choice, in terms of civilian employment, were more limited even than that specified in the list of vital war work mentioned above. Priority was given to getting women into the highly unpleasant and dangerous job of shell-filling in Royal Ordnance Factories. [55] Furthermore, at least until the summer of 1943, those women who opted for industry after being called up under the Act were automatically issued with formal directions, against which their only means of appeal was on the grounds of personal hardship. After that date they were allowed to appeal to the local boards set up under the EWOs but it is not clear whether such women were still automatically issued with formal directions. [56]

The view that the Ministry generally treated people with sympathy and consideration has often been illustrated by reference to the administrative machinery established for dealing with women. Instructions were issued to local offices that women should be interviewed by women and that interviewers should not be much younger than the women they were interviewing. Yet from a more cynical point of view such measures can be seen as an attempt by the Ministry to avoid provoking hostility among interviewees in order to gain their compliance. Parker claims that a further advantage accrued from such machinery. After saying that female officers treated their clients with courtesy and sympathy, he adds 'and perhaps a degree of firmness than most men would have had the courage to apply. The value of this last quality was attested by the results that it achieved.' [57] So it seems that female officers could apply pressure more easily than their male counterparts.

The evidence presented above suggests that the Ministry of Labour used various forms of pressure, including threats of compulsory direction, as a deliberate policy by which workers could be placed in jobs that were considered important. It is unfortunately difficult to estimate the extent to which such a policy was pursued, but the fact that it was pursued at all casts serious doubts on the validity of assessments of the use of labour controls which are principally based on the formal use made of compulsory powers, for instance the number of directions that were issued.

A formal direction warned the individual that failure to comply was an offence and stated:

> In pursuance of regulation 58A of the Defence (General) Regulation 1939, I the undersigned, a National Service Officer...do hereby direct you to perform the services specified in the schedule hereto, being services which in my opinion you are capable of performing. [58]

Once a direction was issued there was no statutory right of appeal, but normally appeals could be lodged with the local appeal boards established under the EWOs, with the exception of women called up under the National Service (No. 2) Act mentioned above.

A breakdown for the number of directions that were issued under regulation 58A is given in Table 6.3. The most obvious point that can be drawn from this table is that there was a massive increase in the use of directions in the latter half of 1942 which was sustained until 1945. Thus, while up to June 1942 some 33,000 directions had been issued, in the following six-month periods from July 1942 until December 1944 an average of 192,000 directions were issued. Although most of these directions were to the building and civil engineering industries, the figures for other directions also show a substantial increase from the latter half of 1942. In accounting for these changes it is necessary to reconsider some of the basic problems facing the government in relation to their manpower strategy.

Until mid-1942 the government were chiefly concerned with expanding the labour force and drawing new workers into the war industries. Thus the Ministry of Labour were often dealing with people who had little experience of work in industry. But from mid-1942 the emphasis of the government's strategy switched from expansion to redistribution. This was particularly true in the building and civil engineering industries in which workers often had to be transferred from one part of the country to another to work on special projects. The quantitative break that occurred in respect of the number of directions issued might therefore be explained either by the fact that it was easier to get people to take up work than it was to get them to tranfer, or else it was easier to gain the compliance of people who had little or no industrial experience. It is also of course possible that the acute labour shortages that had developed by mid-1942, together with the realisation that little in the way of

Table 6.3 Directions to Industry 1941-45

	Men			Women	Total Men and Women
	To building and civil engineering	Other directions	Total		
up to 31/7/41	574	2,218	2,792	151	2,943
Aug - Dec 1941	2,549	7,890	10,439	1,027	11,466
Jan - June 1942	6,515	10,339	16,854	3,745	20,599
July - Dec 1942	189,952	22,811	212,763	8,428	221,011
Jan - June 1943	147,940	25,935	173,875	13,810	187,685
July - Dec 1943	136,106	29,117	165,223	16,363	181,586
Jan - June 1944	127,047	48,690	175,737	16,052	191,789
July - Dec 1944	111,213	54,003	165,216	15,663	180,879
Jan - June 1945	40,145	36,041	76,186	12,554	88,740
TOTALS	762,041	237,044	999,085	87,613	1,086,698

Source: H.M.D. Parker, Manpower, History of the Second World War (UK Civil Series) (HMSO, 1957) p.224

further large scale expansion could be expected, led the government to adopt a stricter policy whereby compulsory direction was to be used much more freely. Finally, the increase in the use of compulsory directions might reflect a general growth of reluctance on the part of workers to succumb to the pressures applied by Ministry officials.

It appears that the total of just over one million directions issued during the course of the war is a tiny figure in comparison with the redistribution of labour that took place. But it is by no means clear that the number of directions was a small figure in relation to the total number of people who could have been directed. Firstly, certain additions have to be made to Table 6.3. Directions to coal mining ballotees (about 22,000) were not included, nor were directions to women called up under the National Service (No. 2) Act. Although no precise figures are available, it is probable that between 50,000 and 150,000 women were so directed. [59] Finally, we must add the number of directions issued under regulation 29BA, which amounted to some 273,000. Thus the total number of directions issued for civilian work may have exceeded 1.5 million. Ideally this figure should then be examined as a proportion of the total number of transfers into, and within, industry which took place and which could have been the subject of directions. Unfortunately no such figures are available and any estimation of the proportional relationship must therefore be speculative. Nevertheless it may be possible to construct a rough and ready guide.

In June 1943, a few months prior to the peak of mobilisation, the total working population stood at about 22 million but many of these people were not liable to be, or else unlikely to be, directed. Of these, the two largest groups were those people in the armed forces - five million - and those who remained working in non-essential industries (with the exception of building and civil engineering) - about six million. [60] Thus the total working population who might have been liable to direction was about 11 million. From this point any reference to figures becomes dubious but two factors were certainly of importance. Firstly, a significant proportion of those who might have been liable to direction, such as those working in agriculture, the police, the civil service etc., would have stayed in their normal peace-time employment throughout the war. They might amount to several million. On the other hand, we know that a considerable number of people changed their employment on several occasions. In the building and civil engineering industries, for instance, the total number of directions to men issued during the course of the war actually exceeds the total number of men working in these industries in 1943 and 1944. [61] If we assume that these two factors cancelled each other out, then the ratio of directions to transfers into or within industry would be about

1.5 to 11 or just over 1 in 7.

Approaching the problem from another angle, we may start with the figures for workers leaving, being discharged or transferred under the terms of the EWOs, which from 1941 to 1945 amounted to some 8.9 million. [62] Some of the people involved undoubtedly left scheduled work in industry altogether (for instance to join the forces, to return home to look after dependents etc). I shall assume however that all of those people involved took other jobs to which they could have been directed. If we then add the numbers of people drawn into work for the first time (2-3 million) the total number of transfers into or within industry which could have been liable to direction would have been as high as 15 million. The ratio of direction to transfers would then be 1.5 in 15 or 1 in 10.

Bcth ways of looking at this problem are riddled with assumptions but we can probably say that the ratio of directions to transfers into and within industry was somewhere between 1 in 7 and 1 in 10. Even if the ratio was 1 in 10, the view that the number of directions issued was almost insignificant is seriously misplaced. It may be argued that the figures for the numbers of directions in the building and civil engineering industries should be treated as a special case and it is undoubtedly significant that about half the total number of directions issued related to these industries. On the other hand, given that the number of directions issued has been used to make judgements regarding the degree to which workers accepted the government's manpower policy, it would clearly be erroneous to omit from the general picture the figures for an industry in which dissatisfaction was rife.

There is little doubt that the Ministry of Labour tried to avoid the use of compulsory directions not for reasons of benevolence, but because it was felt that their widespread use would lead to discontent. Inman gives an example of a shipyard where, at one stage, 95 per cent of the unskilled labour force were working under directions, with what a Ministry of Labour Regional Office described as the obvious results - discontent and desertion. [63] Yet, if the Ministry of Labour did only use directions as a last resort, it is probably accurate to see the number of directions issued not as an indication of workers' willingness to comply with the Ministry's wishes but as the tip of an iceberg of dissatisfaction. Only those workers who positively resisted all forms of indirect pressure would have been directed, and it does not follow that those workers who bowed down to the Ministry's pressure were either willing or satisfied.

For those workers who had been directed there were several common grievances. The question of wages was particularly important. Although under the EWOs a guaranteed wage was payable, in many cases workers directed from one industry to another were forced to accept wage-cuts. This point is well illustrated by reference to the coal industry.

Early in 1941, the Industrial Registration Order was extended to coal mining and in the three months ending on 6 November 1941 some twenty thousand ex-miners had returned to the pits. [64] Many of these men were issued with formal directions and, in a debate on 'Wartime Regulations in Industry', Rhys Davies took up their case. He pointed out that after years of unemployment many miners had found jobs in other industries earning, in some cases, up to seven pounds a week: only to find themselves directed back to the pits for a weekly wage of three pounds five shillings. [65] Bevin seems to have accepted this point for in the same debate he said he had to direct 'all kinds of people, and direct them back into industry, with a loss of many pounds per week'. [66] It is likely that it was precisely in those industries in which wage rates were poorest that the Ministry of Labour had to resort to the use of directions most frequently.

A final point which should be mentioned in relation to compulsory direction concerns the question of conscientious objection to war work. The National Service Acts recognised that people could have a conscientious objection to military service, but at no stage in the war were the government prepared to formally acknowledge, in terms of the law, that individuals could have a conscientious objection to civilian war work or service in the civil defence forces. In practice, however, the Ministry of Labour adopted a rather more flexible approach.

In a letter to the Central Board for Conscientious Objectors early in 1941, the Ministry stated that, 'it was not the Minister's intention, so far as it can be avoided, to direct persons to perform services against which they have genuine conscientious objections' and that, where persons were so directed, they could appeal to the local boards. [67] In a further letter the Ministry added that there was no reason why local boards should rule appeals on grounds of conscience out of order. [68] In 1943, the Ministry of Home Security issued a circular to Local Authorities entitled 'Conscientious Objectors in the Civil Defence (General) Services' which pointed out that Bevin had given an assurance that compulsion would not be used against people who expressed a conscientious objection to making or handling munitions. The circular stated that this assurance had been interpreted liberally and it would not therefore be government policy to force persons in civil defence to do work that was not 'of a civilian character and under civilian control'. As examples it was suggested that conscientious objectors in civil defence should help clear debris but should not be forced to handle munitions, collect iron, or go on parades. [69]

Although the Ministry of Labour may have been prepared to informally recognise certain types of conscientious objection, it remained a question of administrative discretion and Hayes points out that, contrary to the Ministry's view, Local Appeal

Boards often refused to recognise conscientious objection as grounds for appeal. For those people whose conscientious objections were not recognised there were only two alternatives: to undertake the task alloted or to face prosecution. Hayes, working from cases known to the Central Board for Conscientious Objectors, says that, up to the end of 1948, 711 men and 341 women were prosecuted for their conscientious objection to some aspect of civilian service. He also says that 214 female objectors were imprisoned for refusing directions to work. [70]

If we now turn to examine prosecutions in general, the first point to note is that the government's industrial controls created a wide variety of new offences. Most of these, including disobeying directions or contravening the terms of the EWOs, were offences against regulation 58A, but people could also be prosecuted for failing to obey a direction under regulation 29BA or for failing to register or attend an interview under regulation 80B. The maximum penalty on summary conviction for such offences was three months imprisonment, a fine of one hundred pounds, or both. In addition, a person convicted of an offence against regulation 58A by reason of failing to comply with any direction would, if the failure to comply continued, not only be guilty of a further offence but also liable to a fine not exceeding five pounds for every day the failure to comply continued. [71]

It is apparent that there were very few prosecutions until the spring of 1942 but after then the numbers rose substantially. Up to the end of March 1942 a total of 773 workers had been prosecuted for offences in connection with the EWOs, the Restriction on Engagement Order, or for refusing directions under regulation 58A. Of these, 91 people had been imprisoned. [72] But by January 1943, over 8,000 workers had been prosecuted under the industrial regulations [73] and, in February 1944, it was announced that 23,517 workers had been prosecuted for industrial offences that had not existed prior to the war. Of these, 1,807 workers had been imprisoned. [74] If this pattern continued it seems likely that, by the end of the European war, a total in excess of 30,000 workers would have been prosecuted. The steep rise in prosecutions after the spring of 1942 can be partly accounted for by a dramatic increase in the number of prosecutions for absenteeism. It will be recalled that, in March 1942, absenteeism and persistent lateness were made direct offences under the EWOs and, in the twelve months from March 1942 to March 1943, there were 5,403 successful prosecutions for absenteeism. [75] But even if a majority of the prosecutions from 1942 were for absenteeism or persistent lateness, it is clear that the number of prosecutions for other offences under the industrial controls also rose sharply.

By 1944 the number of workers being sent to prison prompted a meeting between officials of the Home Office and the Ministry of Labour. Notes of the meeting state that the Home Office was seriously worried by the number of people being sent to prison for offences against regulation 58A and 80B 'which now exceed the total number of persons sentenced to imprisonment under all the other Defence Regulations put together'. [76] The meeting discussed at least two possibilities - to ask the courts either to make greater use of suspended sentences or to consider adjourning cases where it seemed likely that an offender might be prepared to follow the instructions of the Ministry. Both methods had the dual advantage of keeping offenders out of prison while at the same time threatening them with immediate imprisonment if they continued to contravene orders and directions. In April 1944 the Home Office sent a circular to the Clerks to the Justices pointing out that large numbers of people were being sent to prison under regulations 58A and 80B. The circular noted that courts sometimes adjourned cases to see if the offender would follow directions, and it suggested that this procedure might be used more frequently. [77]

The Home Secretary was asked in Parliament whether the terms of this circular interfered with the independence of the judiciary. He replied that it did not and noted that the practice of issuing circulars to the courts was as old as the Home Office itself. [78] Yet, clearly the circular was designed to have an effect.

A variation of the scheme was also employed in connection with reluctant Bevin Boys. Up to October 1944, 500 young men had been prosecuted for refusing to obey directions to coal mining or for leaving work without permission and 143 had been sent to prison. Parker notes, however, that those offenders who promised in court that they would obey the direction were usually released; as were those youths who had been imprisoned but during their confinement had changed their minds and were prepared to accept their lot. [79]

As with the number of directions that were issued, it might be thought that the number of prosecutions that occurred reflected a general acceptance and satisfaction with the way in which the Ministry of Labour used the industrial controls available to them. But this is not necessarily the case. Certainly, the total number of prosecutions that occured was a minute proportion of the total number of workers covered by the industrial controls, but no specific conclusion can be drawn from this fact. Given that following a conviction workers were still expected to obey the instructions, together with the fact that penalties could be severe, workers would have been reluctant to face prosecution. It seems likely in fact that, for both the Ministry and workers, prosecution was a last resort. At about the same time as the numbers of prosecutions began rising, so too did the level of industrial disputes. It may be that disputes were partly motivated by a growing dissatisfaction with the operation of industrial controls for, as we shall see in the next chapter, it was much more difficult to quell organised industrial unrest than it was to prosecute individual workers.

COMMENTARY

The mobilisation of manpower for the second world war has been lauded as a great success and as an example of what can be achieved through centralised state-planning. Writers such as Parker and Bullock have also argued that the success of the government's policies was largely based on the acceptance of the need for centralised control and the voluntary participation of the vast majority of workers involved.

There is no doubt that the expansion and redistribution of the labour force was a major contribution to Britain's capability to launch and sustain offensive military operations and that it was a remarkable example of intricate administration and complex planning. Yet the machinery of compulsion was an integral and crucial part of that process. Unless the workforce could be expanded and people got to work in the right places at the right time, the most coherent of plans and the most efficient of administrations would have been useless. Without underestimating the large numbers of people who did volunteer for all sorts of war work, it is quite clear that many people did not accept that they should either take up work, change jobs or stay in jobs, (with all the sacrifices that might be involved) in order to fulfil the government's plans. It was, after all, the realisation that voluntary recruitment and methods would not fulfil estimated requirements that led the government to implement compulsory measures in the spring of 1941.

Because labour controls could only be introduced by legislation and because of the very nature of the government strategy, most elements of the manpower policy were publicly acknowledged. What does not appear to have been appreciated at the time, and has received scant attention since, is the extent to which the government pursued a systematic policy of indirect pressure to get people to take specific jobs, join the auxiliary forces or the civil defence services. The more successful this policy, the less the government had to resort to the use of formal directions and thus Bevin could begin to erect the edifice of 'voluntaryism' which dominated government explanations of their strategy.

Bevin's task was made easier by the lack of opposition to these controls in Parliament. Although a few Labour MP's, such as Rhys Davies, attacked the principles of industrial conscription and the wide range of labour controls, the vast majority of MP.'s were largely quiescent. With Bevin as the Minister responsible, Labour MPs apparently had no objection to workers being forced or directed into jobs they did not want, even if it did result in a serious cut in wages.

The introduction of industrial conscription in all but name was, and still is, an unprecedented limitation of a workers ability to choose his or her employment within the economic constraints of society. It was accomplished through a consensus of the political elite and the trade union leadership which agreed that such measures were necessary, and by a series of policies designed to exercise effective control without appearing to do so - the proverbial iron fist in a velvet glove.

The pre-war planners and Chamberlain's wartime Tory government had been loath to introduce extensive control over civilian labour, fearing the reaction of the Labour Party and the trade union movement. As we shall see in the historical postscript, the post-war Labour government were loath to dispense with the powers which enabled them to exercise control over individuals' working lives.

Chapter Six: Notes

1. A.J.P. Taylor, English History 1914-1945, (Oxford, 1965) p.512.

2. PRO CAB 52/3, 'Report of the Interdepartmental Committee on the Emergency Powers (Defence) Bill and the Defence Regulations' dated 21st April 1937.

3. PRO CAB 52/5 WL 7. NS(WL)4, appended. Report of the Manpower Sub-Committee dated 10 December 1937.

4. Ibid.

5. PRO LAB 8/248.

6. Ibid, letter from Ernest Brown dated 13 September 1939.

7. W. Hancock and M. Gowing, British War Economy, History of the Second World War (UK Civil Series), (HMSO, 1949) pp.148-9.

8. see for instance Hancock and Gowing, British War Economy, p.144 and D.N. Chester, (ed.), Lessons of the British War Economy, (Cambridge, 1951) p.36.

9. Hancock and Gowing, British War Economy, p.149.

10. Defence Regulation 58A, in 'Defence Regulations Vol.I', (HMSO, March 1944).

11. A. Bullock has argued that Bevin's distaste for compulsion ensured that compulsory powers were only used in the last resort. See A. Bullock The Life and Times of Ernest Bevin, Vol.II, (Heinmann, 1967) especially Chapters One and Two.

12. Hancock and Gowing, British War Economy, p.311.

13. H.M.D. Parker, Manpower, History of the Second World War (UK Civil Series) (HMSO, 1957) p.105.

14. According to Parker these arrangements were little different from the proposals made in 1936 and, this being the

case, it again illustrates the importance of long term planning. See Parker, Manpower, pp.43-5

15. See for instance, Bullock, Life and Times of Bevin, p.57 & 273-4: Hancock and Gowing, British War Economy, p.306: & Parker, Manpower, p.225.

16. Parker, Manpower, p.113

17. Churchill, The Second World War, Vol. III, (Cassell, 1950) p.455 and see PRO CAB 66/19, WP(41)258.

18. Parker states that, under the terms of the Act, women were allowed to choose between the auxiliary forces, civil defence or industry. While the War Cabinet agreed to allow such options, the Act itself did not provide for them. see Parker, Manpower, p.286 and the 'National Service (No. 2) Act', 5 & 6 Geo 6, Ch.4.

19. PRO CAB 65/20, WM 121.

20. Cmd. 7225, 'Ministry of Labour and National Service, Report for the Years 1939-46', p.29.

21. These figures are compiled from the table of Registrations of Women under the RfEO in Parker, Manpower, Table VII, p.491.

22. PRO LAB 8/346, Memo to Regional Controllers dated 24 January 1942.

23. PRO LAB 8/514, Forms relating to industrial controls.

24. Cmd. 7225, pp.31 & 32.

25. Ibid.

26. I have been unable to discover either how many women were registered under the Act or the number who, once registered, were placed in industry. My suggestion is based on the assumption that the one third who expressed no preference were placed equally in the auxiliary forces and industry. It is a dubious assumption but the best that can be made in the circumstances.

27. Cmd.7225, pp.30 & 32.

28. Parker, Manpower, p.482, Table of distribution of Manpower at June each year, Females aged 14-59.

29. Ibid, p.289.

30. v.386 H.C.DEB 5s col.593-4.

31. Cmd.7225, p.65

32. Figures taken from Parker, Manpower, Table 26 between p.210-11 and Cmd.7225. p.2.

33. Figures taken from Parker, Manpower, Table 26, between pp.210-211.

34. Ibid, Table XIA, p.499.

35. see for instance Bullock, Life and Times of Bevin, p.57 and 273-4 Hancock and Gowing, British War Economy, p.306 & Parker, Manpower, p.225

36. Copy in NCCL archives, Filing Case No. 4 'Wartime' Section 9 'Essential Works Orders 1943-5'.

37. PRO LAB 8/632, Memorandum regarding the enforcement of the EWO provisions.

38. Ibid.

39. Mass Observation, People in Production, (J. Murray, 1942) p.17.

40. v.374 H.C.DEB 5s col.195.

41. PRO CAB 123/27, LP(43)252, dated 12 November 1943.

42. Parker, Manpower, p.255.

43. Ibid.

44. Ibid. Parker does make the point that psychological problems such as claustrophobia were taken into account at this second medical examination.

45. See Cmd 7225, p.4, Bullock, Life and Times of Bevin p.42-6 and Parker, Manpower, Chapter XIII.

46. see for instance, Bullock, ul Life and Times of Bevin, p.142 and Parker, Manpower, p.224.

47. Bullock, Life and Times of Bevin, p.44-6.

48. Cmd.7225, Manpower, p.40.

49. Parker, Manpower, p.224.

50. Ibid, p.295

51. PRO CAB 66/20, WP(41) 285, Circular appended to Memorandum.

52. v.376 H.C.DEB 5s cols.432-3.

53. PRO CAB 66/19, WP(41)257.

54. PRO CAB 65/20, WM 110.

55. Cmd. 7225, p.31

56. Parker, Manpower, p.287 (Footnote). Parker's comments are unfortunately ambiguous.

57. Ibid, p.294.

58. PRO LAB 8/514, forms relating to the industrial controls.

59. 125,000 women were conscripted into the auxiliary forces between 1941 and 1944. On the basis of the statement made in Cmd 7225 that, of the total number called up under the National Service (No. 2) Act up until 1944, one third opted for industry, one third for the forces, and one third expressed no preference, we can speculate that about the same number were placed in industry as in the auxiliary forces. If we add to this those women called up under the Act after the service option was withdrawn (ie, all those would have been placed in industry) this may give an upper limit of 150,000. On the other hand it is not clear whether directions were issued automatically after 1943 (see footnote 56) and if they were not the number of women directed would be far fewer. See also footnote 26.

60. These figures are taken from Parker's table on the Distribution of Manpower in Great Britain, see Parker, Manpower, Table 26, between p.210-11.

61. A total of 762,041 directions to men were issued in respect of the building and civil engineering industries, whereas the total numbers working in those industries in 1943 and 1944 were 700,000 and 600,000 respectively.

62. Parker, Manpower, Table XIA, p.499.

63. P. Inman, Labour in the Munitions Industries, History

of the Second World War (UK Civil Series), (HMSO, 1957) p.138.

64. v.376 H.C.DEB 5s col.154.

65. v.380 H.C.DEB 5s col.416.

66. v.380 H.C.DEB 5s col.424.

67. quoted in D. Hayes, Challenge of Conscience, (George Allen and Unwin, 1949) p.261.

68. Ibid, p.262.

69. PRO HO 208, Circular No. 162/1943.

70. Hayes, Challenge of Conscience, pp. 265, 275 and Appendix C p.389.

71. Defence Regulation 58A, in Defence Regulations, Vol.I.

72. v.379 H.C.DEB 5s col.350.

73. v.386 H.C.DEB 5s col. 265.

74. v.399 H.C.DEB 5s col. 343.

75. v.390 H.C.DEB 5s cols. 29-30.

76. PRO LAB 8/921, Notes of a meeting held at the Home Office 11 January 1944.

77. PRO HO 158/36, Circular to the Clerks to the Justices, No. HO/120/44C.

78. v. 406 H.C.DEB 5s col.729.

79. Parker, Manpower, p.255.

Chapter Seven

CIVIL LIBERTIES IN INDUSTRY

From the latter half of the nineteenth century, industry had been the central arena of class strife as workers fought not only to improve their wages and conditions but also to establish the right to organise at their workplace and the rights to strike and picket. By the 1930s the British political and legal systems had (with some qualifications such as the 1927 Trades Disputes Act) recognised these rights. Yet they remained (as they do today) sensitive and potentially volatile areas.

From the earliest days of wartime planning it had been recognised that domestic production would play an important part in Britain's war effort and, with the opening of the French Atlantic ports to the U-boat fleets in 1940, it became a crucial factor. Many factors can, of course limit industrial production, but one of those which has been persistently emphasised (both in times of war and peace) has been the state of industrial relations, particularly in so far as industrial disputes disrupt the continuity of production. Taken on its most simplistic level an absence of industrial disputes would clearly aid production. But how could this be achieved? The attempts of the wartime governments to solve this problem were both complex and wide-ranging and many of their initiatives go beyond the scope of this book. In this chapter, therefore, I shall concentrate on an examination of the way in which the governments attempted to restrict civil liberties in the industrial sphere, in the context of the more general factors which relate to the introduction and use of those restrictions.

INDUSTRIAL APPEASEMENT TO THE ESTABLISMENT OF TRIPARTISM

The 1937 report on the Emergency Powers (Defence) Bill and the defence regulations recommended, as I noted in Chapter One, that 'no provision should be included in the Defence Regulations to limit the freedom of civilians to strike', and argued that 'So long as it is lawful to strike, those people who promote strikes cannot be properly penalised'. [1]

The report did not explain why these recommendations were made but I suggested that the authors may not have envisaged the formation of an all-party coalition government which would make such prohibitions a political possibility. Certainly, any attempt by a Tory government to place blanket restrictions on the right to strike would have been likely to provoke industrial opposition to a degree whereby industrial peace would be endangered rather than enhanced.

When the first defence regulations were published in September 1939, it appeared that the advice of the Ad-Hoc Committee in 1937 had been forgotten. Regulation 2B made it an offence to:

> do any act with intent to impair the efficiency or impede the working or movement of any vessel, aircraft, vehicle, machinery, apparatus or other thing used or intended to be used in His Majesty's service or in the performance of essential services, or to impair the usefulness of any works, structure or premises used or intended to be used as aforesaid. [2]

Strikes were not excluded from the scope of this regulation and could certainly be construed as impairing the usefulness of a factory or plant. Thus, at the beginning of the war, strikes in essential services were probably illegal. But in a memorandum presented to the Home Policy Committee in November 1939, the Home Secretary stated that regulation 2B had never been intended to cover strikes. [3] The regulation was one of those discussed by the MP's consultative committee in November 1939 and a clause was subsequently added to the regulation, stating that 'a person shall not be guilty of an offence against this Regulation by reason only of his taking part in, or peacefully persuading any other person to take part in, a strike'. [4] None of the other defence regulations threatened to impinge on the right to strike, and it seems likely therefore that the intention of the government had been to follow the recommendations of the 1937 report.

It would be wrong to assume, however, that workers' rights were not threatened by the regulations introduced by the Chamberlain government. Regulations 12 and 14 dealt with activities in and around 'protected places' and regulation 15 made it an offence to be in the vicinity of a protected place, or premises in which essential work was being carried out, for purposes 'prejudicial to the public safety or the defence of the realm'. Most establishments engaged in key war manufacture (such as munitions, aircraft, tanks etc.) were quickly designated 'protected places' and entry to such establishments was subject to the approval of a competent authority, which was usually the firm's management. Perhaps of more importance were the powers given to the Secretary of State and the Admiralty under regulation 14 to make by-laws and directions regulating the conduct of persons whilst in a 'protected place'. It has been difficult to obtain specific details of the by-laws and directions that were made since, according to the Home Office, they were not published in the normal sense of the term, merely exhibited in poster form in appropriate places. [5] But from documents in the Lord President's Secretariat Files it appears that a set of by-laws and directions were made in 1939 and remained in force until at least 1941. [6] I am unable to say whether the original by-laws and directions were amended in 1939 or 1940 but, as they stood in March 1941, they placed important restrictions on workers' activities. By-law number five, for instance, covered literature and stated that no person in a protected place could, without the permission of the approved authority, distribute, deposit or offer for sale any literature, handbills, leaflets or other printed or pictorial matter of any description. Similarly, by-law number six prohibited the display of notices or leaflets without permission, and by-laws numbers ten and eleven prohibited meetings or processions in a protected place without the permission of the approved authority. [7] Although it seems likely that similar if not identical restrictions were in force during the phoney war period, the only evidence I found to suggest that they were being used to any extent came in the form of a parliamentary question from the Communist MP Willie Gallacher. In February 1940 he asked the Home Secretary whether regulations 12 to 15 would be amended to secure the rights of trade unionists and the right to peacefully picket. Anderson replied that those regulations were not meant to be used in that way, but Gallacher retorted that they were being so interpreted. [8] This suggests that some prosecutions had either taken place or had at least been threatened. But most criticism of these regulations during the phoney war period was couched in terms of their potential threat rather than concrete occurrences, and this indicates that there was no widespread use of these regulations at that time. [9]

If this was the case it would be accurate to say that, despite the introduction of regulations 12 to 15 and the protected places by-laws, the Chamberlain government did little to interfere directly with trade union and workers' rights during the first six months of the war.

As I have suggested previously, the Chamberlain government was anxious to retain some degree of consensus among the political elite, and any action to curtail, say, the right to strike, would almost certainly have provoked the Parliamentary Labour Party into serious opposition on that and other issues. Beyond this, however, such actions would also have found the trade unions united in opposition and therefore posing a real threat to industrial stability. In other words, all the time the Chamberlain government laid great importance on the development of consensus and on the continuity of production, they had little option but to appease the labour and trade union movements. Thus, as with manpower controls and the Control of Employment Act, the Chamberlain government chose appeasement rather than confrontation on both a political and an industrial level. It was a choice the coalition government never had to face.

Following the Labour Party's entry into government and the appointment of Bevin as Minister of Labour, the leadership of the trade union movement were increasingly drawn into the governmental process. On a national level this involvement was based on a proliferation of advisory bodies which included representatives of the employers' organisations, the TUC and, in most cases, the government. Two of the most important committees were the National Joint Advisory Council, and the National Production Advisory Council, linked to the Ministry of Labour and National Service and the Ministry of Production respectively. The National Joint Advisory Council consisted of fifteen representatives of the British Employers Confederation and fifteen representatives of the TUC and was usually chaired by Bevin. This committee concentrated on issues related to manpower and industrial relations and attached to it, as a sort of executive sub-committee, was a Joint Consultative Committee consisting of fourteen members equally divided between employers and the TUC representatives. The National Production Advisory Council consisted of eleven vice-chairmen of Regional Boards and twelve representatives equally divided between the employers and the TUC. Joint consultation and representation was also established on a regional and district level. Thus, Regional Boards, which considered all aspects of production in a given area, had parity representation of employers and trade unions, and the Local Appeal Boards established under the EWOs consisted of representatives of the local Ministry of Labour Office, the local employers organisation and the local trade union organisation.

The establisment of 'tripartism' as the formation and work of such joint bodies has become known, was clearly an important feature of wartime administration. Although a detailed analysis of tripartism goes far beyond the scope of this book, one or two points do need to be made.

It might be thought that the establishment of tripartism was a step forward for the industrial labour movement - a step, even if a crude one, towards an industrial democracy where workers, through their representatives, could have an effective voice in planning and running the economy. Now if trade union leaders on national, regional or local bodies represented the views of workers, or at least their members, there would be a good deal of truth in this view. Yet the flow of power and control in the trade union movement has rarely been a one way process from the rank and file to leaders who simply served that rank and file. At best, power and control have flowed in both directions and, in many trade unions, it is firmly located with the leadership of the organisation. [10]

It does not necessarily follow, therefore, that the inclusion of trade union representatives on planning or administrative bodies gave an effective voice to the interests or rights of rank and file workers. Indeed, I would argue that the more removed a trade union representative was from the shop-floor the less likely he would be to represent shop-floor workers. Thus, while shop stewards sitting on joint production committees were usually directly accountable to their fellow workers, there was no similar rank and file control over TUC representatives sitting on the national planning bodies such as the National Joint Advisory Council. If anything, the opposite was the case: TUC representatives who had agreed policy with the government could then use their constitutional and organisational supremacy to try to force their decisions on rank and file trade unionists.

With the vast majority of trade union leaders supporting both the war effort and the coalition government, trade union bureaucracies became an important organ of social control, a point which has been recognised by several writers. Middlemas, for instance, notes that for much of the war Bevin carefully retained a buffer state of union officials between shop-floor and government [11] and, talking of tripartism in general, he says, that the:

> TUC & employers could combine with the War Cabinet to reinforce industrial harmony at the expense of the tertiary level of industrial political activity, which they subsequently labelled as agitators and extremists. [12]

Similarly, Calder notes that the trade unions were permitted to become 'the hand maidens of domination' [13] and Pollard points out that:

> The leaders of the large trade unions, ...became so eager to show a sense of responsiblity for the economy as a whole, that they laid themselves open to legitimate attacks by their own members for neglecting their interests. [14]

In the later years of the war the importance of the trade union leadership's collaboration with the government lay in the use of its power and authority to prevent and limit the spread of strikes. But in 1940 it helped the coalition government to take the step which pre-war planners and the Chamberlain government had shrunk from advocating or introducing - formal powers to limit the freedom of workers to strike.

On 24 May 1940, at the height of the invasion crisis, the Director of the Security Services wrote to the Home Office to 'urge most strongly' that the provisions in the defence regulations safeguarding the right to strike should be removed. The letter does not explain why this was felt necessary, but these particular proposals were effectively quashed after the Ministry of Labour wrote to the Home Office pointing out that such changes would require consultation with the TUC and that they could see no reasons for them. [15]

The Ministry of Labour probably questioned the necessity of these proposals because they were already giving detailed consideration to a rather different strategy. On 28 May, Bevin asked the first meeting of the Joint Consultative Committee to consider how best to remove the question of wages from industrial controversy. Just a week later the representatives of the employers and the trade unions presented a unanimous reply to the Minister which began with a declaration that, during the emergency, there should be no stoppages of work as a result of trade disputes and that those disputes which arose should, if necessary, be settled by compulsory arbitration. [16]

This was what Bevin had hoped for and, on 10 July, a new defence regulation - 58AA - was introduced allowing the Minister of Labour to make Orders prohibiting strikes and lock-outs and to establish the machinery for compulsory arbitration. Eight days later the 'Conditions of Employment and National Arbitration Order' (Order 1305) was made under regulation 58AA. [17] Order 1305 allowed the Minister of Labour to refer any dispute reported to him either to existing arbitration structures or to the National Arbitration Tribunal. In both cases the findings of the arbitration body were to be binding on all parties. Part II of the Order prohibited strikes and lock-outs except in cases where the dispute had been referred to the Minister and he had not, within 21 days of the dispute being reported, referred the case to arbitration. Thus, for all practical purposes, strikes became illegal from July 1940.

The year of 1940 has been traditionally thought of as the year of the 'Dunkirk Spirit' and certainly in the summer and autumn of that year many people worked long hours, often voluntarily, and productivity in essential war industries showed a marked rise, at least until fatigue set in. [18] Furthermore, there were fewer working days lost through strikes in 1940 than in any of the preceding thirty-nine years. [19]

But despite this, a considerable number of strikes took place in the latter half of 1940 without due notice being given to the Minister of Labour. Yet, apparently as a matter of policy, there were no prosecutions under Order 1305 that year. [20] In fact until the early months of 1941 the Ministry of Labour seem to have regarded the clause prohibiting strikes and lock-outs as a deterrent rather than as a punitive sanction. In October 1940 the Lord Advocate explained to Bevin that employers were angry that strikers were not being prosecuted. In a letter dated 1 November, Bevin replied:

> The main object of the Order is to produce the greatest measure of stability in industry and to preserve as far as is practicable the continuity of production...We have already considerable evidence that the main object of the Order is being achieved and the fact that strikes and lock-outs are illegal is having much effect both on the minds of the work people and on the course of negotiations in the many troubles that arise. [21]

Beyond this policy objective there were also fears about the extent to which the Order could be used as an effective sanction. In a note by the Chief Industrial Commisioner in September 1940, it was stated:

> The Order has a substantial deterrent effect but it is an instrument which would probably be shown to be useless if any considerable body of workpeople chose to defy it. It is necessary to avoid such a situation and to maintain the Order's maximum utility by not exposing the impotence of the Government to enforce the prohibition of a stoppage of work. [22]

This was a prophetic statement and in recognising the potential power of organised and committed workers it goes a long way to explaining why the government did not rely on legal controls in the area of industrial relations, using instead the power and authority of the trade union leadership.

In concluding this section further mention must be made of the legislation relating to protected places. In the summer of 1940 a number of prosecutions occurred under regulations 12-15, notably in connection with left-wing activities. In his book 'British Liberty In Danger', Ronald Kidd gives several examples. He says that in June 1940 a man was convicted at Clerkenwell for taking literature (viz. twelve copies of the 'Daily Worker') into a protected place, and that a man was convicted of 'causing and addressing an assembly in a protected place' after, as Kidd put it, having a chance conversation on a political subject with his workmates in the toilets. Kidd also cites a case of two communists who were charged under section 2 of regulation 15 after addressing a meeting outside a locomotive works. Significantly, in this case, Kidd notes that copies of the leaflet 'The People Must Act' were being distributed during the meeting. [23]

As we saw in Chapter Four, there was a wave of action

against leftists and pacifists in the summer of 1940 and this extended into the industrial sphere. In 'Engineers at War' Richard Croucher notes that almost every shop steward who spoke about this period 'mentioned being watched, followed or interviewed formally by the police'. [24] Prosecutions under the protected places regulations were almost certainly part of that campaign. Kidd argues in his book that the protected places legislation was misused in the examples he cited. But, as we shall see in the next section, one of the principal functions of that legislation was to control political, especially communist, activity in industry.

THE INDUSTRIAL IMPERATIVE

Although the groundwork for the government's industrial strategy was laid in the crisis year of 1940, it was not until 1941 that production became of paramount importance. The introduction of manpower controls is the clearest and most obvious example of this development, but it is also reflected in the government's attitude towards industrial relations. In circumstances where large numbers of workers had little or no experience of factory life, or were placed in jobs they disliked or were unsuited to, dissatisfaction among the industrial workforce could be expected to rise. This could produce both an extra potential source for industrial unrest and a fertile soil for propaganda critical of government policy. It is not therefore surprising to find the government attempting to find ways of combating these tendencies. Yet if government action was either too obvious or too harsh there was a danger of a backlash which could also cause industrial unrest. This section therefore is primarily about balance or, put more crudely, what the government could get away with.

I noted that in 1940 the Ministry of Labour had avoided prosecuting strikers under Order 1305. But in 1941 the Ministry began to use the Order more positively and a number of workers were prosecuted. Although there is no evidence directly connecting the introduction of manpower controls and the use of Order 1305 as a sanction, the first convictions under the Order occured in April 1941, [25] only a month after the Registration for Employment Order and the Essential Works Order had been introduced. I would suggest that the government were aware that the imposition of manpower controls was likely to encourage industrial unrest and that they began to test, by way of experiment, the effectiveness of Order 1305 as a punitive sanction: to be used, perhaps, as and when all the informal methods of control had failed to prevent a strike occuring.

The probable criteria used for selecting which strikes to proceed against during this period were set out in an inter-departmental memorandum in October 1941. The writer stated:

> The question...of proceedings under the Order does not, and in my view should not arise until, as a result of our contact with the case, we are satisfied that the stoppage is associated with subversive activities or that there is a malicious intent...or that there is a wilful and obstinate refusal...to accept the discipline of the law and, normally, of their own Trade Union. [26]

It will be noted that the memo laid stress on the attitude of strikers to the authority of the government and - significantly in the context of tripartism - to the authority of the trade unions. There is no reference to the extent to which a group of workers might be justified in taking strike action.

It is not clear whether few strikes lived up to the criteria laid down or whether the Ministry's approach remained cautious. But, up to October 1941, only six strikes had resulted in prosecutions and the number of workers involved was small. [27] Furthermore, it is apparent that the Ministry of Labour were anxious to restrict prosecutions to cases they considered suitable. In December 1941 a Home Office circular to Chief Constables emphasised that it was up to the Ministry of Labour to decide whether proceedings should be instituted and that, although the police should report cases to the Ministry, no further investigations should be made unless a specific request to do so was made by the Ministry of Labour. [28]

In the spring of 1942 far more aggressive tactics were adopted and we may assume that this was a result of a high-level policy decision, given the careful considerations outlined above. It is not clear whether the new policy was an expansion of the experiment of the previous year or whether particular circumstances, such as the political crisis in the spring of 1942, prompted the Ministry to take a tougher line. What is apparent though is that the government suffered an important defeat and the earlier warnings of impotence were shown to be accurate.

On 9 January 1942, miners at the Betteshanger Colliery in Kent struck over the level of allowances payable for working difficult seams. After what Parker describes as abortive attempts by the Mines Department to settle the dispute [29] the Ministry of Labour agreed to prosecute some 1,050 miners for contravening Part II of Order 1305. Three local union officers were imprisoned and those men who had been working on the difficult seam were fined three pounds each. The other thousand or so miners were fined one pound each. Although all the miners had been convicted they decided to continue their strike, and miners in some other pits stopped work in sympathy. On 28 January, possibly after government intervention, the dispute was settled with the miners getting 'substantially what they went on strike to obtain'. [30] At the beginning of February, the Home Secretary agreed to remit the three prison sentences. Moreover, by May, only nine miners had paid their fines. Although warrants for the arrest of the other thousand or so miners were prepared, the impracticality of making so many arrests, combined with the probability that such arrests would provoke further strikes, led the Ministry of Labour to propose that the warrants should be held in abeyance. The Home Office accepted this proposal, [31] and the vast majority of fines were never paid.

If, as I have suggested, the government were experimenting with the use of Order 1305 as a punitive sanction between April 1941 and June 1942, the results were hardly satisfactory. While there was evidence that small isolated disputes might be controlled by using the Order as a sanction, the Betteshanger strike exposed the weakness of the Order when used against large numbers of strikers who were well organised and prepared to stand firm. Parker makes both points when he states:

> Where large numbers decided to take the law into their own hands, they could be fairly confident that no punitive sanctions could be effectively taken against them. On the other hand, where the number of strikers was relatively small and prompt action was taken, an appearance in court had at times salutary corrective consequences. [32]

It was probably the relative impotence of the Order which, in part, led the government to take further measures to control strikes in 1944.

The problem of finding a balance between preventing and provoking industrial unrest can also be discerned in government discussions of the protected places legislation which occurred in 1941 and 1942. In March 1941 the Home Defence (Security) Executive, the HD(S)E for short, received a report from the Security Services [33] which warned that some of the protected places by-laws might be 'ultra vires' defence regulation 14, under which they had been made. It seems the Security Services had obtained information that the validity of the by-laws was to be questioned for, on 13 June, Lord Swinton wrote to Norman Brook noting that the legal powers had been challenged in the courts in the case of a man charged with distributing literature in a protected place. [34] The HD(S)E decided to set up a sub-committee to look into the validity of the by-laws, but its terms of reference also included an examination of 'their expediency on grounds of policy'. [35]

The report of the sub-committee which was submitted to both the HD(S)E and the Lord President's Committee, [36] noted that certain of the by-laws were probably 'ultra vires' and recommended not only that new directions should be made under regulation 12 to replace the doubtful by-laws, but also that the clauses allowing a 'competent authority' to give permission for activities such as literature distribution to take place should be omitted from the new directions. Regarding the role and usefulness of the by-laws and directions, the report, referring to by-law number five, stated that while all sorts of literature was covered by its terms:

> the importance attached to the by-law in practice, however, derives from its use to prevent the circulation in protected places of subversive and in particular, communist publications. [37]

The report added that while the Security Services wished to use new and valid prohibitions to the full and prosecute all distributors of communist literature in protected places, the Home Office had expressed serious reservations about such a strategy. [38]

The Home Office probably felt that such prosecutions would lead to industrial unrest, but despite their reservations it is apparent that the by-laws and directions were seen as a method of controlling critical propaganda and other activities in essential industries.

The sub-committee's recommendations for stricter controls were accepted, but the new directions produced further problems. In March 1942, Lord Swinton wrote to the Lord President saying that the Supply Ministries, Managerial Organisations and Trade Union Executives, all wished to circulate material in protected places but were prohibited from doing so under the new legislation. The HD(S)E had therefore recommended that the following categories of literature and notices should be exempted.

(i) works notices or instructions
(ii) government publications
(iii) journals or similar publications issued by or with the authority of Trade Union Executives
(iv) works magazines or bulletins issued with the permission of an approved authority.

In connection with point (iii) above, Swinton pointed out that such an exemption would help to strengthen the authority of Trade Union Executives. [39]

These proposals were agreed, for the by-laws and directions were suitably amended in May 1942. [40] Yet it remains difficult to assess how these and previous sets of by-laws and directions were used by the government. An NCCL pamphlet published in 1942 says that the by-laws and directions had been rarely used [41] by which they meant that few prosecutions had taken place. It would appear, therefore, that their primary use was as a deterrent rather than as a sanction.

Indeed it appears that, in 1942, the Ministry of Labour had to step in to prevent employers making use of the by-laws and directions in ways which might bring them into disrepute or provoke industrial unrest. In August 1942, a case was reported to the NCCL in which the management of a firm had brought proceedings against a number of workers who had signed a 'circulated request' (presumably a petition) requesting extra milk for an invalid worker. According to the report, however, the police intervened and persuaded the management to drop the case. [42] The police action was probably a result of an intervention by the Ministry of Labour for, in a similar case a month earlier, the Ministry's interest is documented. The management of a firm had caused summonses to be issued against six workers who had been involved with a petition regarding the quality of food in the factory canteen. Although the workers' action was illegal under the by-laws and directions, the magistrate persuaded the firm to drop the case to 'avoid bad blood' as a local newspaper put it. [43] A Ministry of Labour memo discussing this case stated that the regulations had not been intended to be used in such a manner and that such action should be stopped. [44]

What seems likely to have happened is that the Ministry, realising that petty or unjustifiable prosecutions would only serve to damage industrial relations, persuaded the Home Office to issue a circular to Chief Constables and the Clerks to the Justices advising them to try and prevent such prosecutions. Alternatively, Local Offices of the Ministry might have been asked to exert what influence they could to the same ends.

THE RISE OF INDUSTRIAL UNREST

In comparison with the years immediately prior to the war, the number of working days lost through industrial disputes in 1940 and 1941 was significantly reduced and, as I said earlier, in the crisis year of 1940, fewer days were lost through disputes than in any previous year since 1900. I suggested that this probably reflected what has popularly been termed the 'Dunkirk Spirit', but whatever its basis it was a trend that was not sustained. In 1942, the number of working days lost through disputes exceeded the totals for 1938 and 1939, and the figures rose again in 1943. [45] In 1944, there were more stoppages of work than in any previous year since the beginning of the century and, with the exception of 1926 - the year of the General Strike - more workers were involved in disputes than in any year since 1921. Altogether, 3,714,000 working days were lost through disputes in 1944. [46]

It is quite clear that there was a substantial rise in

industrial unrest during the later years of the war, but some writers have sought to discount the importance of this development. Taking the period of the second world war as a whole, Parker draws a comparison with the first world war and points to the fact that there were fewer working days lost and fewer workers involved in disputes than was the case between 1914-18, even though there were far more people employed in industry in the later period. But taking the years of the two wars in isolation is of dubious value, for if strikes during the two wars are placed in the context of the immediate pre and post-war years a very different picture emerges. The number of working days lost through disputes during the first world war was consistently far lower than in the immediate pre and post-war years, whereas in the second world war more working days were lost in 1944 than in any other year between 1933 and 1954. The same figures for 1943 and 1945 exceed the yearly totals for 1938 and 1939 and the period 1946 to 1949. [47]

Another point that has been made is that the average duration of strikes during the second world war was short, and that the vast majority of strikes arose out of disputes about wage rates. Calder, for instance, describes the typical strike during the second world war as a 'swift outburst over piece rates'. [48] What few writers have mentioned are the political circumstances within which strikes during the second world war took place. Yet they are clearly of crucial importance in any assessment of the nature and level of strikes.

After the formation of the coalition government, workers who took strike action not only had to face the hostility of the government and the vast majority of MPs, but also that of the trade union leadership and, after June 1941, of the Communist Party. In other words, in the later years of the war, workers who took strike action were almost totally politically isolated. But perhaps of even greater importance was that the TUC and trade union leaders used their authority and power to prevent strikes. In September 1943 Bevin, replying to a question regarding the number of strikes that had taken place during the preceding month, was able to say that he knew of none that had received the official support of trade unions and added that he had received 'every assistance' from the trade unions. [49] The following month, in reply to a more general question about the trade unions' role in strikes, a junior Minister said 'I am glad to say that almost without exception trade unions have not given official support to stoppages of work.' [50]

By refusing to grant official recognition to strikes, Trade Union Executives had a powerful weapon. Not only did it increase the political pressure on strikers, it was also an important sanction. Without official backing, strikers could not claim strike pay and did not have access to the organisational resources of their national union. If only for these reasons it is not suprising that strikes tended to be of short duration. In relation to comparisons with strikes in the first world war, these points are also of importance for, between 1914-18, sections of the labour and trade union movements opposed the war and were more likely to see strikes in a sympathetic light.

Given the political circumstances described above I would argue that the level of strikes that occured in the later years of the second world war was quite remarkable, and the government were clearly very concerned, both with the possible effect on production and the fact that workers were prepared to defy not only the authority of government but also that of the trade union leadership.

The government's response to the increasing level of strikes was a complex one and is largely beyond the scope of this book, since it involved the relationships of power, pressure and influence both between government and the trade union leadership, and between the trade union leadership and ordinary union members. Yet this is significant, for it points to the difficulties the government faced in employing the sort of powers with which this book has been concerned.

I noted in the previous section that attempts to use Part II of Order 1305 against large numbers of strikers who were committed to their action had not only failed but exposed the weakness of the Order. Not surprisingly, therefore, the Order was not used as a principal weapon in government attempts to prevent strikes in the later years of the war, although there were a substantial number of prosecutions of small groups of workers. From April 1941 (when the first prosecution was brought) until the end of the war with Germany, there were 109 cases of prosecutions under Part II of the Order, but in only twenty of these did the number of workers proceeded against exceed one hundred. [51] Altogether some 6,300 workers were prosecuted for taking part in illegal strikes. [52] In Scotland, where the majority of prosecutions occurred, the Lord Advocate virtually gave up prosecuting in 1944 according to Parker, and he adds that this decision illustrates the weakness of the sanctions in the Order. In England and Wales there were only three prosecutions in 1944, and in two of these the courts dismissed the charges on the grounds that the stoppages of work were not strikes but lock-outs. [53]

Of course the Order may still have acted as a deterrent (although Parker doubts this) and, by a refinement of method, prosecutions under the Order were sometimes used in attempts to ensure that the workers involved did not take part in further strike action. A Ministry of Labour file notes that, in the case of a dispute that arose in October 1943, some workers accepted a scheme of paying a voluntary fine of one pound which was to be refunded if they worked without further stoppages for the next eight weeks. [54] Similarly, following the prosecution and conviction of 160 miners under Order 1305 and regulation 58A, the judgement of the court was suspended for six months to see whether the workers were prepared to work without further stoppages. [55] It is not clear whether advice or instructions were issued to local magistrates to adopt this approach but Parker suggests that, in many cases, there was some liason between the courts and the Ministry of Labour. [56]

Despite the efforts of the government and the trade union leaders, the level of strikes continued to rise. By the autumn of 1943 industrial unrest had reached such a pitch that it was seen as a real threat to the production programmes necessary to support the invasion of Europe. Yet, rather than accept the possibility that many workers in industry could have genuine grievances, Bevin, in line with the view expounded by most of the press and many Tory MPs, saw rank and file action and defiance of the trade union leadership as stemming from political and subversive motives. In September 1943 he spoke of disputes arising 'not from a wages dispute but in order to embarrass the government in the political field' [57] and in other speeches in the autumn he hinted that the government would consider taking further powers. Suspecting that any further powers would be directed towards strengthening the position of the trade union leadership, Aneurin Bevan suggested that such an approach smacked of 'Gauleiter reasoning'. He argued:

> It is not a healthy situation for the unions when their members have to strike both against the union and the employers before they can obtain redress. That is not a situation which calls for the legal strengthening of the unions. It is rather one which demands that the unions should resume their proper function as advocates and champions of the workers. [58]

As far as Bevin was concerned, the early months of 1944 provided further evidence of subversive activities designed to disrupt industry. Following the announcement of a new pay award for miners and a government statement which suggested that this award might not be implemented, an unofficial strike began on a massive scale. In Yorkshire and South Wales alone some 220,000 miners joined the stoppage, and coal production was seriously disrupted. The government moved to appease the strikers and offered a complete overhaul of the wages structure. The miners were persuaded to return to work. At about the same time, however, shipbuilding and engineering apprentices in Tyneside and elsewhere struck in support of a demand that apprentices should be exempted from the Coal-Mining Ballot scheme. Almost 12,000 apprentices were involved in the strike and Bevin theatened the strikers with immediate medical examination and call-up to the Army. [59] After about two weeks the strike was called off without any concessions being obtained.

It was as a result of this strike that four members of the Revolutionary Communist Party were prosecuted under the Trades Disputes Act. But, as I said in Chapter Four, there is no real evidence to suggest that trotskyists or any other so-called subversive elements either caused, or played a significant role in, the growth of industrial unrest. Bevin, however, explained the need for regulation 1AA in these terms to both the Cabinet and other government committees. On 5 April, Bevin told the Cabinet that he had received TUC approval for the new regulation and, on 11 April, the Joint Consultative Committee also endorsed the regulation. [60] After being discussed by the Lord President's Committee and the Home Policy Committee, regulation 1AA was introduced by Order in Council on 17 April 1944. Using the threat of a sentence of up to five year penal servitude, regulation 1AA stated that:

> No person shall declare, instigate or incite any other person to take part in, or shall otherwise act in furtherance of, any strike or lock-out likely to interfere with essential services. [61]

except by reason of either simply ceasing work or refusing to continue to work, or by any act done at a duly constituted and authorised meeting of a trade union to which a person belonged. As a concomitant to regulation 1AA, the clause in regulation 1A which allowed people to take part in, or peacefully persuade others to take part in, a strike was revoked and replaced by a clause which provided that no person should be deemed to have committed an offence against the regulation by reason of having, during the course of a strike, ceased to work, refused to continue to work, or refused to accept employment.

Despite Bevin's explanation that the changes were necessary to curb subversive activities, it is quite clear that the new regulation and the amendments to regulation 1A had much wider implications. Not only did they pose a threat to any workers who might argue for or help organise a strike (except in so far as the did so at a duly constituted trade union meeting) they also appear to have made any form of picketing illegal. Even the apparent safeguard regarding trade union meetings was a double-edged sword, for in at least some unions the national organisation had the authority to determine what was or was not a duly constituted meeting. It also gave the union leaders both the time and the opportunity to organise and argue against a strike should workers try to avail themselves of the safeguard. In a memo submitted to the Home Policy Committee on 17 April, Bevin stated 'I do not desire in any way to weaken the hand of the Unions, but rather to help them maintain discipline amongst their members.' [62]

Ministers and trade union leaders were undoubtedly aware of the scope of the changes in the law and, again as I said in Chapter Four, any measure which might help to control the spread of industrial unrest must have appeared an attractive proposition in the last few months before D-Day.

The introduction of regulation 1AA caused a storm of protest and, on 28 of April, Aneurin Bevan moved a prayer in the House of Commons to annul the relevant Order in Council. [63] He argued the government had stirred up a campaign against trotskyists and agitators in order to win support for the regulation, and pointed out that there were thirteen million workers in Britain who were not members of trades unions and had no protection whatsoever under the regulation. He also referred to the gulf that had developed between the trade union leadership and their membership and stated:

> Do not let anybody on this side of the House think that he is defending the trade unions: he is defending the trade union official, who has arterio-sclerosis, and who cannot re-adjust himself to his membership. He is defending an official who has become so unpopular among his own membership that the only way he can keep them in order is to threaten them with five years in gaol. [64]

Replying for the government, Bevin continued to argue that the recent wave of strikes had largely been the work of subversive elements, but he couched his allegations in general terms and declined to give specific details. [65] On the face of it the vote of 314 to 23 at the end of the debate seemed to be an overwhelming victory for the government and a personal triumph for Bevin. But, in fact, a large number of Labour MPs had failed to support the government. Michael Foot, in his biography of Aneurin Bevan, says that out of a total of 165 Labour MPs only 56 had voted in favour of regulation 1AA, and twenty three of these were either Ministers, Whips, or Parliamentary Private Secretaries. [66] On the basis of these figures, regulation 1AA led to the largest backbench rebellion over a civil liberties issue during the course of the war. An interesting side issue which arose out of this debate (and which reinforces the points made in earlier chapters regarding the limitation of parliamentary control) was that, prior to the debate, Bevan had been warned not to attack the government and was subsequently threatened with expulsion from the Labour Party. [67]

The powers under regulation 1AA were formidable, but the government were still confronted with the basic problem. The rationale behind regulation 1AA was to try to ensure the continuity of production. But, given that 1AA had already caused something of a political storm, it was likely that any attempts to bring prosecutions under the regulation would provoke similar hostility in industry. Certainly the government could not afford to see the regulation used indiscriminately and, at a meeting at the Home Office on 20 April 1944, consideration was given to the instructions which should be issued to the police regarding the operation of the regulation. The meeting agreed that the police should not use their own initiative to bring prosecutions under the new regulation, since policy issues would have to be taken into account. The meeting concluded, therefore, that the police could investigate cases but should take no action until the Director of Public Prosecutions, the Ministry of Labour and other appropriate government departments had been consulted. In cases of picketing where the police felt action was necessary, it was agreed that workers should be warned before being arrested, and, in any incidents where an arrest occurred, a report should be forwarded to the Home Office immediately. [68] A circular along these lines was issued to Chief Constables at the beginning of May 1944. [69] In fact, in the year or so of its existence, there were no prosecutions under regulation 1AA [70] even though there must have been many instances of strikes in respect of which a prosecution was technically possible. Presumably it was consistently concluded that a prosecution under the new regulation would be counter-productive.

This does not mean of course that the regulation was of no use. Croucher says that it 'was perhaps the most important of a number of factors which tended to dampen down the militancy which had flared up in the winter of 1943-44' and that it did have a general deterrent effect. [71] It could also be used as a direct threat. Only two days after the regulation was introduced, a meeting at the Home Office discussed an unofficial bus workers' strike that was taking place at certain London depots. The meeting noted that there was no hint that trotskyists were connected with the dispute but nevertheless agreed that pickets should be warned that they would be contravening regulation 1AA and, if their activities continued, should be arrested, charged and then released on bail. [72] Since there is no indication that prosecutions were brought, we can only assume that the warning to pickets was sufficient to stop their activities. The usefulness of the regulation as a deterrent or threat was the subject of an analogy drawn by the Minister of Labour in response to a parliamentary question in October 1944. Asked whether the regulation was to be withdrawn, Bevin replied 'No, Sir: plenty of things take place in the street when the policeman is not present, which do not happen when he is there.' [73]

COMMENTARY

In most of the questions I have discussed, restrictions on civil liberties affected individuals or groups with comparatively little political or economic power in society. But if large numbers of industrial workers withdrew their labour for any length of time, war production could be rapidly and significantly impaired. To this extent, the question of civil liberties in industry is of a qualitatively different nature from other civil liberties issues, since industrial workers could exercise a direct countervailing power to that of the state. Whether they did so or not was a function of a wide variety of factors, but that a potential sanction against government action existed goes a long way to explaining the circumspection with which the wartime governments took and used powers to restrict civil liberties in industry, particularly the right to strike.

Although the Chamberlain government introduced the legislation relating to protected places, in the absence of a fully operative political consensus they were not prepared to restrict the right to strike and agreed to amend the only regulation which threatened to do so. It was not until the Labour Party joined the government, and the co-operation of the trade union leadership ensured, that it became politically possible to introduce regulation 58AA and Order 1305. I have stressed that the trade union leadership played a crucial role as an organ of social control and one of their functions was to attempt to minimise any industrial unrest that might result from the use of legal powers against workers. I showed that one of the principal roles of the protected places legislation was to curb the dissemination of political - especially communist - propaganda in the war industries. Perhaps one of the reasons why these regulations did not provoke a great deal of industrial unrest or political controversy was because trade union leaders argued that the regulations were not aimed at the ordinary worker but at the political activist. The trade union leadership could not, however, guarantee success in relation to restrictions on the right to strike, which affected any worker who might be involved in an industrial dispute. The Betteshanger miners' strike in 1942 showed that Order 1305 could not be used against large groups of workers who were prepared to defy it without the danger of provoking further, and possibly widespread, industrial unrest. Similarly, any major prosecution under regulation 1AA would have been likely to have the same effect.

The political consensus and the co-operation of the trade union leadership enabled the coalition government to introduce legislation limiting the right to strike. But since the government were pre-occupied with maintaining production, Order 1305 and regulation 1AA could only really be used as a deterrent or a threat to small groups of workers, or in circumstances where the workers themselves were divided. Their importance in this respect should not be underestimated but the practical limitations on their use is clearly illustrated by the number of unofficial strikes that took place in the last two years of the war.

Chapter Seven: Notes

1. PRO CAB 52/3, Report of the Interdepartmental Committee on the Emergency Powers (Defence) Bill and the Defence Regulations, dated 21st April 1937

2. Defence Regulation 2B in Defence Regulations Vol.I, (HMSO, March 1944).

3. PRO CAB 75/3, HPC(39)103.

4. Defence Regulation 2B in Defence Regulations Vol.I.

5. In a letter to the author dated 30 March 1979, the Departmental Record Officer at the Home Office stated that, although the defence regulations were published:

> 'the by-laws and directions made under Defence Regulations 12 and 14 were not so published: they were, of course, exhibited in various appropriate places, in poster form, so that people who needed to know were made aware of their content.'

The basis for this was probably that, by clauses included in relations 12 & 14, any by-laws etc. made under the regulations were exempted from Section Three of the Rules Publication Act of 1893.

6. PRO CAB 123/93, A sub-committee of the Home Defence (Security) Executive was set up in 1941 to '...review the Protected Places By-Laws 1939'. This file also includes a list of by-laws in effect at the end of March 1941.

7. Ibid, By-laws Nos. 5, 6, 10 and 11 in the list of existing protected places by-laws at 31 March 1941.

8. v.356 H.C.DEB 5s cols.1248-9.

9. A letter from Ronald Kidd dated 30 November 1939 said that regulations 12 to 15 'might' be used to restrict trade union activities and the issue of 'Civil Liberty' for January 1940 makes a similar point. NCCL Archives, Filing Case No. 4 'Wartime', Section 6 'Emergency Powers (Defence) Regulation' and Section 5 'Wartime Regulations - Cuttings from 'Civil Liberty'.

10. For a specific discussion of this point see S.M. Lipset, M.A. Trow and J.S. Coleman, 'Democracy & Oligarchy in Trade Unions' in W.E.J. McCarthy, (Ed.), Trade Unions (Penguin, 1972).

11. K. Middlemas, Politics in Industrial Society, (Andre Deutsch, 1979) p.284.

12. Ibid, pp.285-6.

13. A. Calder, *The People's War*, (Panther 1971) p.454.
14. S. Pollard, *The Development of the British Economy, 1914-1967*, 2nd Edition, (Edward Arnold, 1969) p.342.
15. PRO HO 45/19056, letter from the Director of the Security Services to the Home Office dated 24 May 1940 and letter from the Ministry of Labour to the Home Office.
16. H.M.D. Parker, *Manpower*, History of the Second World War (U.K. Civil Series), (HMSO, 1957) pp.133-4.
17. SR & O No.1305, 18 July 1940.
18. Calder, *People's War*, pp.135-6.
19. D. Butler & J. Freeman, *British Political Facts 1900-1967*, Second Edition, (Macmillan, 1968) p.219.
20. Parker, *Manpower*, p.467.
21. PRO LAB 10/118, letter from Bevin dated 1 November 1940.
22. PRO LAB 10/116, Note by Chief Industrial Commissioner dated September 1940.
23. R. Kidd, *British Liberty in Danger*, (Lawrence & Wishart, 1940) pp.205-7.
24. R. Croucher, *Engineers at War*, (Merlin Press, 1982) p.95.
25. Parker, *Manpower*, p.467.
26. PRO LAB 10/153, Interdepartmental memo dated 29 October 1941.
27. Parker, *Manpower*, p.468.
28. PRO HO 158/24, Circular to Chief Constables No. 827723/88 dated 3 December 1941.
29. Parker, *Manpower*, p.461.
30. Ibid, p.462.
31. Ibid.
32. Ibid, p.469.
33. PRO CAB 123/93, Note from Lord Swinton dated 16 June 1941.
34. Ibid, Letter from Lord Swinton to Norman Brook.
35. Ibid, Notes on the Sub-Committee on the Protected Places By-Laws.
36. Ibid, Report of the Sub-Committee on the Protected Places By-Laws, dated 16 June 1941.
37. Ibid, Sub-Committee Report.
38. Ibid, Sub-Committee Report.
39. Ibid, Note from Lord Swinton to the Lord President dated 20 March, 1942.
40. According to an NCCL Pamphlet: A. Tuckett, *Civil Liberty and the Industrial Worker*, (NCCL, 1942) p. 34. Held at Documents section, University of Sussex Library, UKNO (Nat).
41. Ibid, p.29
42. NCCL Archives, Filing Case No. 5, Section 8 'Protected Places 1942-3' Report dated 10 August 1942.
43. NCCL Archives, Filing Case No. 5, Section 8, 'Protected Places 1942-3' cutting from the West Lancs. Evening Gazette, 29 July 1942.

44. PRO LAB 10/432, internal Ministry of Labour memo.
45. In 1938 and 1939 1,334,000 and 1,356,000 working days were lost respectively. The comparable figure for 1942 was 1,527,000 working days and for 1943 1,808,000 working days. Butler and Freeman, British Political Facts, p.219.
46. In 1944, 2,194 stoppages began in the year, involving some 821,000 workers. Ibid.
47. Ibid, p.219.
48. Calder, People's War, p.456.
49. v.392, H.C.DEB 5s.cols.423-4.
50. v.393 H.C.DEB 5s col.389.
51. Figures compiled from Parker, Manpower, p.469.
52. v.463 H.C.DEB 5s col.39.
53. Parker, Manpower, p.469.
54. PRO LAB 10/270.
55. Ibid.
56. Parker, Manpower, p.468 and 469.
57. Quoted in M. Foot, Aneurin Bevan, Vol. I, (MacGibbon and Kee, 1962) p.443.
58. Ibid.
59. Parker, Manpower, p.465.
60. PRO LAB 8/844, Minutes of the Joint Consultative Committee, 11 April 1944.
61. Draft of Regulation 1AA appended to memo submitted to the Home Policy Committee on 17 April 1944. PRO CAB 75/19, HPC(44)29.
62. PRO CAB 75/19, HPC(44)29.
63. for debate see v.399 H.C.DEB 5s cols.1061-1158.
64. v.399 H.C.DEB 5s cols.1071-2.
65. for Bevin's speech see v.399 H.C.DEB 5s cols.1119-1132.
66. Foot, Aneurin Bevan, p.456.
67. for further details see Foot, Aneurin Bevan, pp.450-1 and 456-463.
68. PRO HO 45/19609.
69. PRO HO 158/36, Circular to Chief Constables, No.HO 131/44 G2.
70. Parker, Manpower, p.470.
71. Croucher, Engineers at War, pp. 308-309
72. PRO HO 45/19609, Meeting on the 19th April 1944.
73 v.403 H.C.DEB 5s cols.1912-3.

HISTORICAL POSTSCRIPT: THE END OF THE WAR

On 9 May 1945, only two days after German representatives had signed the instrument of surrender, Morrison announced in the House of Commons that an Order in Council had been signed revoking a large number of defence regulations. These included regulations 1AA, 2C, 2D, 18AA, 18B, 29BA, 39BA, 39E, parts of regulations 39B and 88A. The Home Secretary said that:

> The regulations which have been revoked include those to which Parliament has rightly given especially vigilant attention because of their effect on the general field of civil liberties

and that he was happy to announce:

> the return to those traditional British freedoms which all of us who hold the democratic faith are zealous to maintain. [1]

Yet the return to 'traditional British freedoms' was by no means complete. In fact, it was to be a further fourteen years before the last of the wartime powers affecting civil liberties was revoked.

Significantly, those regulations which were kept in being for any length of time (with the exception of 39A - the incitement to disaffection regulation) were all related to controls in the industrial sphere. It had been recognised by the coalition government that the transition from war to peace would place great strains on the economy and that the abandonment of all industrial controls at a stroke would create further serious economic dislocation. In 1943, a memo to the Emergency Legislation Committee recommended that regulations 58A and 58AA should be revoked six to twelve months after the cessation of all hostilities, which at the time was expected to be some eighteen months after the end of the war in Europe. [2] In order to continue a wide range of industrial regulations, the coalition government prepared a 'Supplies and Services (Transitional Powers) Bill' to last for two years after the expiration of the Emergency Powers Acts. [3]

The 'Emergency Powers (Defence) Acts' were due to expire in August 1945, but Churchill's caretaker government introduced a Bill to extend the EP(D)A'S for six months, that is until February 1946. In October 1945, the new Labour government introduced the 'Supplies and Services (Transitional Powers) Bill' but, rather than lasting for two years, the Act was to continue in force for five years and could be extended if an address was passed by Parliament. [4] The Bill became law in December 1945 and regulations 58A, 58AA and 80B were continued until December 1950. In February 1946, prior to the expiration of the EP(D)A's, the government also introduced an 'Emergency Laws (Transitional Provisions) Bill', which allowed for the continuance of certain defence regulations, not covered by the main Act, until December 1947. Among those continued, were regulation 39A and regulations 12 and 14 relating to protected places. [5] In 1946 an 'Emergency Laws (Miscellaneous Provisions) Act' replaced the 'Emergency Laws (Transitional Provisions) Act' and, although regulation 39A was revoked at this stage, regulations 12 and 14 were continued until December 1950. [6]

After five years of peace and with the Supplies and Services Act and the Emergency Laws Act due to expire in December 1950, it might have been anticipated that this would mark the end of the wartime emergency powers. But this was not the case. In the autumn of 1950 and each subsequent year until 1959, first the Labour government and then its Conservative successors, asked Parliament to continue parts of both Acts for further periods of one year. Parliament duly obliged. [7] It was only in 1959, fourteen years after the end of the war, that both Acts were repealed by the 'Emergency Laws (Repeal) Act, 1959'. The period from 1950 to 1954 did, however, see the gradual revokation of all but one of the remaining regulations affecting civil liberties. In 1950, regulations 12 and 14 were allowed to lapse and, in 1952, the sections of regulation 58A which had provided for the Essential Works Orders were revoked. A year later the power to direct individuals to specific employment was abandoned. [8]

The one exception to this process was regulation 58AA which was kept in being until 1959. Throughout the 1950s, therefore, the Minister of Labour retained the power to make an Order by which strikes and lock-outs could be prohibited. But Order 1305 was replaced in 1951 by an Industrial Disputes Order which did not prohibit strikes or lock-outs and it was probably the usefulness of this Order that led to the continuance of regulation 58AA.

Having described the legislative basis for the continuance of emergency powers in post-war Britain, it remains to consider briefly how those powers affecting civil liberties were used. In this context, regulation 58A, which provided most of the powers for the control of civilian labour, was undoubtedly the most important.

The period from the end of the European war until 1947 saw a gradual relaxation of labour controls. Although a new and comprehensive 'Control of Engagement Order' was introduced in May 1945, [9] registrations under the 'Registration for Employment Order' were suspended in July 1945 and the number of directions issued to workers was drastically reduced. [10] In December 1945 the Minister of Labour announced that there was to be a review of the Essential Work Orders and that direction to work would no longer be applied to women, or to men over the age of 30. Similar limitations were to be applied to the 'Control of Engagement Orders' with the exception of a few key industries. Thus, large numbers of people were to be freed from controls on their employment. But the Minister warned 'I should make it clear that it is the Government's intention that the limited controls which will remain in force should be strictly enforced, if necessary by the institution of proceedings against offenders.' [11]

One of the most noticable results of the government's policy was a rapid de-scheduling of firms and industries that had been covered by the EWOs. In September 1945, some 8.7 million workers were still employed in scheduled undertakings but, by May 1946, this figure had fallen to 2.9 million. [12] By June 1947 all the EWOs had been revoked, although in coal-mining and agriculture they were replaced by 'Control of Engagement Orders' by which workers could not move out of those industries without the permission of the Ministry of Labour. Further relaxations occurred in the first half of 1947. The use of directions was limited to keeping workers in coal mining and agriculture, and general controls over men up to the age of thirty under the 'Control of Engagement Orders' were revoked. [13] Thus, by mid 1947, the only large groups of workers still covered by industrial controls were men aged 18-50 who worked in agriculture, coal-mining and the building and civil engineering industries.

This process of relaxation came to an abrupt halt in the summer of 1947 at a time of major financial and economic crisis. On 6 August the Prime Minister warned that certain labour controls would have to be re-introduced. [14] A new 'Control of Engagement Order' came into effect on 6 October 1947 and, with certain specific exceptions, men aged 18-50 and women aged 18-40 had, once again, to obtain new work through the labour exchanges or other approved agency. [15] The use of directions was also resumed and, in November 1947, the Minister of Labour stated in the House of Commons that people coming to the labour exchanges would be given a choice of four jobs and that, if none of these were accepted, directions might be issued. [16] Another measure introduced in the summer of 1947 was a new 'Registration for Employment Order' which could be applied to men aged 18 - 50 and women aged 18-40. By April 1948, people engaged in street trading, or connected with amusement arcades, betting or football pools were required to register. In total 37,072 men and 58,893 women registered, of which about 8,000 were placed in new employment. [17]

Despite the re-imposition of wide ranging controls the number of directions issued was very small. Between October 1947 and March 1950, only 29 people were directed to new employment and 668 workers directed to continue working in coal-mining and agriculture. [18] In addition, between 300 and 400 people had been directed to attend interviews and medical examinations under regulation 80B. Yet, as we saw in Chapter Six, the advantages of labour controls lay not so much in the use of compulsion, rather it enabled the government to pressurise people to take specific jobs, the threat of direction operating as a potential sanction. In 1947, the Minister of Labour euphemistically described this process as one of 'guidance'. [19]

The Conservative Manifesto for the General Election of 1950 promised to abolish the direction of labour, and, only a month after the election in which the Labour Party scraped home with a tiny majority, it was announced that the 'Control of Engagement Order' was to be revoked and the use of directions discontinued. [20] Although the powers of direction under regulation 58A were not dispensed with until 1953 no further attempts were made to control civilian labour by the use of wartime emergency powers.

In comparison with regulation 58A, the other preserved powers affecting civil liberties led a very quiet life. Regulations 12 and 14 were continued until 1950, but the number of protected places was drastically reduced. Although it is likely that the by-laws restricting various forms of trade union and political activity remained in force, I found no indication that they were widely used. The final regulation which needs to be mentioned is 58AA, under which Order 1305 had been made in 1940. The Order remained in force until 1951 and so strikes remained effectively illegal for six years after the end of the war. As we saw in Chapter Seven, the Order had not prevented large numbers of strikes taking place, yet the Labour government and the trade union leadership considered it sufficiently useful (perhaps as a peripheral potential weapon, or as a moral stick with which to beat unofficial strikers) to continue its existence. Between 1945 and 1949 no-one was prosecuted under the Order but, in October 1950, after an unofficial strike among gasworkers, ten strikers were prosecuted for taking part in an illegal strike and sentenced to one month's imprisonment. [21] Although the sentences were reduced on appeal, the prosecution prompted protests from rank and file trade unionists who were angered further in 1951 when seven dockers' leaders were charged with conspiracy to incite dockers to strike in contravention of Order 1305. As far as I am able to ascertain, this was the first time a conspiracy charge had been connected with Order 1305. When the case went to court the jury failed to reach a verdict on this charge, although the men were found guilty of conspiracy to incite dockers to break their contracts. [22] The use of Order 1305 had only succeeded in provoking a storm of protest and, in August 1951, it was revoked and replaced by an 'Industrial Disputes Order' which, although preserving a system of compulsory arbitration, did not restict the right to strike. [23] Following the revocation of Order 1305 there were no further attempts to restrict or prohibit strikes by means of wartime emergency powers, although, as I noted earlier, regulation 58AA remained in force until 1959.

Although for much of this section I have discussed those regulations which were continued after the end of the war, it should be reiterated that most of the defence regulations with which this book has been concerned were revoked either at the end of the war in Europe or shortly after the end of hostilities in the Far East. To this extent the coalition and Labour governments fulfilled the pledges given in 1939 and 1940, that restrictions on civil liberties would only be maintained for the duration of the wartime emergency. But this was not the case in the industrial sphere, even though the regulations that were continued were kept in being by post-war legislation rather than the Emergency Powers Acts.

Undoubtedly it would have been extremely difficult to completely abandon the powers under regulation 58A as soon as the war ended. Thus the wartime government's plan to revoke regulation 58A two years after the end of the war in Europe, together with the relaxation of these controls between 1945 and 1947, was perhaps the best that could be expected. On the other hand, the Labour government's decisions to continue regulation 58A and 58AA until 1950 and the reimposition of labour controls in 1947 are rather different matters. Although Britain was gripped by serious economic and financial difficulties in the post-war years, it is hard to see that these problems were greater than those faced between September 1939 and May 1940; a period when regulations 58A and 58AA did not exist. Furthermore, the continuance of reg.58A may not simply have been motivated by immediate economic difficulties, for there are indications that the leadership of the Labour Party gave serious consideration to the possibility of making the controls over civilian labour a permanent feature of the peacetime economy. [24] I would argue that the Labour government's attitude to labour controls was both expedient and a function of a belief in centralised economic planning. In both cases, the Labour government were prepared to disregard individual workers' rights. A similar case could be made for the government's retention of Order 1305 for six years after the end of the war, except that, as a concrete restriction on the right to strike, Order 1305 had proved to be something of a paper tiger.

Although all the wartime restrictions on civil liberties were eventually ended, the preservation of regulation 58AA into the late 1950s and the consideration given to permanent enactment of powers to control civilian labour stand as a reminder that, throughout modern history, governments have made permanent legislation and powers which were originally justified in terms of a specific and temporary need. The danger that present or future restrictions on civil liberties might follow this pattern should never be discounted.

Postscript: Notes

1. v.410 H.C.DEB 5s cols.1908-12.

2. PRO CAB 71/29, EL(43)10.

3. Lord Morrison of Lambeth, Government and Parliament, 3rd Edition (Oxford, 1964) p.305.

4. 'Supplies and Services (Transitional Powers) Act', 9 Geo 6, Ch.10.

5. 'Emergency Laws (Transitional Provisions) Act', 9 & 10 Geo 6, Ch.26.

6. 'Emergency Laws (Miscellaneous Provisions) Act', 11 & 12 Geo 6, Ch.10.

7. see for instance the Address to extend the Acts in 1950. v.478 H.C.DEB 5s cols.2494-2637. Also, from 1950, the government published annual White Papers explaining what legislation had been revoked and what was to be continued. See for example the 1950 White Paper, Cmd.8069 'Continuance of Emergency Legislation'.

8. see Cmd. 8893 and Cmd. 9207, Annual Reports of the Ministry of Labour and National Service for 1952 and 1953, Cmd.8893, pp.22-3 and Cmd.9207, p.21.

9. see Cmd. 7225, 'Ministry of Labour and National Service, Report for Years 1939-46' p.170.

10. see Cmd. 7225, pp.167-9.

11. v.417 H.C.DEB 5s col.618.

12. v.416 H.C.DEB 5s col.726 and v.423 H.C.DEB 5s col.157 (written replies).

13. Cmd. 7559, 'Ministry of Labour and National Service, Report for the Year 1947', p.30-1.

14. v.441 H.C.DEB 5s cols.1500-1.

15. see Cmd. 7559, pp.32-4.

16. v.443 H.C.DEB 5s cols.1362-5.

17. Cmd. 7559, p.36 and Cmd. 7822, 'Ministry of Labour and National Service, Report for the Year 1948', pp.19-20.

18. v.475 H.C.DEB 5s col.187 (written replies).

19. v.443 H.C.DEB 5s cols.1357-8.

20. v.472 H.C.DEB 5s cols.470-2.

21. D.N.Pritt, The Labour Government 1945-51, (Lawrence and Wishart, 1963) pp.369-70.

22. Ibid, p.438.

23. Cmd. 8640, 'Annual Report of the Ministry of Labour and National Service for 1951', p.vii.

24. In November 1947, the Labour MP, Rhys Davies, attacked the Labour Party's philosophy regarding industrial conscription. He implied that some sections of the Party, including the leadership, believed that industrial conscription and the direction of labour should be a permanent feature of a peacetime economy moving towards socialism. See v.443 H.C.DEB 5s cols. 1343-53. Certainly the Labour government were considering passing a Bill which would make certain aspects of the powers under the Supplies and Services Act permanent. See Lord Morrison of Lambeth, Government and Parliament, pp.305-6.

CONCLUSIONS

GOVERNMENT PRACTICE AND CIVIL LIBERTIES

What is clearly evident throughout this book is that the factors influencing government policy towards civil liberties issues were both numerous and variable. But they can be usefully divided into two types; motivating factors, which encouraged or led the government to take certain measures to restrict civil liberties, and constraining factors, which tended to discourage them from taking such steps. These two types are not necessarily mutually exclusive, nor should they be regarded as mechanistic forces. Often, motivating and constraining factors were interactive and the case of the requirements of war production is an example of a process which might best be seen as incorporating both motivating and constraining factors.

With these qualifications in mind it is possible to list most important motivating and constraining factors affecting policy determination.

<u>MOTIVATING FACTORS</u>	<u>CONSTRAINING FACTORS</u>
The perceived military threat.	Lack of political consensus.
The desire to control and limit the expression of opinions and views.	Potential political opposition.
The requirements of war production.	The maintenance of a liberal democratic image.
	Potential industrial opposition.

This list is by no means exhaustive, and I shall discuss further factors below. But if we consider the above factors in more detail their fundamental importance will be illustrated.

<u>Motivating Factors</u>

<u>The Perceived Military Threat</u>. The importance of this factor is most clearly seen in respect of many of the measures taken

in the crisis months of 1940. The military and security authorities argued successfully that the general internment of enemy aliens was an absolute necessity from a military point of view. Similarly, the detention of members of the British Union and the banning of that organisation in the summer of 1940 was at least partly based on the fear that British fascists might operate as a fifth column in the event of invasion. The general tightening of the defence regulations between April and July 1940 can also be linked to the threat of invasion and it should also be borne in mind that, had invasion occurred, the legislative framework existed for setting up special courts and giving complete authority to Regional Commissioners. Prior to the war, the anticipation of air bombardment had resulted in far wider powers being made available under draft regulation 18B and this was probably also the case with other regulations. Finally, this factor also influenced the application of censorship. One of the principal objects of censorship was to prevent information of military value reaching the enemy and it was even argued that some control over the expression of opinion was necessary to safeguard information of military value.

<u>The Desire to Control and Limit the Expression of Opionions and View</u>. As I showed in Chapters Four and Five, this factor is clearly visible throughout the war, but underlying it are several subsidiary factors. I have just mentioned the view that the expression of opinion could convey information of military value to the enemy, and this came to the fore explicitly in the summer of 1940 when the government were considering the introduction of compulsory press censorship. But this was a relatively minor point; of far greater importance was the question of morale and a commitment to a policy of political discrimination. These two factors are not always easy to distinguish, but the policy of political discrimination is shown most clearly in respect of actions taken against the Communist Party after they had pledged support for the government following the Nazi invasion of the Soviet Union. But even in earlier government discussions, evidence that dissident political propaganda was having a negligible effect on morale did little to dampen the desire of Ministers to suppress it. The question of morale is most prominent in government discussions of the national press but, as Ian McLaine has shown, what constituted morale was never clearly defined [1] and what was argued to be undermining morale was often little more than the expression of criticial opinions. In view of the continual campaign against the Communist Party and measures taken against the trotskyists in the later years of the war, it is significant that the national newspaper which provoked the most extreme reaction was the 'Daily Mirror' which, unlike most of the national

press, often analysed British society in terms of class relations and sometimes adopted a left-wing stance.

Although most of these issues are discussed in Chapters Four and Five, this factor had an impact in other areas too. In the summer of 1940, the Home Secretary assured an MP that interned enemy aliens who were communists would not be eligible for release under the category which provided for release from internment on the basis of an individual's proven hostility to fascism. It is likely that many interned enemy aliens who held dissident political views found it particularly difficult to obtain release. Similarly, as I said in Chapter Three, at least some communists and pacifists were detained under regulation 18B, and there is no doubt that the continued detention of members of the British Union was designed to prevent the recurrence of fascist propaganda. Finally, in the industrial sphere, one of the principal objects of the protected places legislation was to prevent the dissemination of left-wing, particularly communist, propaganda. This point is however also tied in with the final motivating factor discussed below.

The Requirements of War Production. The most obvious results of this factor were the controls imposed in the area of civilian employment discussed in Chapter Six, but the introduction of regulation 58AA and Order 1305 were also based on the view that they would aid the continuity of production. The protected places legislation was designed to have a similar effect by restricting workers' rights to discuss and organise and to limit the dissemination of left-wing propaganda. Finally, as I mentioned in Chapter Two, the fact that interned enemy aliens were an untapped source of labour at least partly explains the more rapid rate of release that occurred in 1941.

Constraining Factors

Lack of Political Consensus. Between September 1939 and May 1940, the Chamberlain government was trying to establish a consensus among Britain's political elite over the major issues of the war, since it was believed that without political unity it might prove impossible to unify the country to the extent necessary to fight a total war. Thus, political opposition that did, or might, occur during the phoney war period was of particular significance since it threatened to hamper further developments towards consensus. This had important repercussions in the area of civil liberties despite the government's majority in the House of Commons.

The importance of this factor is most clearly seen in the government's decision to amend the defence regulations in November 1939. But it also explains why the government allowed the Control of Employment Bill to be emasculated and, in part, why no attempt was made to provide for industrial conscription in the original Emergency Powers Act or restrict the right to strike by means of the defence regulations. In this context it is significant that such powers were quickly taken by the coalition government after May 1940.

Potential political opposition The added significance of political opposition in Parliament during the life of the Chamberlain government was reversed in the later years of the war. With the political consensus structurally based, parliamentary opposition to restrictions on civil liberties was usually reduced to a rump. Even when a considerable number of MPs did oppose measures taken by the government - as in respect of policy towards enemy aliens or the use and scope of regulation 18B - they were unable to force any significant changes in policy. In other words, once the government had decided upon and taken a certain course of action political opposition in Parliament was largely impotent. Yet curiously, what Ministers saw as potential political opposition appears to have had a constraining influence, noteably in the field of the control of expression of opinion. A wide draft regulation to control propaganda was dropped in favour of regulation 2C because the small committee of representative MPs had objected to it. A similar fate probably befell draft regulation 2DA at the beginning of 1941. One of the arguments against banning the 'Daily Mirror' in 1942 was that such a step would provoke strong political opposition both in and outside Parliament. Similarly with the proposals to introduce compulsory press censorship in the summer of 1940.

If potential opposition sometimes constrained the government but actual opposition failed to force the government to change its policies, what was the difference between them? One possible answer which I suggested in Chapter Four was that, where the government took action, it was correctly calculated that opposition would not be strong enough to force a change of policy. Whereas, in the instances mentioned above, it was calculated that opposition might be sufficiently strong to force them to retreat and that it was therefore better not to take those particular measures at all.

It seems that political opposition was considered potentially strongest in respect of formal restrictions on the expression of opinions, and outside Parliament this was true to the extent that the national press was consistently opposed to compulsory restrictions and had considerable political and social influence. Yet this does not explain why the government was wary of introducing a regulation to control other forms of propaganda, such as leaflets. In the light of the general inability of parliamentary opposition to force changes of policy after the formation of the coalition government, it is unlikely that opposition to an extension of formal controls over the expression of opinion would have been an exception. This suggests that it may not have been the strength of political opposition which constrained the government so much as the arguments such opposition might raise. This point leads and is directly related to the next factor I wish to discuss.

The Maintenance of a Liberal Democratic Image In attempts to justify their public actions to limit the activities and propaganda of political organisations, government spokesmen stressed a general commitment to democracy and freedom of expression, but argued that the government could reasonably curtail activities and propaganda which they claimed were an abuse of that freedom. But because what were seen as abuses were often little more than opposition to the war or government policy, the government had difficulty in operationalising this view while at the same time preserving a democratic image. This I think explains why potential political opposition in this field acted as a constraining factor - because opponents of a wide regulation controlling propaganda would have questioned whether the government was really committed to democratic freedoms.

There were important reasons why the government had to maintain a democratic image, which stemmed from the fact that the war had been depicted, both by the government and the media, as a war to preserve democracy and freedom. Thus any explicit or apparent abandonment of a commitment to liberal democratic freedoms would raise serious doubts about why Britain was fighting the war. This could have had far reaching implications, not only in terms of public opinion in Britain, but also in terms of American reaction to, and involvement in, the war effort.

Given that throughout the war the government had a strong desire to control and limit the expression of dissident opinion, the requirement of maintaining a democratic image had important implications and explains why many of the government's actions discussed in Chapter Four were taken on a covert or quasi-covert level. Similarly, attempts to control the expression of opinion in the national press by means of informal contacts and pressure can be seen as a function of these two factors. Finally, the policy of indirect pressure pursued in relation to the government's manpower strategy can also be related to the maintenance of a democratic image since, in the absence of outright and universal compulsion, Bevin could argue that the governments's policy of expanding and redeploying the labour force was based on 'voluntaryism'.

Potential Industrial Opposition This factor is closely linked with the motivating factor I called the 'requirements of war production'. Indeed, it might be more accurate to see potential industrial opposition as a constraining aspect of that motivating factor. Its importance is most apparent in Chapter Seven in respect of the government's difficulties in using Order 1305 and regulation 1AA as punitive sanctions because they might lead to a greater disruption of production than they were intended to prevent. But worries about industrial opposition had wider implications. The decision to lift the ban on the 'Daily Worker' was taken because the continuance of the ban was threatening to sour relations between the government and the labour movement. More directly, the fear of industrial opposition was almost certainly another reason why the government's manpower policy was based on the use of indirect pressure rather than the widespread and naked use of compulsory powers which could have been easily identified and thus more easily opposed.

Although the motivating and constraining factors outlined above appear to have been the most important influences on government policy, other factors undoubtedly played a part. The precedent of the first world war DORA regulations and the planning of emergency legislation during the inter-war years were a significant determinant of the form of the Emergency Powers Act and the defence regulations at the beginning of the war. Another point that should be mentioned is the role of parliamentary opposition in raising individual cases, most notably in respect of interned enemy aliens and detainees under regulation 18B. Although parliamentary opposition was unable to force significant changes of policy, MPs casework brought to light particular iniquities which might otherwise have remained undisclosed. In this way they effected changes in the administration of overall policies. Finally, mention should be made of the possible part played in policy determination by individual or collective prejudices. The demands of the military and security authorities to continue general internment in the autumn of 1940 may well have been based more on prejudice than military requirements. Bevin's apparent obsession with trotskyists played at least a small part in the decisions to prosecute members of the Revolutionary Communist Party and introduce regulation 1AA. Similarly, Churchill's undoubted hostility towards the 'Mirror' newspapers at least ensured that they were frequently discussed by the Cabinet. The importance of such points should not be overestimated, but neither should they be ignored when arbitrary powers are placed in the hands of a small number of people.

Despite the differing impact of the factors discussed above it is possible to make a number of points by way of a general assessment of government practice towards civil liberties. Firstly, the emergency powers taken during the second world war encroached a very long way into traditional civil liberties. Furthermore, with the exception of the concessions made in the autumn of 1939, the government were able to resist all demands to relinquish those powers until 1945, even though many of the regulations had originally been justified in terms of the perceived military threat which, by 1942 at the latest, had evaporated. Barry Cox in 'Civil Liberties in Britain' mostly discusses the wartime period in terms of the emergency powers and their use, and he says 'that authority could give itself very special powers indeed and then largely feel constrained not to use them'. [2] Unfortunately, Cox appears to have fallen into the trap of only seeing usage in terms of the formal and legal use made of emergency powers - the concrete examples of government exercising its powers under the defence regulations. Now while the formal use of emergency powers was of course important, the impact of emergency powers on civil liberties was designed to go, and indeed went, far beyond this. As we have seen, many of the regulations were intended to have a deterrent effect and there is evidence to show that they did so. Furthermore, where the existence of a regulation was not itself a sufficient deterrent, the government could threaten to make use of it. I have given a number of examples where the government made such threats. Thus the use of the emergency powers must be analysed not only in terms of constraints on the government, but must also take into account the extent to which individuals or groups complied with the regulations rather than face the possibility of action being taken against them. Examined in this way it is difficult not to conclude that the emergency powers imposed real and significant restrictions on civil liberties beyond the formal use made of them.

Even then, to concentrate on the emergency powers only gives us one side of the picture, for civil liberties were restricted in many other ways. The internment of enemy aliens is an obvious case, but perhaps of greater significance are some of the methods employed to control political activities. Ordinary peace-time legislation such as the Public Order Act was used, at least for a time, as a tool in a policy of controlling dissident political opinion. The government were also able to use their vast resources and influence to the same ends. Indeed, most of the government's covert strategy was based on powers which were not derived from emergency legislation. Similarly, the use of informal contacts with owners and editors lay at the root of the government's attempts to control the expression of opinion in the national press. The relationship between the use of emergency powers and other powers, whether legal or informal, was largely determined by the motivating and constraining factors discussed above. But government policies can be seen as a unified whole in the sense that they were based on expediency.

The government documents at present available do not show

an explicit desire to restrict civil liberties as such - for the sake of doing so. On the other hand, neither do these documents indicate any reluctance to restrict civil liberties from the basis of a deep commitment either to civil liberties or to democracy. Although, in public, government spokesmen stressed their concern with both civil liberties and democratic values, government documents suggest that such statements were, at best, window-dressing. Restrictions on civil liberties were always discussed in relation to specific objectives and those objectives were usually determined by the main motivating factors I listed above. The notion of expediency is important here because, having defined the specific problem to be solved, the government usually looked for the most expedient solution. Whether that solution restricted civil liberties was not itself considered important. It had an impact only in so far as such a restriction might raise problems in respect of the constraining factors I discussed. Being based on expediency, government policies towards civil liberties issues can be summed up in terms of attempts to maximise military, political or economic control with the minimum of inconvenience.

DEMOCRACY AND CRISIS GOVERNMENT

Although this study has been primarily concerned with an examination of government practice towards civil liberties, it has necessarily looked at several other important aspects of government and the political process in Britain during the second world war. In the introduction I argued that the study of crisis government could be expected to tell us a good deal about the nature of a political system, and that this might have important implications for the idea of democracy. What then does the evidence of this study suggest? To begin, it is necessary to summarise some of the features of wartime government which have been discussed in this book.

The first point concerns what I have called the structural political consensus. In the British political system, the possibilities for influencing the policy of a government with a clear majority in the House of Commons are, at best, limited. But the activities of opposition parties and organised groups outside Parliament can substantially challenge the validity of government thinking on the level of public debate, and pressure on the government sometimes succeeds in forcing a change of policy. In part, these processes continued to function during the life of the Chamberlain government. But things were very different during the period of the coalition. As we have seen, there was not one example of that government being forced to change its public stance on any civil liberties issue.

The structural political consensus was essentially an

alliance of Britain's political elite. Once that alliance had been formed, many of the normal channels for opposing government policy were effectively closed off. There was no longer any sizeable opposition in Parliament and the government's majority became a virtual monopoly. When parliamentary opposition did develop, the government could resort to the use of party discipline and the whipping system to keep it to a minimum. From outside parliament, pressure groups like the NCCL could do little more than try to persuade MPs to fly in the face of political realism. Furthermore, with the leadership of the trades union movement also incorporated into the structural consensus, the recognised path for the articulation of working class dissatisfaction was cut off in certain key areas. Instead, the trade union structure became an important organ of social control. One of the most important effects of the structural consensus was that there was no longer any recognised political opposition to challenge the goverment in the arena of public debate. While the press and radio might report the views of leaders of the different political parties and the trades union movement, these views were invariably all part of the structural consensus. This is not to say that there was no debate within the consensus. Rather, that public debate was largely limited by the terms of that consensus. Indeed, as we have seen, it was sometimes considered unpatriotic or even treacherous to challenge the policy of the coalition government. When political opposition did arise it seems to have obtained scant coverage in the media. Public opinion was necessarily restricted and, in this sense, manipulated by the existence of the structural political consensus.

The formation of an alliance within the British political elite does not guarantee that the resultant government is either democratic or representative. What it did guarantee during the second world war was that, in the areas covered by this book, political opposition was minimised and official ideology strongly reinforced.

Perhaps reinforcement of official ideology and manipulation of public opinion was a by-product of the structural consensus. But another important feature of wartime government was the extent to which direct attempts were made to manipulate public opinion. Virtually any dissident political activity or criticism of government policy could become the subject of attempts to suppress it. Throughout the war, government maintained that certain forms of criticism and opinion were irresponsible and could reasonably be curtailed. It was pronounced illegitimate to try to influence public opinion in a manner prejudicial to the war effort, or to systematically foment opposition to the war. In other words, the most fundamental areas of potential debate - the nature of the war, whether Britain should be fighting that war - were precisely those areas in which it was claimed that the expression of opinion could be curtailed. In practice, critical opinion in those areas was never subject to blanket suppression. But neither were attempts to restrict the expression of opinion confined to these fundamental questions. A significant factor influencing policy in this area was the extent to which such activity or criticism was making itself felt on public opinion or was believed likely to do so. In other words, activity and criticism believed to be harmless was allowed to continue unhindered (helping to maintain a democratic image) but activities and criticism which were seen as a threat were subjected to a variety of restrictive measures. Furthermore, public consideration of policy in this area was itself limited, and thus manipulated, by the use of covert or informal strategies specifically designed to avoid public discussion.

If these points are considered alongside the use of intensive official propaganda during the war years, [3] it is hard to avoid the conclusion that, throughout the war, government was systematically engaged in attempts to ensure its own ideological hegemony. Far from trying to represent the will of the people, the wartime governments attempted to control what the will should be.

Another feature of wartime government which has figured prominently in this study is the role of the military and security authorities. In a period of war one would expect to find them having a greater influence on policy. What is less obvious is that they should have a significant, and sometimes determining, influence on policy towards civil liberties. Yet it was the military and security authorities who forced through the policy of general internment and they were probably instrumental in the decision to detain a large number of fascists under regulation 18B.

Furthermore, the Home Defence (Security) Executive appears to have been active in most of the areas discussed in this book. Because of continuing official secrecy it is impossible to make a thorough analysis of the role of this committee or the influences upon it. But the indications are that it was heavily influenced by military thinking and the attitude of the security services. Given its status as a Cabinet Committee it was almost certainly responsible for the development and execution of specific policies. Evidence so far available shows that it strongly favoured further restrictions on civil liberties. I would suggest that it probably initiated covert operations carried out by MI5 and Special Branch designed to impede the activities of dissident groups in the political and industrial sphere. To sum up, it seems that the military and security authorities played an important part in determining policy towards civil liberties - certainly far beyond anything which could reasonably be described as a threat to military or national security.

A final area which has been touched on in this study is

the relationship between the executive and the judiciary. The normal structure of the judicial system was unaffected by the war. Yet there were not many signs of judicial independence in the area of civil liberties. On the contrary, in the case of Liversidge vs Anderson, the courts consistently upheld the government's interpretation of 'reasonable cause' in regulation 18B. The Law Lords decision has subsequently been discredited but, even in 1941, it prompted Mr. Justice Stable to comment that the stature of the judiciary had been reduced to that of 'mice squeaking under a chair in the Home Office'. [4] We have also seen that the Home Office sometimes advised the courts by the use of circulars to the Clerks of the Courts. The Home Secretary implied that there was nothing unusual about this. That may be so, but such advice was clearly designed to have a political effect. In so far as it did so, the courts performed a political function on behalf of the executive.

These features of wartime government have only been discussed in relation to the main subject of this study, and cannot therefore be regarded as conclusive. Nevertheless, taken in conjunction with the restriction of civil liberties during the period they add up to a picture of a society which can hardly be described as democratic.

Despite constitutional continuity and government concern with maintaining a democratic image, the crisis government of Britain during the second world war exhibited important political features normally associated with authoritarian regimes. The military and security authorities were an influential force in areas beyond the requirements of military and national security. The judicial system, if not dependent on the executive, was at least prepared to aquiesce to their political leadership. More importantly, government made serious attempts to manipulate public opinion by restrictions on civil liberties, a reliance on secrecy and its own propaganda. Finally, the political system was, in many respects, a closed one after the formation of the coalition government and came to resemble a one-party state.

Set against the usual conclusions of popular history, this assessment of British government during the war may seem radical and unnecessarily harsh. Yet the only other substantive study of crisis government came to a similar conclusion. Clinton Rossiter's comparative study of 'Crisis Government in the Modern Democracies' - first published in 1948 - concluded that the forms of government adopted by the western allies during the second world war were 'constitutional dictatorships' and he argued that 'No form of government can survive that excludes dictatorship when the life of the nation is at stake.' [5]

Having concluded that Britain was not a democracy during the second world war and that the political system exhibited a number of authoritarian features, does this tell us anything about the British political system in general? We can start with a simple question. Can any political system which adopts such forms during a period of crisis be properly described as a democracy at all? Most democratic theorists have ignored this question, but Rossiter implied an affirmative answer when he wrote 'No sacrifice is too great for our democracy, least of all the temporary sacrifice of democracy itself'. [6] But to sacrifice democracy in times of crisis necessarily means more than just suspending it - it means limiting its application. It is limited to the extent that there is a threat to the survival of the economic, social and political system. In other words, democracy is subordinated to the requirement of system survival. By its very nature, a period of crisis raises fundamental questions. Indeed, an internal crisis may only exist because fundamental questions are being asked. Thus, a period of crisis is a time when substantial change might be most likely to occur or to be demanded. If that potential for change is eliminated by the adoption of the methods and structures described in this book then I would argue that such a political system cannot properly be described as democratic. Rather, the existence of democratic forms during periods of peace and stability serves to mask an important aspect of that system - the extent to which it will attempt to protect itself from the people it is supposed to serve when it is under threat.

This view will undoubtedly be challenged, but the evidence of this study suggests we must go further - to question the extent to which democracy can really be said to exist in Britain even during periods of relative peace and stability. One of the most remarkable points demonstrated by this study is the extent to which wartime government was not dependent on a break with constitutional tradition or the use of emergency powers. This raises the question of the extent to which the same or similar features might have a more general application.

Take the question of consensus. I have argued that the structural consensus closed off areas of the political process and reinforced the consensual ideology. Structural consensus in the British political system has only occurred at times of severe crisis, but it has not been uncommon for there to be a looser form of consensus among Britain's political elite. Consider the case of Northern Ireland. Since the late 1960s the major parties at Westminster have pursued what has been termed a 'bi-partisan approach' - the main opposition parties generally supporting the policy of the governing party. It seems that, compared with the rest of Europe and the United States, public debate of the question in Britain has been stifled and there has been little chance for any group to get its views across unless it has accepted the basic terms of the bi-partisan approach. Equally high degrees of consensus have been exhibited for many years in the areas of foreign and defence policy with, I would argue, similar results. In other words, there does seem to be a case for arguing that it is the existence of consensus, rather than the establishment of structural consensus, which can restrict political access and limit public debate. Perhaps the stronger that consensus the more substantial such effects can be. Examined in this way, the wartime structural consensus can be seen as a strong and explicit form of a more general tendency towards consensus within the British political system, particularly as a response to crisis. [7] While it would be difficult to argue that the existence of consensus among the political elite is itself undemocratic, this study has shown that the effects can be. On the face of it, such effects may occur whenever a consensus is formed.

This study has also shown that the wartime governments made extensive use of covert or informal strategies to restrict civil liberties and attempt to manipulate public opinion. But these strategies were rarely based on the possible use of emergency powers. They relied on the ability of government to intervene in more discreet, subtle ways. There is no evidence to suggest that Ministers or senior officials saw these wartime activities as being unusual or an unpalatable necessity in wartime. So are they common practice? Some recent studies have suggested that government attempts to control the expression of opinion by the media occupy an important and permanent place in the less public reality of British politics. [8] Similarly, some studies have suggested that covert strategies have been used to restrict civil liberties and impede legitimate political activity. [9] In this case though, evidence relating to the post-war period is indicative rather than conclusive. Furthermore, it has not been suggested that such strategies have been employed as conscious and deliberate policy by Ministers and central government departments. Rather it has been argued that state agencies such as the police and security services have been able to employ such methods because they can act with a good deal of autonomy. While this may be true, perhaps it is too generous. During the second world war, Ministers and certain departments were aware of, and responsible for, at least some of the covert strategies described in Chapter Four. If it were shown conclusively that central government consistently used such strategies to restrict civil liberties and attempt to manipulate public opinion it would be impossible to continue describing Britain as a democracy.

This leads to the final point I wish to raise because the greatest obstacle to thorough study of government practice towards civil liberties is official secrecy. This study has shown that government policies towards civil liberties cannot be properly assessed solely by reference to a government's public position. Yet any use of covert and informal strategies is largely protected from public view for at least 30 years.

Even after this span of time, the public availability of documents is dependent upon official decision, and important areas of secrecy can be maintained. During the second world war such secrecy served to deceive the public about the true nature and extent of government interference with civil liberties. The same could be true today. We cannot tell because research is impeded by the extent of official secrecy. Civil liberties are supposed to be a crucial element of democracy. It is a strange democracy which makes it impossible to make a thorough study of government practice towards civil liberties.

Conclusions: Notes

1. Ian McLaine, Ministry of Morale - Home Front Morale and the Ministry of Information in World War II (George Allen & Unwin, 1979) pp. 7-11.

2. B. Cox, Civil Liberties in Britain, (Penguin, 1975) p.36.

3. see McLaine, Ministry of Morale.

4. quoted in R.F. Heaston, 'Liversidge vs. Anderson in Retrospect', in Law Quarterly Review, vol. 86, January 1970, pp. 33-68.

5. C. Rossiter, Constitutional Dictatorship, Crisis Government in the Modern Democracies, 2nd edition (Harbinger Books, 1963) p.vii.

6. Ibid.

7. In his recent book, Middlemas makes the point that a loose form of consensus was made in the decade 1916-26 and that this survived until the mid-1960s. See K. Middlemas, Politics in Industrial Society (Andre Deutsch, 1979).

8. see J. Margarch, The Abuse of Power, (W.H. Allen, 1978) and A. May and K. Rowan, (eds.), Inside Information - British Government and the Media (Constable, 1982).

9. For example see T. Bunyan, The History and Practice of the Political Police in Britain, (Quartet Books, 1977).

BIBLIOGRAPHY

PRIMARY SOURCES

Public Record Office

CAB 16/211 Committee for Imperial Defence, Sub-Committee on the control of aliens in war
CAB 23 Cabinet Minutes, 1916-1939.
CAB 52 Committee for Imperial Defence, War Legislation Committees
CAB 65 War Cabinet Minutes
CAB 66 War Cabinet Memoranda, WP Series
CAB 67 War Cabinet Memoranda, WP(G) Series
CAB 68 War Cabinet Memoranda, WP(R) Series
CAB 71 Lord President's Committee, Minutes and Papers.
CAB 73 Committees on Civil Defence, Minutes and Papers.
CAB 75 Home Policy Committee, Minutes and Papers.
CAB 76 Committees on Imperial Communications and Censorship
CAB 98/18 Committee on Communist Activities
CAB 123 Lord President of the Council, Secretariat Files
CAB 128 Cabinet Minutes, 1945-7
PREM 1-4 Prime Minister's Personal Papers
HO 45 Home Office, Registered Papers
HO 158 Home Office, Circulars
HO 202 Home Office, Weekly Home Security Reports
HO 208 Ministry of Home Security, Circulars
FO 371/29172-29192 Foreign Office, General Correspondence Files
LAB 8 Ministry of Labour and National Service, General Files
LAB 10 Ministry of Labour and National Service, Files on Industrial Relations
INF 1 Ministry of Information, General Files
MEPOL 2 Office of the Commissioner of the Metropolitan Police General Correspondence

Nearly all of the above files contain items which are

unavailable to the public. Below are listed files which are completely unavailable, although their titles suggest they should have been used in this study.

CAB 93/2 Home Defence (Security) Executive, Minutes of Meetings
CAB 93/3 Home Defence (Security) Executive, Papers
CAB 113 & 114 Home Defence Committees (including Security), Secretary's Files
CAB 121 Special Secret Information Files
HO 214 Aliens Supplementary Registered Papers
HO 215 Internees Registered Papers
DEFE 1 A selection to illustrate the work of the postal and telegraphic censorship
MEPOL 3 Files dealing with special police duties
MEPOL 7 Police Orders, general and confidential, to be brought to the attention of all ranks
MEPOL 8 Office of Commissioner, confidential books and instructions
MEPOL 10 Senior Officers' Papers

Archives of the National Council for Civil Liberties Held at the Library of the University of Hull

Modern Records Centre at the University of Warwick

Tarbuck Papers (MSS 75) Documents relating to the Workers International League, the Revolutionary Socialist League and the Revolutionary Communist Party, including copies of Socialist Appeal
HMSO Press (Harrow) Federate Chapel, (MSS 77), Minutes and Correspondence
National Union of Journalists, (MSS 86) Minutes of National Executive Committee and other Committees
Howard League for Penal Reform (MMS 16) Minutes of the Executive Committee and other Committees

Records of the Peace Pledge Union
Held at Dick Sheppard House, 6 Endsleigh Street, London

Mass Observation Archive, University of Sussex
Mary Adams Papers

Command Papers
Cmd. 6162, 'Defence Regulation 18B, Instructions issued by the Secretary of State with regard to the detention in prison establishments of persons detained in pursuance of Regulation 18B.'
Cmd. 6217, 'German and Austrian Civilian Internees, Categories

of Persons Eligible for Release from Internment and Procedure to be Followed in Applying for Release.'
Cmd. 6223, 'Civilian Internees of Enemy Nationality, Categories of Persons Eligible for Release from Internment and Procedure to be Followed in Applying for Release.'
Cmd. 7225, 'Ministry of Labour and National Service, Report for the Years 1939-46.'
Cmd. 7559, 'Ministry of Labour and National Service, Report for the Year 1947
Cmd. 7822, 'Ministry of Labour and National Service, Report for the Year 1948.'
Cmd. 8069, 'Continuance of Emergency Legislation.'
Cmd. 8640, 'Annual Report of the Ministry of Labour and National Service for 1951.'
Cmd. 8893, 'Annual Report of the Ministry of Labour and National Service for 1952.'
Cmd. 9207, 'Annual Report of the Ministry of Labour and National Service for 1953.'

House of Commons Debates
Fifth Series, (H.C.DEB 5s)

House of Lords Debates
Fifth Series, (H.L.DEB 5s)

All England Law Reports
1939-45

Labour Party Annual Conference Reports
1939-45

Newspapers & Periodicals
Including 'The Times', the 'News Chronicle', the 'New Statesman and the Nation', 'The Listener' and 'Peace News'

SECONDARY SOURCES

This list only includes those books and articles which are cited in the text. Many other books and articles were of course consulted while this study was being prepared.

P. Addison, The Road to 1945, (J. Cape, 1975)
C.K. Allen, Regulation 18B & Reasonable Cause in The Quarterly Law Review, Vol. 58, 1942.
BBC, Propaganda With Facts - Notes for Tutors and Students (B.B.C., circa 1978)
R. Benewick, The Fascist Movement in Britain, (Allen Lane, 1972)

A. Briggs, The History of Broadcasting in the United Kingdom, Vol. III War of Words, (Oxford, 1970)
A. Bullock, The Life and Times of Ernest Bevin, Vol. II, Minister of Labour, (Heinemann, 1967)
T. Bunyan, The History and Practice of the Political Police in Britain (Quartet Books, 1977)
D. Butler, and J. Freeman, British Political Facts, 1900-67, (Macmillan, 1968)
A. Calder, The People's War, (Panther, 1971)
D.N. Chester, ed., Lessons of the British War Economy, (Cambridge for the National Institute for Economic and Social Research, 1951)
Sir W. Churchill, The Second World War, Vols. I-VI, (Cassells, 1948-1954) and (Reprint Society, 1950-1954)
B. Cox, Civil Liberties in Britain, (Penguin, 1975)
C. Cross, The Fascist Movement in Britain, (Barrie & Rockcliff, 1961)
J.A. Cross, Sir Samuel Hoare - A Political Biography, (J. Cape, 1977)
R. Croucher, 'Engineers at War', (Merlin, 1982)
W.P. Crozier, Off the Record - Political Interviews 1933-1943, edited A.J.P. Taylor, (Hutchinson, 1973)
H. Cudlipp, Publish and Be Damned, (Andrew Dakers, 1953)
B. Donoughue and G.W. Jones, Herbert Morrison - Portrait of a Politician, (Weidenfeld & Nicolson, 1973)
M. Foot, Aneurin Bevan, Vol. I, (MacGibbon & Kee, 1962)
P. & L. Gillman, Collar the Lot, (Quartet Books, 1980)
W.K. Hancock and M. Gowing, British War Economy, History of the Second World War (UK Civil Series), (HMSO, 1949)
A.H. Hanson, and M. Walles, Governing Britain, (Fontana/Collins, 1970)
T. Harrisson, Living Through the Blitz, (Collins, 1976)
D. Hayes, Challenge of Conscience, (George Allen & Unwin, 1949)
R.F. Heaston, 'Liversidge vs. Anderson in Retrospect' in Law Quarterly Review, Vol. 86, Jan. 1970, p.33-68
HMSO, Defence Regulations Vol.I, 15th Edition, (HMSO, 24th March 1944)
P. Inman, Labour in the Munitions Industries, History of the Second World War (UK Civil Series) (HMSO, 1957)
G.W. Keeton, 'Liversidge vs. Anderson' in The Modern Law Review Vol.5, 1941.
R. Kidd, British Liberty in Danger, (Lawrence & Wishart, 1940)
C. King, With Malice Towards None - A War Diary, ed., W. Armstrong, (Sidgwick & Jackson, 1970)
F. Lafitte, The Internment of Aliens, (Penguin, 1940)
Mass Observation, People in Production, (Mass Observation, 1942)
A. May & K. Rowan, eds., Inside Information - British Government and the Media, (Constable, 1982)
W.E.J. McCarthy, ed. Trade Unions - Selected Readings,

(Penguin, 1972)

I. McLaine, Ministry of Morale - Home Front Morale and the Ministry of Information in World War Two, (George Allen & Unwin, 1979)

K. Middlemas, Politics in Industrial Society, (Andre Deutsch, 1979)

Lord Morrison of Lambeth, Government and Parliament, (Oxford, 1964)

Lord Morrison of Lambeth, Herbert Morrison - An Autobiography (Odhams, 1960)

S. Morrison, I Renounce War - The Story of the Peace Pledge Union, (Sheppard Press, 1962)

L. Mosley, Backs to the Wall, (Weidenfeld & Nicolson, 1971)

M. Panter-Downes, London War Notes 1939-45, ed. W. Shawn, (Longmans, 1972)

H.M.D. Parker, Manpower, History of the Second World War (UK Civil Series), (HMSO, 1957)

S. Pollard, The Development of the British Economy, 2nd edition, (Edward Arnold, 1969)

D.N. Pritt, The Autobiography of D.N. Pritt, Part One, From Right to Left (Lawrence and Wishart, 1966)

D.N. Pritt, The Labour Government 1945-51, (Lawrence & Wishart, 1963)

C. Rossiter, Constitutional Dictatorship, Crisis Government in the Modern Democracies, 2nd edition, (Harbinger Books, 1963)

W. Rust, The Story of the Daily Worker, (Peoples Press Printing Society, 1949)

R. Skidelsky, Oswald Mosley, (Macmillan, 1975)

A. Stevens, The Dispossed - German Refugees in Britain (Barrie & Jenkins, 1975)

A.J.P. Taylor, English History 1914-15, (Oxford, 1965)

E.P. Thompson, The Secret State, State Research Pamphlet No. 1 (Indpendent Research Publications, 1979)

R. Titmuss, Problems of Social Policy, History of the Second World War (U.K. Civil Series) (HMSO, 1950)

E. Trory, Imperialist War - Further Recollections of a Communist Orgniser, (Crabtree Press, Brighton, 1977)

A. Tuckett, Civil Liberty and the Industrial Worker, (NCCL, 1942)

H.W.R. Wade, Administrative Law, 4th Edition, (Oxford, 1977)

B. Wasserstein, Britain and the Jews of Europe 1939-45, (Institute of Jewish Affairs/Oxford U.P., 1979)

INDEX